P9-DMG-929

The De-Valuing of America

THE FIGHT FOR OUR CULTURE AND OUR CHILDREN

William J. Bennett

A TOUCHSTONE BOOK
Published by Simon & Schuster
New York   London   Toronto
Sydney   Tokyo   Singapore

TOUCHSTONE
Rockefeller Center
1230 Avenue of the Americas
New York, New York 10020

Copyright © 1992 by William J. Bennett

First Touchstone Edition 1994
TOUCHSTONE and colophon are registered trademarks of
Simon & Schuster Inc.
Designed by Irving Perkins Associates
Manufactured in the United States of America

1   3   5   7   9   10   8   6   4   2

Library of Congress Cataloging-in-Publication Data

Bennett, William John
    The de-valuing of America : the fight for our culture and our
children / William J. Bennett.
        p.   cm.
    Includes index.
    1. Social values.   2. United States—Social conditions—1980–
3. United States—Moral conditions.   4. Education—United
States.   5. Education and state—United States.   6. Drug abuse—
United States—Prevention.   7. United States—Race
relations.   8. United States—Religion—1960–   I. Title.
HM216.B3   1992
306′.0973—dc20   91-42629
                                                              CIP

ISBN: 0-671-68305-5
ISBN: 0-671-79719-0 (PBK)

To Elayne, John, and Joseph.
To Be Loved By People So Precious Is A Daily Encouragement.

CONTENTS

PREFACE

In the fall of 1991, during the Senate Judiciary Committee's interrogation of Clarence Thomas, I was debating former Vice Presidential candidate Geraldine Ferraro at Pacific University in Forest Grove, Oregon. Representative Les AuCoin, a liberal Democrat, was moderating the event. Prior to my opening remarks, AuCoin opined that while it was all well and good that American values have triumphed in Eastern Europe, it would be great if those values triumphed in the United States.

After Representative AuCoin introduced me, I said I could sum up my evening's remarks in a single sentence. "Now that American values have prevailed in Eastern Europe, we should work to see to it that the same values prevail in *Washington, D.C.*" I then added, "The American people are fine. Washington is not. The patient is in better shape than the doctor."

We are in the midst of a struggle over whose values will prevail in America. This book is about that struggle.

What follows is my account of what has fairly been described as a "controversial" public career. It is about politics in the 1980s and my involvement in some of the most hotly debated, passionately felt domestic and social issues of our time. But it is, finally, a book about America as seen through my eyes—about that which is profoundly good and right and decent about this nation on the one hand, and about some of what has gone very wrong on the other.

This volume chronicles my decade of service in the Reagan and Bush administrations, as chairman of the National Endowment for the Humanities, Secretary of Education, and director of the Office of National Drug Control Policy. In it I lay out many of the obstacles I encountered, ranging from entrenched bureaucracies, to belligerent lobbies, to a recalcitrant Congress, to an often hostile academy, to a skeptical but ultimately persuadable press.

11

Throughout I attempt to offer insights into my style of governing—my efforts to go on the offensive; to seize the attention of the public; and to engage in a national debate on the issues I believed to be central to the well-being of the country.

This book incorporates substantial amounts of anecdotal material. This is not simply because the anecdotes make for (I hope) interesting and sometimes amusing reading. The broader purpose is heuristic: behind almost every political disagreement or story there is a *moral,* a broad sentiment, a mind-set that influences and often dictates the judgments made about particular issues. I trust that the anecdotes and experiences I recount help to illuminate my discussion of public policy—the arguments behind the arguments. I discovered a long time ago that you will save a lot of time and energy if early on you identify the underlying philosophy and world view that animates and informs public policy debates. I have tried to do that here, particularly in the context of discussing the debates in which I was a participant.

I describe what I believe to be the troubling condition of our children and our culture, the connection between the two, and explain why and how they came to be that way. I set out my views on how these things have come to such a pass, what I've tried to do about them, and where we need to go from here.

This is what I have tried to achieve. At the same time, it is important to say what this book is *not.* It is not a collection of tracts that outline neat public policy prescriptions for our social woes. It is not a definitive work on American culture. Others have written, and written well, on these subjects. Rather, this is a chronicle of *my* story and what I believe it reveals about pressing domestic and social issues, the modern-day political establishment, and the battle for our culture and our children.

In one important regard this book is different from many other recent political memoirs. While offering frank insights and reflections on prominent political figures, the reader will not find any intentional score-settling toward former colleagues and associates. Every public-official-turned-author knows that there are headlines to be made and books to be sold if he writes a "kiss-and-tell" memoir, particularly if it "reveals" something that casts former colleagues or even (and perhaps especially) presidents, in a bad or embarrassing light. Ironically, it often occurs among individuals who have most benefited personally

and professionally from their associations, who have basked in
the reflected light and achievements of others. People in search
of that kind of book should look elsewhere. When you agree to
serve in an administration, you become part of a team. And
there are certain things you owe your teammates. Loyalty is one
of them. There should be no statute-of-limitations on that particular virtue, even in Washington.

The Reagan and Bush teams were ones on which I was proud
to serve. I came away from public life as I went in—encouraged
and hopeful, reassured in my belief that it is possible to make a
positive difference. In that sense, I remain an unreconstructed
advocate of the possible. I hope this book captures that spirit.

Many of the individuals I met whose stories I recount in this
volume lived outside of Washington. This is because few Cabinet
members have traveled the country as extensively as I have during the last decade. None has benefited more. Visiting America's
classrooms, universities, public housing projects, street corners,
and town halls has helped me see the everyday reality behind
government reports, newspaper accounts, and statistics. It was an
indispensable means for me to gauge the convictions and sentiments of the public.

Working in Washington and still being able to engage in a conversation with the American people was illuminating. One striking impression I came away with is this: elite and mainstream
America now adhere to profoundly different sets of beliefs and
values. The skepticism toward this country that once characterized many intellectuals and their ideological soulmates has turned
to antipathy. Over the last two decades they have waged an all-out
assault on common sense and the common values of the American
people. We now stand at a crossroads.

America, then, is engaged in an ongoing and intensifying cultural war. It is a conflict that I actively participated in during the
last ten years. I brought to it strong views and deep convictions.
For that I make no apologies. The judgments made herewith may
cheer some. They will undoubtedly infuriate others. That's fine,
and in fact that would be very much in keeping with the reaction
I evoked during my years of service in government. My real hope
is to do with this book what I tried to do during my public career:
stimulate a true national discussion over some of the most consequential issues of our time. If it succeeds on that count, it will
alone have been worth the effort.

*   *   *

There are many people who have made this book possible, in ways large and small.

I would first like to express my thanks to Presidents Reagan and Bush. They gave me, a former professor of political philosophy, the rare privilege to fight in the public arena for things in which I believe. That I was able to do so directly on behalf of two presidents whom I like, respect, and admire is a rarer privilege still. To each I owe a debt of gratitude which I can never fully repay.

No public official has worked with more intelligent, hardworking, and principled colleagues than I have over the last ten years. To have been supported by men and women of such extraordinary talent was my great good fortune. These were people dedicated to ideas and ideals; their hard work was in the service of good and noble ends. I am extremely grateful to them.

In writing this book I benefited from the help of many friends and colleagues. Among those who reviewed early drafts of individual chapters were Gary Bauer, Mark Blitz, John Cribb, Midge Decter, Edwin Delattre, John DiIulio, Terry Eastland, Emily Feistritzer, Chester Finn, Jr., William Kristol, Robert Lichter, Lyn Nofziger, Terry Pell, Stanley Rothman, Ted Smith, and John Walters. While this book surely is not what each of them thought it ought to be, it is a better book because of their thoughtful criticisms and input. I thank them all.

My agent, Robert Barnett of Williams & Connolly, guided me through a new frontier, the world of publishing, with his usual skill, patience, and sound counsel.

My thanks to the John M. Olin Foundation for its support of my work, and to its president, William Simon, whose support, encouragement, and advice have always been steady and sure.

I am grateful to the Hudson Institute and to its president, Les Lenkowsky. He provided me with a post-government place to land and made me feel welcome.

Before I undertook this project with Simon & Schuster, a number of friends told me that Robert Asahina is an outstanding editor. It turns out he is better than advertised. I benefited greatly from his sharp editorial eye and his sharp red editorial pencil. Bob understood from the beginning what this book should do and be, and he kept me on the straight-and-narrow throughout.

Special thanks are due to Bill Schulz and Bill McGurn, who allowed me to impose on their friendship and tap into their considerable editorial talents. They demonstrated both, in spades, during the writing of this book. I am deeply indebted to both men.

In this project, as in so many others, Noreen Burns was a great source of encouragement and assistance. Her standards are invariably high and her memory of events is invariably right; this is a better book because of her efforts.

A very special debt of gratitude is owed to Peter Wehner. Over the years, I have come to respect and rely on him in many ways, but this was never more so than when I embarked full-time on this enterprise. During the writing of this book, Pete was indefatigable; his insights, judgment and advice were always on target; and his skills were invaluable.

Finally, I want to thank Elayne. When you lead as "controversial" a public life as I have, you are inevitably going to be the subject of a lot of criticism. Often, she took the criticisms harder than I. But Elayne was unwavering in her support and she never lost faith in the things I was trying to achieve. She was my closest and most constant companion throughout, and made all parts of the journey worthwhile. I am also grateful to her for giving me the single best piece of advice I received while I was serving in government. She told me to get out of Washington and visit the rest of America.

INTRODUCTION
THE CULTURE WARS

When I came to Washington in 1981, I was curious about the state of my soul and how much pressure would be put on it. So I sought the counsel of former New York Senator Jacob Javits, a man whom I often disagreed with on policy matters but whose integrity had always impressed me. "Make no deals," he told me. "You will, after a time, be left alone." He then added: "If you dance with someone, you will have to dance with the whole crowd." Ten years and three government jobs later, I can say on matters of principle, I did not dance. Many people said a lot of tough things about me, but they didn't say that.

It was March 1981, and I was brand-new to Washington. President Reagan had just named me chairman of the National Endowment for the Humanities, a federal agency that at that time distributed $130 million a year for scholarly work, museums, and educational and television programs in the areas of history, philosophy, and literature. One of the things I intended to do was begin a systematic review of grants funded by NEH.

Before that could happen, however, by happenstance I came across the broadcast of "From the Ashes . . . Nicaragua." I was watching an installment of the PBS series "Middletown" and "From the Ashes . . . Nicaragua" was broadcast immediately after it. I was astonished by what I was watching. "From the Ashes . . . Nicaragua" was produced with the help of an NEH grant. It turned out to be not an educational documentary, but a politically tendentious pro-Sandinista film. It portrayed life in Nicaragua from the point of view of a shoemaker's family and showed poor laborers and children toiling, with bent backs and sad countenances, until the Sandinista "liberators" moved into town. Their arrival had a tonic effect; everyone perked up and started rejoicing because of the dawning of an enlightened new day. The film reminded me of a more sophisticated version of the kind of Marxist propaganda that had spewed forth for decades from Moscow.

It's somewhat difficult now, more than ten years after Daniel Ortega came to power and unleashed the Sandinista reign of terror on the Nicaraguan people, to recall the infatuation many intellectuals and academics had with the Sandinistas when they took power ("the beautiful revolution," some called it). In the late seventies and eighties the Sandinistas were viewed by a lot of people as political liberators of the first order, "popular revolutionaries" who would unshackle the victims of oppression. Some church groups saw the Sandinistas as ushering in the Kingdom of Heaven on earth ("the reign of God has arrived in Nicaragua, the reign of truth, hope, and justice," is how one Catholic priest put it). Nothing in the film suggested that those utopian hopes were to be crushed, as they ultimately were, by totalitarian coercion.

"From the Ashes . . . Nicaragua" had no business posing as a documentary. And it certainly had no business receiving taxpayer funds to produce and distribute it. I decided to set down some markers and went public with my criticism. I denounced the film, describing it to *The New York Times* as

unabashed socialist-realism propaganda. There was not a scintilla of evidence of perspective. It is political propaganda, not the humanities. Why are we financing propaganda? The program was a hymn to the Sandinistas.

At those words many in the arts and film community went apoplectic. No chairman had ever done anything like this before. My predecessor, Joseph D. Duffy, asserted "the endowment is not a moral pulpit." There were ominous warnings from the director of the film of "political and artistic censorship"; my actions were having a "chilling effect" on free speech and the free expression of ideas; I was violating the First Amendment.

So began my entry into the culture wars.

The charges leveled against me were nonsense. (During a question-and-answer session with leaders of humanities councils from various states, one person charged that my sharp criticism might have a "stifling effect" on filmmakers. "For me to say that this is a piece of junk violates your creative freedom?" I replied.) While I was chairman, the NEH supported many quality, nonpolitical works in humanities filmmaking. For example, we supported a young filmmaker in a project that traced the history of the building of the Brooklyn Bridge. It turned out to be a good film. Seven years later the recipient of the grant came up to me on an airplane and thanked me for giving him, as he put it, "my start in show business." The man was Ken Burns, producer of the extraordinary television series "The Civil War."

What I was trying to do in the case of "From the Ashes . . . Nicaragua" was to put a halt to the taxpayers' subsidizing of left-wing, anti-American propaganda, and to send a signal that it wouldn't happen again. "You may not use . . . the humanities or the name of the humanities or the name of the National Endowment or the name of state committees as a pretext for partisan, political tendentiousness," I said in a speech before the fifty state humanities councils. Worse yet in the eyes of some of the liberal elite, I had spoken out against—and taken action against—the stifling political climate within the academic and intellectual world. The word was out; I was to be watched. I was in the fight, the first of many cultural fights I found myself in during my years in the Reagan and Bush administrations.

In the fall of 1981, in the Oaks Apartments in Chapel Hill, North Carolina, I was waiting—and hoping—for a call from the White House. Months before, I had interviewed in Washington for the position of chairman of the National Endowment for the Humanities. There were three finalists for the job: Robert Hollander, a professor of comparative literature at Princeton; Melvin Bradford, a professor of English at the University of Dallas; and myself.

At the time I was the thirty-seven-year-old director of the National Humanities Center, a think tank for scholars in the humanities, located in the Research Triangle Park in North Carolina. I had assumed the directorship of the center two years earlier, following the death of its first director (and my close friend and mentor), Charles Frankel. Frankel and his wife were brutally murdered in their suburban New York home by three men looking for money to pay for their drug habits. A philosopher committed to reason, Frankel was shot repeatedly in the head at close range.

Although I had been a lifelong Democrat, I thought I had a good chance of being named chairman. I had pretty good academic credentials, having earned a Ph.D. in political philosophy from the University of Texas, a law degree (focusing almost exclusively on legal philosophy and jurisprudence) from Harvard, and having taught philosophy at a number of universities. I also had the support of others whose opinions carried some weight in the Reagan White House—including the social commentator Irving Kristol; the editor of the conservative magazine *National Review*, William F. Buckley; and the nationally syndicated columnist George Will.

I had one other thing working strongly in my favor: I was a moderately well known academic who supported Ronald Reagan. Now, the reader may wonder why this was at all significant. After all, Ronald Reagan won the 1980 election in a landslide; he carried forty-four states and won by well over 8 million votes. One would assume that there was a pool of academics well qualified for presidential appointments, academics who supported Ronald Reagan.

In fact, that was *not* the case, at least not in the field of the humanities. In November 1980 we did a straw poll of the Humanities Center's scholars. As I recall, there were thirty-one votes for Jimmy Carter, seven votes for John Anderson (who was running as an independent), and three votes (including my own) for Reagan.

A colleague's wife who worked at the University of North Carolina library described hearing the chairman of one of the academic departments say the day after the 1980 election (echoing film critic Pauline Kael's famous comment), "I voted for Carter. Most of my colleagues voted for Carter. And a few voted for Anderson. But Reagan got elected. Who in the hell voted for Reagan?" This typical academic myopia helps explain why I was a good candidate for the job—the "pool" was not very large.

The phone rang on Friday night and when I answered, a woman with a heavy Austrian accent said, "Hello, is this Mr. Hollander?" A couple of thoughts flashed through my mind. I knew immediately, from her accent, that the caller was Helene von Damm, the Director of Presidential Personnel. I assumed that the White House had decided on a new chairman of the National Endowment for the Humanities—and it wasn't me. I also assumed that any future prospects of public life had gone up in smoke.

"No, this is not Mr. Hollander," I answered. "This is William Bennett." She said, "I'm very sorry. I meant to call you Mr. Bennett, not Mr. Hollander." We both laughed nervously—she because of embarrassment, I because of a sense of relief. I then proceeded to hear her out.

Mrs. von Damm said that President Reagan had decided to nominate me and she hoped that I was as excited and pleased about the choice as the President. I told her that I was, and she said that she would be in touch in a few days to discuss procedures and protocol. I thanked her and hung up. I was eager.

Over the next couple of days, I read through my "Commonplace Book"—a collection of my favorite quotations—and found a quote from Oliver Wendell Holmes, Jr. "The place for a man who is complete in all powers is in the fight," Justice Holmes wrote. "The professor, the man of letters, gives up one-half of life that his protected talent may grow and flower in peace. But to make up your mind at your peril upon a living question, for purposes of action, calls upon your whole nature." I knew I wasn't anywhere near "complete in all powers." But I had a clear sense I was about to enter in the fight, and would soon be making up my mind at some peril.

Mrs. von Damm called the following week. While there was enthusiasm on the part of the President and others for my nomination, she told me that the White House faced an almost unprecedented problem with my candidacy. Both my home-state senators, Jesse Helms and John East, were opposed to my nomination. Von Damm told me that I faced some tough sledding ahead because a candidate of a Republican president not supported by his two Republican home-state senators would be hard to overcome. She told me that I needed to persuade Senators Helms and East—two of the guardians of the conservative movement—to change their minds and support me.

I was certainly willing to try, but I didn't know precisely what the obstacles were. It turned out that Senator East had once been a student of Mel Bradford, and very much wanted to see him ascend to the chairmanship of NEH. Jesse Helms, a loyal same-state senator with no horse of his own in the race, was willing to support Bradford. Also, I was still a registered Democrat; growing up, I had most closely identified with the John F. Kennedy and Hubert H. Humphrey wing of the Democratic party. A number of people had been telling Senators East and Helms that I was not only a Democrat but also a left-leaning liberal—this despite my support for Reagan, my public stance against a variety of liberal articles of faith, and my writings for conservative journals. One item kept reappearing in most of the arguments made to Senators Helms and East: I had a picture of Dr. Martin Luther King, Jr., hanging in my office. I didn't know then—and I still don't know—what importance that story held for either senator; it never came up in any conversation with them. It was true that in my office I had a picture of Dr. King resting during the civil rights march to Montgomery. I had been a long-time admirer of the public Dr. King and believed that he made an enormous contribution toward advancing the cause of equality and improving American society.

During my undergraduate and graduate school days, I had spent a lot of time studying the works of three American figures—James Madison, Abraham Lincoln, and Martin Luther King, Jr. Each exercised political and intellectual leadership and each profoundly affected a different century in our nation's life. These men also demonstrated something else that I would take as my credo into public life: it is ideas and ideals that ultimately move society—ideas and ideals contained in the great works of Western civilization, and which students should encounter through education.

In any case I faced an uphill battle. I was being whipsawed by conservatives who thought I was a liberal and by liberals who knew (based on my record and my writings) I was conservative. A lot of my critics loved the fact that my nomination was being held up by my own conservative senators, and they tried to draw me into criticizing Helms and East. I wouldn't, for reasons laid out in *The Federalist Papers*. According to James Madison, senators have a right, even a duty, to look at national and not simply provincial interests. If Helms and East thought there was a better candidate than one from North Carolina, it was their right, even their duty, to say so.

I tried to set up meetings with both senators to find out what their objections to me were. My task was complicated when the influential conservative columnist Patrick J. Buchanan wrote that

Helms and East were right to object to my nomination because, from my résumé, I looked like a standard academic liberal.

I was surprised at the criticism from Buchanan. We are both graduates of Gonzaga College High School in Washington, D.C., a Catholic high school known for its academic excellence and strong school loyalty. About two months after I had been confirmed for the job, I ran into Buchanan at a reception. He said, "Hey, fella, you're doing a good job."

I told him, "You should have expected it, Pat. I'm a Gonzaga man." Buchanan seemed taken aback and was momentarily speechless. I added, "In fact, I was on the last city championship football team." Pat then said, half-jokingly, I thought, "If I'd known that, I never would have taken that shot at you."

During the first of my several meetings with Senator Helms, he said that he had no real philosophical objections to me, he was simply deferring to his colleague Senator East. But Bradford's candidacy was derailed when *The New York Times* revealed that his scholarly work included harsh criticisms of Abraham Lincoln. Understandably, the White House did not want to get involved in a long, contentious confirmation hearing in which senators from both parties would be grilling a Reagan administration appointee on his criticisms of Lincoln, who was not only one of this country's two greatest presidents, but also the first Republican president, the real founder of the party.

But the collapse of the Bradford candidacy did not mean that Senators East and Helms were ready to embrace me. The word was that East in particular was not warming to me. I wanted a chance to talk with him to see if I could respond to his objections, or whether his objections were something visceral or so deeply held that I couldn't overcome them.

When I finally met Senator East, he behaved in an impressive, high-minded fashion. He told me that he had hoped that Mel Bradford could have been confirmed, but he now realized that that wouldn't occur. Inasmuch as I was President Reagan's choice, he was prepared to get behind my nomination—if I could satisfy him on a couple of points. I nodded, swallowed hard, and wondered what the points were. He asked me whether I was prepared to run a fair, impartial, nonideological agency. I said, "Yes, of course." He then asked me if that meant that I would be sure that when the applications of conservative scholars were evaluated and reviewed, they would be evaluated and reviewed by the same standard as the applications of liberal scholars. That was a fair request; I assured Senator East that would in fact be the case. And that was the end of the conversation. Senator East had been caricatured as holding some of the most rigid and ideological views known to man, yet the only concerns he expressed to me were about procedural due process. The interview went well and I left thinking that I would now be confirmed with relative ease.

A day or two later, however, I heard that Senator Helms was having additional doubts about me. The King issue had surfaced again, and material was being sent to Senator Helms indicating that a good number of the scholars at the National Humanities Center were liberal. I was asked about this by White House personnel and I explained that the "charge" was true; I had no interest in running an academic institution that had no political variety, and in any event it is virtually impossible to run an academic center for the humanities and *not* have a lot of liberal scholars. In each of the first two years at the Center we had three or four conservative scholars out of forty. This led one of the Center's professors to march into my office one day and ask if we were trying to make the Center "a conservative coven."

Friends again sought to intervene on my behalf. I was told that I should meet with Edwin J. Feulner, president of The Heritage Foundation, the influential public policy organization in Washington to which conservatives look for guidance. I was told that he was very influential with Senator Helms and I would help my cause if I could convince Feulner that I would do a good job. The meeting with Feulner didn't begin nearly as well as the one with Senator East. Feulner (now a friend) was, I thought, distant, even a little suspicious. Given what he had heard, I couldn't blame him. He said there were "worries" about me and that he didn't feel he could recommend me unless I could give some hard evidence that I merited conservative support.

I told Feulner that my conservative views were matters of public record, but he needed to judge that for himself. He then asked me whether I had ever read any material from his organization. I told him that I had not only *read* some Heritage Foundation material, but I also had actually *written* some of it. The Heritage Foundation had reprinted an article I had coauthored with Ed Delattre called "Moral Education in the Schools." It was a scholarly criticism of moral relativism and the "values clarification" movement that took hold in many American schools in the late 1960s and 1970s. Our article turned out to be a popular Heritage Foundation reprint.

Surprised, somewhat taken aback, and then relieved by what I said, Feulner said, "Yes, I remember. You're *that* Bennett." He then told me that he had been very much impressed with my article, thought he knew of some of my other writings, and would have no problem supporting me for chairmanship of the NEH. Feulner then called Senator Helms, and I was finally on my way. From that point on the nomination proceeded smoothly and I was appointed chairman of the National Endowment for the Humanities by President Reagan on December 21, 1981 (I was confirmed by the Senate on February 8, 1982). On the day the President appointed me, I called Joseph Duffy and told him to stop any grant-approval letters. I knew the direction of the work at the NEH, and I wanted to set a new course.

The new course began with "From the Ashes . . . Nicaragua." This was my baptism into politics, the first of many conflicts that can best be understood as a fight for the culture, the social and moral environment in which we raise our children, and the government's responsibility and limitations in this effort. The battle lines are being drawn and redrawn, even now.

The battle for the culture refers to the struggle over the principles, sentiments, ideas, and political attitudes that define the permissible and the impermissible, the acceptable and the unacceptable, the preferred and the disdained, in speech, expression, attitude, conduct, and politics. This battle is about music, art, poetry, literature, television programming, and movies; the modes of expression and conversation, official and unofficial, that express who and what we are, what we believe, and how we act. Christopher Dawson, a noted intellectual historian, put it well in his 1947 Gifford Lecture:

A social culture is an organized way of life which is based on a common tradition and conditioned by a common environment. . . . It is clear that a common way of life involves a common view of life, common standards of behavior and common standards of value.

Why is there a battle about our culture? Part of the answer lies in understanding that there is a fundamental difference between many of the most important beliefs of most Americans and the beliefs of a liberal elite that today dominates many of our institutions and who therefore exert influence on American life and culture.

The elite are most often found among academics and intellectuals, in the literary world, in journals of political opinion, in Hollywood, in the artistic community, in mainline religious institutions, and in some quarters of the media. They exercise disproportionate influence because many people look to them (at least historically they have done so) as opinion makers and trendsetters. They write articles and books, give speeches, make movies, report stories, make news, and often interpret events; in short, they are the filter through which many Americans are informed about events. They exert a considerable amount of influence in official Washington—on the people who shape public discourse, who govern, who legislate, and who lead.

According to Stanley Rothman, S. Robert Lichter, and Linda Lichter, perhaps the nation's leading authorities on the study of American elite attitudes and authors of the forthcoming *Elites in Conflict: Social Change in America Today* (New York: Praeger, 1992):

> The cultural establishment, which includes academics, the creative elite of television and motion pictures, and the leaders of the new public interest groups, are more liberal and alienated from traditional institutions and values than are traditional elites. . . . Social and cultural changes in American society and culture have produced a new secular, liberal and cosmopolitan sensibility which partially rejects traditional bourgeois emphases on work, frugality, sexual restraint, and self-control.

The authors go on to say, "The traditional elites of America used to be the repository of the bourgeois values of family, community, freedom, and self-restraint. Perhaps the impact of the new strategic elites is clearest in the erosion of the bourgeois values among those who have always been its keepers. . . . We thus appear to be witnessing the gradual abdication of the . . . traditional underpinnings of American society."

Elections underscore the vast political differences separating elites and the rest of the American people. In presidential elections the elite usually vote overwhelmingly liberal and Democratic. For example, 96 percent of the "public interest elite" (key individuals publicly identified with public interest movements in lobbying, in law, in academia, and in foundations) voted for George McGovern in 1972; 93 percent voted for Jimmy Carter in 1976; and 92 percent voted for Jimmy Carter or John Anderson in 1980. This remarkable uniformity is but one example of how distant they are from the political beliefs (as well as the moral and philosophical underpinnings of those beliefs) of the rest of the electorate.

Make no mistake. By elites I do not mean registered Democrats. The elite are people who, unlike the rank-and-file Democratic party that I came from, are often *not* at home with the traditional beliefs of most Americans; they tend to be skeptical and mistrustful of American society. Their measure is not simply the extent to which our society falls short of realizing its ideals, but sometimes the wholesale *rejection* of American ideals. Marked by alienation, suspicion, and doubt, the liberal elite call into question what is commonly thought of as "the American dream."

From what I have observed, the liberal elite proceed from a certain social and political predisposition. The predisposition tends to be an adopted orientation, not a conclusion based on evidence and argument. When you sift through the arguments, you will often find that modern-day academics and intellectuals (which many elites fancy themselves to be, or long to be) have arrived at their position not, ironically, through intellect, through open-ended, disinterested thinking and inquiry, but through disposition, sentiment, bias, and ideology. Many intellectuals are predisposed to accept certain premises and arguments—a preconceived reality. They search for facts to sustain their political position. The approach is (as philosopher Karl Jaspers said of Marx's writings) "one of vindication, not investigation." Serious public debate is therefore a casualty, since they are not likely to change their minds on the basis of compelling empirical arguments. Their starting point is not evidence but ideology. They are undeterred by what Thomas Huxley called "the tragedy of a fact killing a theory."

Another motivation of critics of American practices is status. They hope to achieve reputations, among other elites especially, for being original, deep, thoughtful, and *unconventional. Odi profanum vulgus* ("I hate the vulgar crowd") is a fitting slogan. If the middle class likes it—be it conventional morality, patriotism, Ronald Reagan, or even *Rocky,* light beer, cookouts, or Disney World— that alone is enough for many of the elites to disdain it, often with an aura of self-assured moral and intellectual superiority. The goal of life is the acquisition of "advanced" attitudes, in contrast to (in their view) the more crass, unsophisticated, simplistic attitudes of the middle class, of most Americans.

At a gathering of the elite, an often performed ritual is to mention a derided object or individual, followed by a superior laugh and roll of the eyes. As the novelist Tom Wolfe has pointed out, oftentimes in the eighties when elites met they didn't make arguments against Ronald Reagan or his policies; they simply mentioned his name and snickered.

These deep divisions go a long way toward explaining differences in public policy and the tenor and shape of contemporary public discourse. By virtue of their influence, the elites have increasingly shaped the popular culture; they influence much of the debate on social and domestic policy, including matters such as education, drugs, AIDS, abortion, sexual norms, race relations, welfare and poverty, economics, law, and the arts. This confluence has had its effect. "Elites abandoned the ethic of character," George Will has written, "an ethic that encouraged and even enforced right conduct." This abandonment has consequences.

The liberal elite derive from, and draw support from, many quarters. The academy is the one I know best, and it is symptomatic of many of the attitudes to which I am referring. The fundamental convictions and even aspirations of the majority of the American electorate are not at home—indeed they are most unwelcome— among humanities and social science faculty on many university campuses. Many academics have walled themselves off from the rest of America.

Much of this academic world operates on a different set of assumptions as to what constitutes correct social and moral norms. There is often an outright hostility toward the middle class and the values it holds, which academics condescendingly view as those of a philistine "bourgeois" society.

There is of course something inherent in intellectuals that asks uncomfortable questions and challenges common assumptions; indeed, that is one of the intellectual's time-honored tasks, from Socrates, Aristotle, Aquinas, Descartes, Locke, and Hume, to Burke, Mill, Jefferson, Madison, and Lincoln. The ideas advanced by intellectuals have often played a constructive role in history. Their task is to think critically, constructively, with respect for the evidence, and in pursuit of wisdom.

Unfortunately many of today's intellectuals have overstepped the bounds of common sense and seem to have given up on the disinterested pursuit of truth. They have hitched their intellect to the service of ideology. It seems that for many their whole purpose is to stand in opposition to what most Americans believe. But that is not being an intellectual; it is being a crank. The social critic Lionel Trilling coined the phrase "adversary culture" to describe the disdain many intellectuals hold toward the rest of society. And the would-be intellectuals follow suit.

For example, the American people overwhelmingly elected and reelected Ronald Reagan president. Most Americans saw him as a strong, able leader whose view of the world was steady and whole. I don't think most Americans cared whether he was a man of overpowering intellect. They cared more that he was a man of correct *beliefs,* of right *sentiments.* What James Barbour, a former governor and senator from Virginia, wrote of James Madison is what many Americans felt toward Ronald Reagan: "The good genius of his country was in him personified."

Many academics, on the other hand, viewed Reagan as a reactionary, unsophisticated, racist, insensitive, trigger-happy Cold Warrior who wanted to lead America back to the Dark Ages. It was not uncommon to hear on a university campus the term "fascist" used to describe Ronald Reagan.

If Reagan was unpopular among most liberals—and he was—he was the absolute bane of the intellectuals. The things that he and his supporters stood for, the values he tried to embody, his pride in this nation, were an affront to virtually everything that most intellectuals hold dear. Their hostility was particularly fierce against other academics who supported Reagan; there was a sense that we academic Reagan supporters should have "known better" because we were more "sophisticated," more "cultivated," and more knowledgeable. These same intellectuals—furious because of the many good things that happened on Ronald Reagan's watch—are now engaged in an all-out effort to trash his presidency and his legacy.

The art community is another example of those whose opinions are both of, and help shape, the attitudes of the liberal elite. Perhaps nowhere is there a more unremittingly hostile view of middle-class life and values than among the artistic community and their spokesmen. Jerry Muller, who teaches modern European history at the Catholic University of America in Washington, D.C., tells us how far we have fallen (*Commentary*, February 1991):

> If we had an Index of Leading Cultural Indicators, the level to which our public culture has dropped might be charted by the fact that in the summer and autumn quarters of 1990, our dominant cultural elites were unable or unwilling to explain why the exhibition of photographs of a man with a bull whip in his anus [Mueller is referring here to the famous, or infamous, Robert Mapplethorpe exhibit] should not be subsidized by the national government. Indeed, those who insisted that this was not an achievement worthy of collective support were angrily and contemptuously characterized by most of the cultural establishment as intellectual Neanderthals, too primitive to comprehend the nature of culture, which we were told must necessarily be committed to the exploration of ever-new areas of experience. This reveals a deficit of moral resources far deeper and more troubling than our more noted budget and trade deficits.

Tom Wolfe has described the ridiculous scene of thousands of artists *screaming* for taxpayer money, but with no strings attached, all in order to shock, abuse, and ridicule taxpayers' most deeply held convictions and values. They think they have a constitutional right to be subsidized. As Wolfe has said, "I think the National Endowment for the Arts is one of the great comic spectacles of our time. You only have to imagine some poor, rejected former NEA artist going to Voltaire or Solzhenitsyn, and saying, 'They're attaching strings to my money! I went to the government for money for my art and they're attaching strings to it!' The horse laugh that even Solzhenitsyn—who is not given to horse laughs—would have given them would be marvelous to hear."

Most of the art that has been the subject of the great public funding controversies of the late eighties and nineties is nothing we would grieve at losing. In fact, we ought to cheer its passing. The "controversial" art so often heard about is often a bad joke. But it is not a harmless bad joke; it has serious repercussions. Irving Kristol has pointed out that "what the 'arts community' is engaged in is a politics of radical nihilism; it has little interest in, and will openly express contempt for, 'art' in any traditional sense of the term."

Yet when some sensible people say that bad art does not deserve to be funded out of the public kitty, they are criticized. Here's the usual sequence in Washington: A piece of "controversial" art is funded by the National Endowment for the Arts. Someone finds out about it and, if it is not too graphic, publishes a picture in the paper. (If it is too offensive to publish, it is usually described euphemistically as "provocative" or "explicit.") Average citizens are properly troubled by this revelation and shake their heads in bewilderment. In response a few conservative congressmen get together and say an end should be put to public financing of the art piece in question.

Artists, liberal representatives, some journalists, and pseudo-sophisticates of every stripe react with outrage. Charges are repeated like an incantation; cries of "censorship," "violation of free speech," and "Jesse Helms" are heard throughout the land. They would have you believe that Orwell's *1984* has arrived.

The expressed outrage of the art community lacks any sense of propriety, or proportion, or reality. Perhaps that is because its members are not living in reality. They're talking in ridiculously solemn terms about how America is about to become a fascist state. The official arts lobby of Washington and its apologists decry the public's intolerance—and in the process they utter some of Washington's greatest foolishness.

And they usually draw support from the media. Researchers at the Center for Media and Public Affairs analyzed 234 news and opinion pieces—in *The New York Times*, *The Washington Post*, and on the ABC, CBS, and NBC evening newscasts—dealing with "controversial" art. They found almost unanimous negativity toward congressional Republicans who criticized NEA funding of pornography or spoke out against 2 Live Crew–type obscenity. Typical was columnist Anthony Lewis of *The New York Times*, who wrote that "a small band of religious zealots and right wing opportunists is trying to show the world that America is an intolerant puritan country, contemptuous of artists."

Early in my government career I clashed with some members of President Reagan's Committee on the Arts and Humanities for their questioning the almost unchallenged assumption that the arts and humanities were severely underfunded. It amazed me to see how many well-intentioned supporters of Ronald Reagan had been so easily co-opted by the liberal elite. The Achilles' heel of some members of the Reagan crowd was the invitation to serve on an exclusive arts committee. They forgot conservative principles and were swept off their feet by the "prestige" of being associated with the arts lobby.

During a meeting with top Reagan assistant Michael Deaver, I objected to a medal designed by a New York artist consultant to the Presidential Commission on the Arts and Humanities. The medal, meant to commemorate the twentieth anniversary of federal support for the arts and humanities, bore the likeness of a nude woman with her limbs stretched out in an awkward, "inviting" pose. It was ugly, obscene, and not the sort of thing with which I thought Ronald Reagan should be associated. I told Deaver so. He thought I was being prudish; I thought he was being trendy and juvenile. Fortunately, the medal got lost in the process. It never saw the light of day.

If the arts and humanities are not receiving the kind of money they should, it is mainly because of what artists and humanists have done to their craft. They have debased the currency. In fact, generous government grants are responsible for much of the undistinguished art littering the landscape. If we had less government subsidy we would have less of it.

There is, of course, good art, music and painting, but sometimes you need to search to find it. My wife Elayne and I and our friends and neighbors enjoyed wonderful evenings at the John F. Kennedy Center for the Performing Arts, watching Les Miserables, listening to the National Symphony, and taking our children to The Nutcracker. But we were also on more than one occasion dismayed by some of what we saw at this revered center of Washington cultural life.

*   *   *

The arts matter not only because they matter to people of prominence and power, or because there is a heated debate in Washington about art funding; they matter also in a far more fundamental way—because they are among the instruments, the bearings and trappings of civilization that are a means of educating the young. They matter because on canvas, in paint, and in photographs they say something about who we are, what we think, and what we believe. Because these things are public, children see them and take something away from them.

If we believe that good art, good music, and good books will elevate taste and improve the sensibilities of the young—which they certainly do—then we must also believe that bad music, bad art, and bad books will degrade. As a society, as communities, as policymakers, we must come to grips with that truth.

The battle over culture reaches beyond art, music, poetry, photography, literature, cinema, and drama. The broader issue has to do with a growing realization that over the last twenty years or so the traditional values of the American people have come under steady fire, with the heavy artillery supplied by intellectuals. This all-out assault has taken its toll. In our time, too many Americans became either embarrassed, unwilling, or unable to explain with assurance to our children and to one another the difference between right and wrong, between what is helpful and what is destructive, what is ennobling and what is degrading. The fabric of support that the American people—families especially—could traditionally find in the culture at large became worn, torn, and unraveled.

In this period, many of us lost confidence in our right and our duty to affirm publicly the desirability of what most of us believe privately. We allow our social and cultural institutions to drift away from their moorings; we allowed the public square to become, in Richard John Neuhaus's term, "naked." We ceased being clear about the standards which we hold and the principles by which we judge, or, if we were clear in our own minds, we somehow abdicated the area of public discussion and institutional decision making to those who challenged our traditional values. As a result, we suffered a cultural breakdown of sorts—in areas like education, family life, crime, and drug use, as well as in our attitudes toward sex, individual responsibility, civic duty, and public service.

We have much to worry about when we consider the environment, the public *ethos* in which we raise our children. Our society is made up of a network of institutions, cultural beliefs, mores, and habits. Individuals live in environments in which certain ideas prevail, certain messages are sent. And these messages act to encourage or discourage particular attitudes and behaviors. It makes an enormous difference, for example, whether children get messages from television telling them that honesty is the best policy, and to honor their fathers and mothers—or messages telling them that adultery is the norm, and that the breakup of a family is an expected thing. Likewise, if schools, churches, elected officials, community institutions, and neighborhoods are reinforcing parents' efforts, it makes their jobs easier. If the institutions of society work at cross-purposes (as they often have over the last two decades), the job is harder.

No man is a good citizen alone, Plato teaches us in his dialogue *Gorgias*. And so individuals and families need support, their values need nourishment, in the common culture, in the public arena. Our common culture is not something manufactured by the upper stratum of society in the elegant salons of Washington, New York, or Cambridge. Rather, it embodies truths that most Americans can recognize and examine for themselves. These truths are passed down from generation to generation, transmitted in the family, in the classroom, and in our churches and synagogues. They reside in what Burke called the "moral imagination" of the nation. And today, the moral imagination of most Americans is, I believe, sound.

But far too many decent Americans still remain, in effect, on the moral defensive before their own social and cultural institutions. We cannot hope to reclaim our culture until we reclaim these institutions. This task will be a central—perhaps *the* central—political debate of the 1990s.

Can Americans be confident that their children are going to inherit the habits and values they themselves honor? Are we confident they will be raised in an environment that properly nurtures their moral and intellectual qualities? Can we have confidence in the cultural signals our children receive from our educational institutions, from the media, from the world of the arts, even from our churches? Are we confident that our society is transmitting to our young the right messages, teaching them the right lessons, about the family, drug use, respect for religious beliefs, and our meaning as a nation and our responsibilities as individuals? Is the public air conducive to moral and intellectual health? I believe that most Americans would still answer "no" to these questions.

Even social scientists now recognize the importance of sound values and moral norms in the upbringing of children. Empirical studies confirm what most people, because of their basic common sense, already know. What determines a young person's behavior in academic, sexual, and social life are his deeply held convictions and beliefs. They determine behavior far more than race, class, economic background, or ethnicity. Nature abhors a vacuum; so does a child's soul. If that soul is not filled with noble sentiments, with virtue, if we do not attend to the "better angels of our nature," it will be filled by something else. These matters are of overwhelming importance to our children. As the Roman scholar Pliny the Elder put it, "What we do to our children, they will do to society." Looking today at what we see many kids doing to themselves, to others, and to society at large, we need to reflect on what society collectively is doing to them in the critical task of inculturation, the passing on of our values, in an often hostile atmosphere.

I started my career in government as a philosophical conservative. Conservativism as I understand it is not essentially theoretical or ideological, but rather a practical matter of experience. It seeks to conserve the best elements of the past. ("What is conservatism?" Lincoln once asked. "Is it not adherence to the old and tried, against the new and untried?") It understands the important role that traditions, institutions, habits and authority have in our social life together, and recognizes many of our national institutions as products of principles developed over time by custom, the lessons of experience, and consensus. Conservatives are interested in pursuing policies that will better reinforce and encourage the best of our people's common culture, habits, and beliefs. Conservatism, too, is based on the belief that the social order rests upon a moral base, and that what ties us together as a people—the *unum* in *e pluribus unum*—is in constant need of support.

I remained conservative, outspokenly and proudly so. Because of this I was subjected to a steady drumbeat of criticism by the liberals and the elites. I'm reporting here, not complaining. It was bearable and I hit back. And I believe it's a fair judgment to say that I refused to adjust my views to the prevailing elite dogmas; I didn't "grow" (meaning become more liberal) in office. In fact, as time went on—having heard all the arguments of the liberals and the elites—I left government more conservative than when I started. The old saw that a neoconservative is a liberal who has been mugged by reality applies to me. I'm more conservative today, not because of an allegiance to an abstract political theory, but because of what I have seen with my own eyes, traveling up and down and back and forth across America and visiting hundreds of cities and schools over nine years.

Public policy differences among liberals and conservatives, between elites and nonelites, involve far more than chalking up debate points over abstract issues. Lives are literally at stake. And I believe the sheer bankruptcy of so many liberal solutions (a number of which will be discussed in this book)—the social and cultural cost they have exacted, the children who have suffered—is the most compelling case against contemporary liberalism.

After nine years of public service and heading up three government offices, I have come to the conclusion that the issues surrounding the culture and our values are the most important ones. The convictions and principles that guide us are the most important factors in the improvement of our life together. They are at the heart of our resolution of the knottiest problems of public policy, whether the subject be education, art, race relations, drugs, crime, or the raising of children. In a country "dedicated to a proposition," dedicated to self-evident truths and self-government, the ideas of the mind and the "habits of the heart" (in de Tocqueville's phrase) determine almost all important issues. One function of public policy, then, is to recognize the importance of these things, to encourage their development, and to make sure that they are at the vital center of our national life.

The critical cultural questions we need to ask are: Are our social and cultural institutions worthy of the American people? Do they promote the qualities and habits and values we would wish? If they do not, we need to see to it that they are reformed. This task requires appropriate government policies, but it goes beyond government.

Contrary to much of the conventional wisdom in Washington, no amount of public policy tinkering with structures, programs and approaches can substitute for these values. We must develop a fair appreciation for the real strengths and limitations of government effort on behalf of children. Government, obviously, cannot fill a child's emotional, spiritual, or moral needs. Government is not a father or a mother. Great as it might be, government has never raised a child. And it never will.

This does not absolve government of its responsibilities. Government, through law, discourse, and example, can legitimize and delegitimize certain acts. In a free society, where the people decide, leaders must understand that few things they do matter more than speaking about the right things in the right way. I believe (with qualification) that statecraft is soulcraft. But we need to remember that families, churches, schools, and individuals are the primary agents in the development of a people's moral disposition. Government is an auxiliary. The state does not, cannot, and even should not always pick up where families and individuals leave off. In the end, whether a decent society will flourish or decay depends more on what families, churches, and schools do than on most of what goes on in congressional committees, the courts, state houses, or even the White House. Regeneration comes from within.

After certain necessary functions of government are performed—providing police protection, ensuring basic order and safety, providing for highways, a social safety net, and the like—the American people understand that the institutions of family, church, and neighborhood will bring about more positive change than is within the power of governments—federal, state, or local—to do.

As PBS film critic Michael Medved has said (Shavano Institute, November 1990):

> What matters ultimately in the culture wars is what we do in our daily lives—not the big statements that we broadcast to the world at large, but the small messages we send through our families and our neighborhoods and our communities. . . . The future will depend not so much on the movers and shakers in the centers of power, but on the hopes that we generate in our own communities, our schools, our churches, synagogues, and families.

The lessons I have learned over and over again in the last decade are the theses of this book. The American people's sense of things is in most instances right; the liberal elite's sense of things is in most instances wrong. Still and all, the elite exercise enormous influence in shaping public policy and the terms of public debate (for reasons I will elaborate on later). In this book, I will candidly spell out the differences in thinking on critical issues: drugs, education, race relations, religion, and the common culture.

Too often, the American people have deferred to the views of the elite on these matters. When they have done so, they have for the most part hurt themselves, their interests, their beliefs, and most important, their children. When they have heeded the elites, things have gotten worse—sometimes a lot worse. The cultural debate is fundamentally important to the life of the nation. Our institutions, practices, and policies—in education, drugs, racial matters, and other issues—will not improve until we get the underlying principles right. That's what this book is about—getting cultural issues right, explaining why they matter and why getting them right involves one hell of a fight.

1

CRISIS IN AMERICAN EDUCATION

There's a Chuck Berry song that goes in part, "I got a chance, I oughta take it." Well, I got my chance when President Reagan asked me to be Secretary of Education in 1985, and I was going to take it. I didn't want to leave that job and say to myself, "Boy, when I was Secretary, I wish I had said such and such." I've always tried to say what I really thought while I held a post, not later; to speak truthfully and not to leave with a lot of "I should have saids." I hate it when you don't find out what government officials really think until after they leave office and write a "revealing" memoir. "Retirement candor" cheapens the currency; it makes people suspicious of what people say when they are in the job. At least I can say that when I had my chance I took it.

"How can anyone who [cares] about children not feel terrible about Chicago schools?" This was the question I put to the city during a November 1987 visit while I was Secretary of Education. For about $4,000 per student per year, Chicagoans were supporting a public school system in which nearly half of the children who entered the public school system dropped out before graduating from high school, many to become involved in lives of welfare dependency, drugs, or violent crime. When the scores of the American College Testing (ACT) Program (a standard college-entrance exam) were disclosed, more than *half* of the city's public schools reported high school senior scores in the *bottom 1 percent* of schools nationwide.

The Chicago public school system—the nation's third largest

39

after Los Angeles and New York—was "the worst in the nation," I said. "You have an educational meltdown." (An employee of the Chicago public school system later insisted, "We are not the worst public school system in America. Detroit is worse." I told him that he was guilty of what Justice Holmes called "low aspirations.")

And practically everyone in Chicago—parents, employers, other teachers, and the schoolchildren themselves—knew it. In recent years we've seen some efforts at improvement, but the seventies and eighties in Chicago saw countless thousands of young lives ruined, and still today, tens of thousands of children are not being educated. According to the *Chicago Tribune* (in a full-page editorial written at the end of a tough, unflinching investigative series in 1988), "The Chicago public schools are so bad, they are hurting so many thousands of children so terribly, they are jeopardizing the future of the city so much that drastic solutions must be found."

The *Tribune* series charged school administrators with "institutional child neglect."

Here are but a few of the many horror stories documented:

- All 22 students in Grace Currin's 4th-grade class were supposed to attend summer school in 1988 because, their principal said, Currin did not teach the children enough to pass to the next grade. Currin did not hand in a lesson plan all year. Four principals tried unsuccessfully to have Currin fired. "It's a terrible shame," said Dyanne Dandridge-Alexander, a principal. "Those children have suffered because they have a totally inept teacher that no one has been able to fire." Parents who sat in on her classes said they were at a point where they thought it was hopeless. Currin said she did not deserve the negative ratings. "I still think they did not really get to know me as a teacher," she said. "I am part of the problem, but remember, you can't expect miracles when you have low achievers." Currin told the *Tribune* that her career goal was "to retire at full pension."
- Deborah Harris was suspended from Chicago's Shoop Elementary School after she consistently refused to go to her 7th-grade classroom. Each day she gave the principal a doctor's note saying that she should be given "light duties." Harris was told daily, in writing, by the principal and the district

superintendent, to report to class. She hid in the boiler room, according to testimony. The hearing officer ordered Harris reinstated because the board had not given her written notice that she would be fired if she did not go to class. Harris took a leave of absence the day she was reinstated to Curtis Elementary School and never returned. The board appealed the ruling but lost. "We were shocked," one attorney said. "Hearing officers view this as a man's or woman's livelihood. The hearing officer barely mentioned the children."

· In 1987, ten weeks into the first semester, typing students at Du Sable High School had gone through four substitutes, none of them trained to teach typing or certified in any business subject. During the 11th week, a certified typing teacher arrived, and only then did the students learn where to place their hands on the keyboard. Four weeks later, she took a job in private industry. "It's a shame that we have been in this class a whole semester and they still can't find us a teacher," according to one fifteen-year-old, who spent most of one teacherless class putting on makeup and fixing her hair. "We'll probably have to take it over again." Chicago School Superintendent Manford Byrd, Jr., was surprised that such a situation existed. "I'm not aware of that kind of imbalance," he told the *Tribune*. "Our aim is to get regular certified teachers in all the openings. But I don't know if we've ever been in a better shape than we are now."

· The Chicago Board of Education headquarters, called "Pershing Gardens" by school critics, is in a former warehouse that was renovated at a cost of $22 million. The nearly 3,000 people who worked at the offices on the South Side listened to piped-in music, walked on thick carpets, and enjoyed a panoramic view of the city from their 5th-floor cafeteria.

The late Harold Washington, then mayor of Chicago, was outraged by my criticisms of the city's public school system. "Mr. Bennett has a lot of gall to be criticizing Chicago public schools—or any other school system," he said. Chicago Board of Education president Frank Gardner added, "We hope the impact of his statements do [sic] not further demoralize teachers, who are doing an excellent job."

Jacqueline Vaughn, president of the Chicago Teachers Union (CTU), one of the most powerful teacher unions in the country, told a group of teachers, "I resent your efforts being taken for granted and [people] saying we are responsible for the ills in education because, without us, they would have none.

"We are tired of being given mandates, dictates, instructions and directions from everybody when we are not asked to give our input," she said. "We don't tell them [parents and others] what to do in their kitchens, so why should they tell us what to do in our classrooms?" Vaughn elicited frenzied applause from the assembled school employees.

During a joint press conference with Vaughn, I said I'd be more impressed with her union if it made some effort, any effort, to get rid of its bad teachers while rewarding its good ones.

Her reply was Chicago didn't have *any* bad teachers.

In 1983 the National Commission on Excellence in Education released the landmark report *A Nation at Risk,* the closest thing we have had to a national education grievance list. It cited among other problems, poor performance by American students on a variety of international education tests; a decline in scores on most standardized tests; and a decline in student knowledge in crucial subjects such as English and physics. It gave voice to the growing public sense of crisis about our children and their schools. "The educational foundations of our society are presently being eroded by a rising tide of mediocrity that threatens our very future as a nation and a people," the report said. "We have, in effect, been committing an act of unthinking, unilateral educational disarmament." Countless reports since 1983—some issued by me—have further documented a performance that can only charitably be described as mediocre. "American education is to education what the Soviet economy is to the economy," according to Chester E. Finn, Jr., one of the most insightful commentators on American education.

Our students score last in math and science in comparison with students of other industrialized nations. A 1989 international comparison of mathematics and science skills showed American students scoring at the bottom and South Korean students scoring at the top (South Korean students perform at high levels in math at *four times* the rate of U.S. students). Ironically, when asked if they are good at math, 68 percent of American students thought they were (the highest percentage of any country) compared to 23 percent of South Korean students (the lowest percentage of any country), which demonstrates that this country is a lot better at teaching self-esteem than it is at teaching math.

According to the 1991 National Assessment of Educational Progress (NAEP) study, 72 percent of our fourth-graders can do third-grade math, only 14 percent of our eighth-graders can do seventh-grade math, and only 5 percent of our high school seniors "showed an understanding of geometry and algebra that suggested preparedness for the study of relatively advanced mathematics," i.e., for college-level math.

Math and science aren't the only subjects where American students are left in the backwaters of education. Finn and Diane Ravitch, authors of *What Do Our Seventeen Year Olds Know?*, have shown that 43 percent of our high school seniors could not place World War I between 1900 and 1950. More than two-thirds of them did not know even the half-century in which the Civil War took place. And more than 75 percent were unable to say within twenty years when Abraham Lincoln was President.

One-third of high school students tested in 1986 did not know that the Declaration of Independence marked the American colonists' break from England. Sixty percent did not know that *The Federalist Papers* was written to urge ratification of the Constitution, and 40 percent could not say even approximately when the Constitution was written and ratified. Only three students in five were able to recognize a definition of the system of checks and balances that divides power among the three branches of our federal government.

According to an NAEP-based survey of 21-to-25-year-olds conducted in 1986, fewer than 40 percent were able to interpret an article by a newspaper columnist. And the situation is worse among minorities; just one in ten black young adults and two in ten Hispanic young adults can satisfactorily interpret the same newspaper column. In 1989, *National Geographic* did a survey of geography knowledge. Americans aged eighteen to twenty-four finished *last* among ten countries, including Mexico.

Yet in Chicago and in cities and state capitals all across America, instead of rolling up their sleeves and beginning the hard task of improving education, the education establishment—that wide array of professional organizations putatively representing teachers, administrators, and other educators—by and large offers a steady stream of defenses, denials, ultimatums, and repeated calls for more money. Many of these education bureaucrats, or "edu-crats," have abdicated their responsibility; they should abdicate their authority as well. The few who occasionally break rank and point to problems in the system are usually quickly brought back into line or punished. Too often this education establishment it-self is the single greatest obstacle to sound education reform.

When I was in Chicago, I said it was time to challenge the unions, and to "explode the 'blob' "—the bloated education bu-reaucracy, that ever-increasing population of nonteaching per-sonnel. Whether enrollment declines or increases, the blob always grows—setting new guidelines, rules, procedures, and thereby helping to destroy the capacity of schools and communities to run their own schools free of interference. All school districts have a blob, and together they make the American Education Blob. It may be staffed by fine, well-intentioned people, but when they act together, it is a powerful obstacle to educational achievement and school and parental autonomy.

Unfortunately, much of the education establishment, which in-cludes the unions and other "professional" educational organiza-tions, opposes every common-sense reform measure: competency testing for teachers, opening the teaching profession to knowl-edgeable individuals who have not graduated from "schools of education," performance-based pay, holding educators account-able for how much children learn, an end to tenure, a national examination to find out exactly how much our children know, and parental choice of schools. These are reforms most Americans endorse and are all initiatives that I endorsed or proposed legis-latively while I was Secretary of Education. It should come as no surprise, then, that I found myself in constant friction with the education establishment. If you cut through all of the cant and self-justifying rhetoric, you will confront this hard reality: the education establishment opposes reform because it is interested in maintaining *power*. It will fight to expand that power, and it will fight ferociously any attempt to rein it in. In the end, our children pay the highest price. That I would clash with these special inter-ests was thus inevitable. Our clashes became a major feature of my tenure.

On January 29, 1985, the day after my Senate confirmation hear-ing, Mary Hatwood Futrell, the president of the National Education Association (NEA), and some of her colleagues came to my office. The NEA is the largest union in America (with 2 million members and an operating budget of $135 million) and the most influential and powerful force in the education establishment. The NEA initiated the meeting in order to "establish a dialogue" with the Reagan administration. According to a spokesman, the NEA realized that President Reagan was very popular and they were trying to "relax the confrontational attitude that characterized its view of [Reagan's] first term."

Mrs. Futrell indicated that she and her colleagues hoped we would work together. Surely we would disagree from time to time, she told me. Then came the *real* reason for the meeting. Mrs. Futrell told me that she hoped that if we did disagree, we wouldn't do so publicly. Working through our differences privately would be much better than a loud public debate. This is a time for cooperation, she said, not confrontation.

I told Mrs. Futrell and her colleagues that it was in the public's interest for such a debate to occur, and that it was important for the people who could fix the schools—the American people—to have a candid conversation about what was wrong and what needed to be done. I told her that I wanted to lead that conversation.

I went further than etiquette requires, certainly a good deal further than normal Washington etiquette extends, and told her that the NEA was a big part of the problem. Then came the thinly veiled threat: if there was going to be a public debate, Mrs. Futrell warned, it would certainly have its unpleasant moments.

I told her that we should lay out our differences and let the American people decide with whom they agree. (Following our meeting, Mrs. Futrell told reporters: "If he is as honest and frank with the President as he has been with us, I have no doubt about him.")

The meeting was over. But the battle over American education was just beginning. It was inevitable. And it was a fight very much worth having. The whole world of elementary, secondary, and higher education had become complacent and sloppy and needed nothing less than shock therapy. I appointed myself the hot wire, and I would not be shy about zapping a number of targets at once.

What I had not fully anticipated was the degree of fury that my recommendations, proposals, and ideas would generate. According to a *Washington Post* article that appeared early in my tenure (with a headline that proclaimed, to my pleasure, "Education Chief Rapped for Supporting Parents"), "Some of the nation's established education organizers sharply criticized Education Secretary William J. Bennett . . . for his support of federal rules giving parents more control over 'sensitive' subject areas taught in public schools."

In a news conference, I said, "It's not hard, if one looks at the last fifteen years of education, to understand why parents are distressed. . . . Parents have been burned in the past [and] there are a lot of things in schools that don't belong there."

Claudia Mansfield, of the American Association of School Administrators, was shocked. "I don't believe it," she said of my comments. "That is not good news."

Nancy Young, speaking for the NEA, said, "It's not what we expected. . . . A national person should not be imposing their [sic] views on local parents."

Clearly the education establishment was not prepared for a public debate on what was wrong, who was responsible, and how to fix it.

Instead, the education establishment had insisted that any education reform must be done in consultation with, and ultimately the approval of, the pedagogical organizations they dominated. A September 1985 editorial in a leading education journal, *Phi Delta Kappan,* complained:

> An ideology that is out of touch with those who administer public education may get in the way. Bennett talks about his "Three C's"—content, character, and choice—but as he talks he looks past the leadership of public education. He brings his crusade to the American public, citing public opinion polls, but overlooking the channels that must inevitably convey his message.

I entered the Cabinet believing that if the education reform movement was to succeed, it had to rest on the conviction that the public schools belong to the public, not the experts, not social scientists, not professionals, not an education establishment, not the elite. "I do not work for the education establishment," I said in an interview. "I work for the American people."

That may have surprised some in the education establishment. The anticipation was that because of my work in the humanities I would be an intellectual standard-bearer for education. Certainly I tried. But I think they also expected a Secretary who would mainly travel the commencement circuit and not ruffle any feathers, a kind of Alistair Cooke-as-Education Secretary. Polite nudging, exhortations to improvement, and gentle invocations—along with a lot more money—were what many in the establishment expected of me. They thought I was there to do their bidding, in a conventional, nonconfrontational way. (Ironically, my former teacher John Silber was my chief competitor for the job of Education Secretary. I later heard that one of the reasons I was chosen over Silber was the fear that John would turn out to be "too controversial.")

But what was needed was not exhortation or lectures. What was needed was more on the order of a demolition squad. My target was the entire mediocre education enterprise in America, and my goal was to replace it with a better one. That meant going head-to-head with the guardians of the education system—its powerful interest groups, its political protectors on Capitol Hill, its assumption of full entitlement to the public purse, and its pathetic performance record.

It's worth recounting briefly here a summary of the creation of the Department of Education as described by a Democrat, Joseph Califano, the former Secretary of Health, Education, and Welfare, in his book *Governing America*. Califano wrote about his experience with the NEA in 1977:

> The NEA representatives were more immediately interested in money and a Cabinet-level Department of Education. I told them that I intended to seek substantial increases in federal funds for education, but that I saw little hope of achieving, in four years, the NEA goal of raising from 9 to 33 percent the federal share of the total cost of elementary and secondary education. (I did not express my own reservations about the desirability of the objective.) They nodded their understanding. "What about a Department of Education?" McFarland [Stan McFarland, a top NEA representative] then asked.
>
> "We may not agree on that," I responded. McFarland immediately reminded me of Carter's commitment to the NEA. "That's why the NEA, for the first time in its history, endorsed a candidate for President."

This was political muscle. A *quid* had been given (the endorsement of Carter), and it was time to collect the *quo* (a Cabinet department and an increased share of the federal budget). The assumption had been that the Department of Education would be a wholly owned subsidiary of the education establishment and the special-interest organizations. The people who had the most to do with creating the department had been assured that it would work hand-in-glove with the education powers that be. In particular, they believed the Secretary of Education would be *their* spokesman, *their* representative, *their* creation.

With big money pouring into education and with the rise of unionism, the special interests began to control American education. The teacher unions (especially the NEA) and the professional associations increasingly began to show their muscle. Power was slipping away from parents and individual schools and toward them, which was fine as far as the unions were concerned. According to reporter Robin Wilson of *The Chronicle of Higher Education*, the NEA "has attacked parents' moves to gain more control, saying that they have gone overboard and that teachers cannot be effective under parental veto power."

Some of the largest education interests also increasingly aligned themselves with the political philosophy of the left, with the notion that education problems, like most other social issues, were amenable to solutions from Washington. This meant ever more and ever larger programs created and controlled by Washington, and guided and fine-tuned by those who "knew best"—the education establishment itself.

The modern-day NEA is primarily a political action organization. It routinely takes liberal and even left-wing stands on political candidates and on many national and international affairs. In recent years, the union's Representative Assembly went on record in favor of teacher strikes; school-based clinics dispensing contraceptives; a nuclear freeze; gay rights; the Equal Rights Amendment; D.C. statehood; and Jimmy Carter, Walter Mondale, and Michael Dukakis for president. It has voted against merit pay for teachers; parental choice; voluntary school prayer; state takeovers of bad schools; home schooling; English as the official language; drug, alcohol, and AIDS testing; nuclear power plants; aid to the Nicaraguan resistance; the nomination of Judge Robert Bork to the Supreme Court; and Ronald Reagan and George Bush for president. And at the 1991 NEA convention, while adopting a measure calling on its members and union publication to monitor attacks on First Amendment rights such as freedom of speech, the NEA invoked a separate policy adopted by the board of directors which ousted the Boy Scouts of America from the convention exhibition hall. Some delegates were also prohibited from displaying anti-abortion material. Asked to explain this contradiction, NEA president Keith Geiger said it was a "paradox."

"I don't apologize for it," he said. "I don't try to explain it."

The record then is clear and beyond dispute: the NEA is an organization embodying the philosophy of modern-day liberalism. When power is seized by, or ceded to, an organization of this political and philosophical temperament, it has consequences.

In my visits to schools all over the country, I met and saw many fine teachers; some were members of the NEA who felt that the increasing politicization of their union was doing a tremendous disservice to their profession. Many teachers do not want to get involved in politics in general and liberal political activism in particular, but they feel powerless to resist it. According to C. Emily Feistritzer, director of the National Center for Education Information, "In recent years . . . the NEA's agendas have seemed to veer further and further away from representing the interests of teachers. It is spending millions of dollars annually to support political positions and candidates representing views that increasingly seem at odds with those of teachers." For example:

- More than half of the NEA membership voted for Ronald Reagan both in 1980 and 1984. (The NEA hasn't released data about how its membership voted in the 1988 election.)
- Two-thirds of teachers polled by the NEA in 1985–86 classified their political philosophy as conservative or leaning toward conservative.
- Despite the official positions of the NEA, 79 percent of public school principals, 82 percent of private-school teachers, and 69 percent of teachers in public schools believe "paying teachers based on job performance in addition to seniority and level of education" would strengthen teaching as a profession.
- In addition, 88 percent of public school principals, 84 percent of private school teachers and 80 percent of teachers in public schools agreed that having "upward mobility within the ranks of teaching, i.e., career ladders," would strengthen teaching as a profession.

I found many teachers to be much better and a lot more sensible than what one would guess from listening to some of their union leaders. Soon after I took over at Education, for instance, Albert Shanker, president of the American Federation of Teachers, told a conference, "You can raise salaries and improve some conditions, but if teachers are isolated and locked in a room with a bunch of kids for 25 years, that's not exactly an appetizing prospect for adults." I knew Shanker's statement constituted a false representation of teacher attitudes and was a disservice to the profession, and I said so. When Americans hear

> the head of the teachers' union saying something about the unappetizing prospect of spending six hours a day with children—when emergency room nurses and cops and firefighters hear this, they say, "Give me a break!" If the education reform movement is simply to constitute one great excuse for the leaders of teacher unions to gripe on a massive scale, then it's going to hurt the education reform movement and it's going to hurt . . . teachers. Sooner or later, Americans get tired of people who are always complaining.

When the National Education Association released a report that showed inflation-adjusted teacher salaries had risen more sharply in 1985–86 than at any time since the 1950s, NEA president Mary Futrell expressed the union's cash-register mentality when she said she was "gloomy" about the financial condition of the nation's schools.

"There they go again," I said in response. "Only the NEA could be gloomy in reporting that teachers' salaries have increased by 7.3 percent while the rate of inflation is only 3.2 percent. Most Americans will think this is good news. Teachers' salaries are increasing, education reform is continuing, and the NEA should stop moaning, cheer up, and help out in the effort for better schools and teachers."

Because of the effects that the guiding philosophy of the NEA and other large education organizations have had on traditional American educational practices, many of our schools lost their focus, their confidence, and a clear sense of their mission. This helped open the way for an all-out assault from the Far Left, and our schools were systematically, culturally deconstructed. Many of the things which mattered most in our schools were removed, and they were set adrift. As a result, today many schools (and many education spokesmen) are no longer able to answer the basic institutional, existential questions: Who are we? Why are we here? And where are we going? I heard these questions endlessly, constantly, in many places, especially in summer programs for high school teachers which I had conducted in the early seventies, and in many visits to schools from 1975 to 1988.

Although there are many reasons for America's educational decline, none is more important than the fact that many educators have forgotten the answer to the basic question: What is the purpose of school? My view, to put it simply, is that the purpose of school is to make students both smarter and better, to develop intellect and moral character. When the American people are asked what they want from our schools, they consistently put two tasks at the top of their list: first, teach our children how to speak, write, read, think and count correctly; and second, help them to develop reliable standards of right and wrong that will guide them through life.

Last year I was at an education conference in California and repeated this view. It was promptly criticized by four state commissioners of education. They had other, more complicated missions in mind: to make America a more "just" society; to help students "cope" with life; to increase "global awareness"; and change the shape and focus of America. These are individuals who have the major responsibility for administering their states' public education programs and they are not in sync with the public that put them there, and for whom they work. At a break in the conference, many teachers in attendance came up to me and voiced their agreement with what I said. They told me that their jobs would be a lot better if they were free to focus on the two areas the public wants them to address.

What, then, to do? We must give greater attention to a sound common curriculum emphasizing English, history, geography, math, and science. To do this we have to understand why these subjects were thrown out or weakened in the cultural deconstruction of our schools of the last twenty-five years.

In the late sixties and seventies we saw a sustained attack on traditional American values and the place where those values had long had a comfortable and congenial home—the school. Many of the elite correctly understood that civilization's major task is the upbringing of children; if they could alter the ways we raised children by changing the way we teach them, they could then alter American society to suit their view of the world. Academics provided much of the intellectual heavy artillery—citing how endemically corrupt and sick America is. Once the traditional teachings were discredited and then removed, the vacuum was filled by faddish nonsense, and the kids lost.

The gradual watering down of the high school curriculum was one result of this then-fashionable elite critique of America. Schools, like so many other institutions of our society, were seen as "repressive, coercive" institutions, the curriculum as an instrument of oppression, and their students as little better than prisoners. This attitude was summed up by the then liberal critic Neil Postman, who co-authored a book in the late 1960s, *Teaching As a Subversive Activity*. At the time he believed, "The institution we call school is what it is because we made it that way. If it is irrelevant; if it shields children from reality; if it educates for obsolescence; if it is based on fear; if it induces alienation; if it punishes creativity and independence"—and Postman clearly believed at the time that it did all these things—"it must be changed." (Postman later wrote another book, *Teaching As a Conserving Activity*, in which he recanted his original views.)

According to this view, it was wrong to make students do things they didn't want to do, whether math, homework, or other distasteful pursuits like sitting quietly in a classroom. Testing "dehumanized" students and reduced them to mere "statistics." Basic courses gave way to trendy courses; homework was thought to be outdated and unnecessary.

Too few adults stood their ground to answer the challenge, and to answer the question "Why?" Why, for example, are English, history, math, and science important subjects? Adults sitting on school boards or state boards of education became reluctant to articulate what was academically important and what was not, and lost clarity about what we expected our schools to do. These doubts were of a piece with the reluctance to answer questions like "Why not?" take drugs and "Why not?" occupy the offices of college presidents to protest the Vietnam War. Many in positions of responsibility forgot the answers to these questions—or lost the courage to offer them.

This confusion and diffidence had particularly damaging effects on school curricula, effects we still feel today. According to *A Nation at Risk*:

> Secondary school curricula have been homogenized, diluted, and diffused to the point that they no longer have a central purpose. In effect, we have a cafeteria-style curriculum in which the appetizers and desserts can easily be mistaken for the main course.

English, history, math, and science gave way to a curriculum lacking substance, coherence, or consistent structure; it was replaced by faddish, trivial, and intellectually shallow courses. If you give the average fifteen-year-old the choice of trigonometry or, say, "Rock and Roll as Poetry" and "Baja Whale Watch," many will opt to take the latter—not because they're stupid or bad kids, but simply because they're teenagers. So schools became laboratories, and students guinea pigs. If there was a bad idea in the land, often the first place it was tried was in the school. If we had problems of order in the classroom, the solution was an open classroom and no order at all. If our students weren't learning history, the solution was not to teach them history but to teach them social studies, often a sloppy amalgam of half-baked, "politically correct" sociological theories.

Increasingly, parents became alienated or disenfranchised from their schools and yielded to the cult of "expertise," the authority of superintendents, "education judges" or administrative bodies. And, as the teachers tell us, more and more parents dropped their children at the doorstep of the school and were gone to pursue their own interests. So parents disenfranchised themselves. When serious teachers are asked the single most important improvement that could be made in education, they invariably say greater involvement and cooperation on the part of parents.

On issue after issue the common sense of the public was pushed aside for the agenda of the experts. Few issues illustrated this better than the debate about bilingual education. In September 1985 I proposed new federal policies for bilingual education— "one of the most controversial issues in American education," according to *The New York Times*. In a speech to the Association for a Better New York, I called for deregulating federal bilingual education programs to give local school districts more flexibility in choosing teaching methods, and I strongly advocated making students fluent in English, rather than promoting knowledge of their native languages and cultures. Over the years, government programs in bilingual education gradually had become confused as to purpose and overbearing as to means. As a result, too many children failed to become fluent in English. Before federal money and federal programs became available, many immigrants learned English early, quickly, and well. Now, with a special federal program, fewer were learning English. We were moving backward. After $1.7 billion of federal funding, I concluded, we had no evidence that the children whom we sought to help—the children who deserve our help—had benefited.

I outlined the underlying rationale for changes in federal policies:

> To be a citizen is to share in something common—in common principles, common memories, and a common language in which to discuss our common affairs. Our common language is, of course, English. And our common task is to ensure that our non-English speaking children learn this common language. . . . The responsibility of the federal government must be to help ensure that local schools succeed in teaching non-English speaking students English, so that every American enjoys access to the opportunities of American society.

Following my remarks, the bilingual education groups reacted with sound and fury. The National Association for Bilingual Education called the proposals "a smokescreen for cutting bilingual programs." The executive director of Aspira of New York, a Puerto Rican community group, described his reaction as "one of despair and frustration and anger." The chairman of the Congressional Hispanic Caucus said the Hispanic community viewed my policies as "an act of war" on children whose primary language is not English, and that they reflected a "record of calculated indifference and callous neglect" toward minority-language children.

I pointed out that many foreign-language minorities, particularly Asian-Americans, don't *want* bilingual education because they want their children to learn English. "So, I think, do Hispanic parents, but some of the pressure groups just won't have it," I said. The vast majority of Hispanic parents believe their children should learn English as quickly as possible.

When I visited a Tucson, Arizona, school later that year, some of my critics "arranged" to have the third-grade students read essays to me about the importance of the "native language" to them. "Please, Mr. Bennett," one eight-year-old wrote, "don't take our heritage away from us." My opponents were using the children for crass political purposes, in an attempt to embarrass me and to make their point. But many Hispanic citizens encouraged me to stick to my guns, and I did.

So it went. For three and a half years, my efforts to challenge American education met well-organized institutional resistance, most often from the educational establishment: teacher unions, education lobbyists, and bureaucrats—all groups skilled at the exercise of narrow, self-interested political power. Early on, their opposition appeared as a form of denial—the schools were not so bad as they seemed. A little later, the opposition took a different tack, admitting that things might be bad, but insisting that they could not be fixed in or by the schools—that first "society" or "the system" must be altered. More recently we heard what might be called opposition by extortion, the false claim that fixing our schools would require a fortune in new funding.

But the fundamental problem with American education today is not lack of money; we do not underspend, we underproduce. A review of some 150 studies shows no correlation between spending and educational achievement. The American people have been remarkably generous in their contributions to our schools. In 1990 we spent $414 billion on education, roughly $140 billion more than on national defense. In the international competition on education spending, the United States wins the gold medal. In absolute terms we spend more on education than any other nation in the world. And expenditures keep climbing. In 1950, we spent (in 1989 dollars) $1,333 per student. In 1989, we spent $4,931. As John Silber, the president of Boston University, has written, "It is troubling that this nearly fourfold increase in real spending has brought no improvement. It is scandalous that it has not prevented substantial decline." During that period we probably experienced the *worst* educational decline in our history. Between 1963 and 1980, for example, combined average Scholastic Aptitude Test (SAT) scores—scores which test students' verbal and math abilities—fell 90 points, from 980 to 890.

*   *   *

Improving American education requires not doing new things but doing (and remembering) some good old things. At the time of our nation's founding, Thomas Jefferson listed the requirements for a sound education in the Report of the Commissioners for the University of Virginia. In this landmark statement on American education, Jefferson wrote of the importance of calculation and writing, and of reading, history, and geography. But he also emphasized the need "to instruct the mass of our citizens in these, their rights, interests, and duties, as men and citizens." Jefferson believed education should aim at the improvement of both one's "morals" and "faculties." That has been the dominant view of the aims of American education for over two centuries. But a number of changes, most of them unsound, have diverted schools from these great pursuits. And the story of the loss of the school's original moral mission explains a great deal.

Starting in the early seventies, "values clarification" programs started turning up in schools all over America. According to this philosophy, the schools were not to take part in their time-honored task of transmitting sound moral values; rather, they were to allow the child to "clarify" his own values (which adults, including parents, had no "right" to criticize). The "values clarification" movement didn't clarify values, it clarified wants and desires. This form of moral relativism said, in effect, that no set of values was right or wrong; everybody had an equal right to his own values; and all values were subjective, relative, personal. This destructive view took hold with a vengeance.

In 1985 *The New York Times* published an article quoting New York area educators, in slavish devotion to this new view, proclaiming that "they deliberately avoid trying to tell students what is ethically right and wrong." The article told of one counseling session involving fifteen high school juniors and seniors. In the course of that session a student concluded that a fellow student had been foolish to return one thousand dollars she found in a purse at school. According to the article, when the youngsters asked the counselor's opinion, "He told them he believed the girl had done the right thing, but that, of course, he would not try to force his values on them. 'If I come from the position of what is right and what is wrong,' he explained, 'then I'm not their counselor.' "

Once upon a time, a counselor offered counsel, and he knew that an adult does not form character in the young by taking a stance of neutrality toward questions of right and wrong or by merely offering "choices" or "options."

In response to the belief that adults and educators should teach children sound morals, one can expect from some quarters indignant objections (I've heard one version of it expressed countless times over the years): "Who are you to say what's moral and what's important?" or "Whose standards and judgments do we use?"

The correct response, it seems to me, is, are we really ready to do away with standards and judgments? Is anyone going to argue seriously that a life of cheating and swindling is as worthy as a life of honest, hard work? Is anyone (with the exception of some literature professors at our elite universities) going to argue seriously the intellectual corollary, that a Marvel comic book is as good as *Macbeth*? Unless we are willing to embrace some pretty silly positions, we've got to admit the need for moral and intellectual standards. The problem is that some people tend to regard anyone who would pronounce a definitive judgment as an unsophisticated Philistine or a closed-minded "elitist" trying to impose his view on everyone else.

The truth of the real world is that without standards and judgments, there can be no progress. Unless we are prepared to say irrational things—that nothing can be proven more valuable than anything else or that everything is equally worthless—we *must* ask the normative question. This may come as a surprise to those who feel that to be "progressive" is to be value-neutral. But as Matthew Arnold said, "the world is forwarded by having its attention fixed on the best things." And if the world can't decide what the best things are, at least to some degree, then it follows that progress, and character, are in trouble. We shouldn't be reluctant to declare that some things—some lives, books, ideas, and values—are better than others. It is the responsibility of the schools to teach these better things.

At one time, we weren't so reluctant to teach them. In the mid–nineteenth century, a diverse, widespread group of crusaders began to work for the public support of what was then called the "common school," the forerunner of the public school. They were to be charged with the mission of moral and civic training, training that planted its roots in shared values. The advocates of the common school felt that the nation could fulfill its destiny only if every new generation was taught these values together in a common institution.

The leaders of the common school movement were mainly citizens who were prominent in their communities—businessmen, ministers, local civic and government officials. These people saw the schools as upholders of standards of individual morality and small incubators of civic and personal virtue; the founders of the public schools had faith that public education could teach good moral and civic character from a common ground of American values.

But in the past quarter century or so, some of the so-called experts became experts of value neutrality, and moral education was increasingly left in their hands. The commonsense view of parents and the public, that schools should reinforce rather than undermine the values of home, family, and country, was increasingly rejected.

There are those today still who claim we are now too diverse a nation, that we consist of too many competing convictions and interests to instill common values. They are wrong. Of course we are a diverse people. We have always been a diverse people. And as Madison wrote in *Federalist* No. 10, the competing, balancing interests of a diverse people can help ensure the survival of liberty. But there are values that all American citizens share and that we should want all American students to know and to make their own: honesty, fairness, self-discipline, fidelity to task, friends, and family, personal responsibility, love of country, and belief in the principles of liberty, equality, and the freedom to practice one's faith. The explicit teaching of these values is the legacy of the common school, and it is a legacy to which we must return.

People often say, "Yes, we *should* teach these values, but *how* do we teach them?" This question deserves a candid response, one that isn't given often enough. It is by exposing our children to good character and inviting its imitation that we will transmit to them a moral foundation. This happens when teachers and principals, by their words and actions, embody sound convictions. As Oxford's Mary Warnock has written, "You cannot teach morality without being committed to morality yourself; and you cannot be committed to morality yourself without holding that some things are right and others wrong." The theologian Martin Buber wrote that the educator is distinguished from all other influences "by his *will* to take part in the stamping of character and by his *conscious-ness* that he represents in the eyes of the growing person a certain *selection* of what is, the selection of what is 'right,' of what *should* be." It is in this will, Buber says, in this clear standing for some-thing, that the "vocation as an educator finds its fundamental expression."

There is no escaping the fact that young people need as exam-ples principals and teachers who know the difference between right and wrong, good and bad, and who themselves exemplify high moral purpose.

As Education Secretary, I visited a class at Waterbury Elemen-tary School in Waterbury, Vermont, and asked the students, "Is this a good school?" They answered, "Yes, this is a good school." I asked them, "Why?" Among other things, one eight-year-old said, "The principal, Mr. Riegel, makes good rules and everybody obeys them." So I said, "Give me an example." And another an-swered, "You can't climb on the pipes in the bathroom. We don't climb on the pipes and the principal doesn't either."

This example is probably too simple to please a lot of people who want to make the topic of moral education difficult, but there is something profound in the answer of those children, something educators should pay more attention to. You can't expect children to take messages about rules or morality seriously unless they see adults taking those rules seriously in their day-to-day affairs. Cer-tain things must be said, certain limits laid down, and certain examples set. There is no other way.

We should also do a better job at curriculum selection. The research shows that most "values education" exercises and sepa-rate courses in "moral reasoning" tend not to affect children's behavior; if anything, they may leave children morally adrift. Where to turn? I believe our literature and our history are a rich quarry of moral literacy. We should mine that quarry. Children should have at their disposal a stock of examples illustrating what we believe to be right and wrong, good and bad—examples illus-trating that what is morally right and wrong can indeed be known and that there is a difference.

What kind of stories, historical events, and famous lives am I talking about? If we want our children to know about honesty, we should teach them about Abe Lincoln walking three miles to re-turn six cents and, conversely, about Aesop's shepherd boy who cried wolf. If we want them to know about courage, we should teach them about Joan of Arc, Horatius at the bridge, and Harriet Tubman and the Underground Railroad. If we want them to know about persistence in the face of adversity, they should know about the voyages of Columbus, and the character of Washington during the Revolution and Lincoln during the Civil War. And our youngest should be told about the Little Engine That Could. If we want them to know about respect for the law, they should understand why Socrates told Crito: "No, I must submit to the decree of Athens." If we want our children to respect the rights of others, they should read the Declaration of Independence, the Bill of Rights, the Gettysburg Address, and Martin Luther King, Jr.'s "Letter from Birmingham Jail." From the Bible they should know about Ruth's loyalty to Naomi, Joseph's forgiveness of his brothers, Jonathan's friendship with David, the Good Samaritan's kindness toward a stranger, and David's cleverness and courage in facing Goliath.

These are only a few of the hundreds of examples we can call on. And we need not get into issues like nuclear war, abortion, creationism, or euthanasia. This may come as a disappointment to some people, but the fact is that the formation of character in young people is educationally a task different from, and prior to, the discussion of the great, difficult controversies of the day. First things first. We should teach values the same way we teach other things: one step at a time. We should not use the fact that there are many difficult and controversial moral questions as an argument against basic instruction in the subject. After all, we do not argue against teaching physics because laser physics is difficult, against teaching biology or chemistry because gene splicing and cloning are complex and controversial, against teaching American history because there are heated disputes about the Founders' intent. Every field has its complexities and its controversies. And every field has its basics, its fundamentals. So too with forming character and achieving moral literacy. As any parent knows, teaching character is a difficult task. But it is a crucial task, because we want our children to be not only healthy, happy, and successful but decent, strong, and good. None of this happens automatically; there is no genetic transmission of virtue. It takes the conscious, committed efforts of adults. It takes careful attention.

Americans know that we have problems; the issue is on the table. We must regain control of our schools so that they can serve their time-honored purpose of educating children. I believe that to be effective, reform should attack three fundamental flaws in public education: a soft curriculum, a general lack of accountability for results, and a lack of parental choice.

We have recently begun to make some progress in the curriculum. *A Nation at Risk* recommended in 1983 that every high school graduate have at least four years of English, three of math, three of social studies and three of science. In 1982, only 13 percent of U.S. high school graduates could meet these *bare-minimum* requirements. In 1987, we were up to 29 percent. But this is still a dismally low percentage for graduating seniors—and of course we can assume that 100 percent of our dropouts do not meet this minimum. We have successfully raised the "floor" of American education. According to Barbara Lerner, an expert on education reform, "The good news is, first, that minimum competence—literacy and numeracy, basically—is now nearly universal among our high-school graduates. And, second, while the SAT scores of American students in general have stayed pretty much the same for a decade, those of minority students have not. From 1980 to 1989, Hispanic and Asian scores on such advanced tests rose" (*Commentary*, March 1991). But overall achievement is still far too low. In 1990–91, verbal SAT scores for blacks were 351 (out of a possible 800). This figure is up from previous years, but it is still dismally low. Every high school student in an American school should have four years of English, and at least three years each of math, science, history, and geography. If these years include of serious, solid study, scores will rise and education will improve.

Solid and meaningful years of study means the study of the essentials of these disciplines. Acquiring "skills" should not come at the expense of acquiring knowledge. Students should finish high school knowing not just the "method" or "process" of science or history; they should actually know some science and history. They should know fractions and decimals, and percentages and algebra and geometry. They should know that for every action there is an equal and opposite reaction, and they should know who said "I am the state" and who said "I have a dream." They should know about subjects and predicates, about isosceles triangles and ellipses. They should know where the Amazon flows, and what the First Amendment means. They should know about the Donner party and slavery, and Shylock, Hercules, and Abigail Adams, where Ethiopia is, and why there was a Berlin Wall. They should know how a poem works, how a plant works, and the meaning of "If wishes were horses, beggars would ride." They should know the place of the Milky Way and DNA in the unfolding of the universe. They should know about the Constitutional Convention of 1787 and about the conventions of good behavior. They should know what the Sistine Chapel looks like and what great music sounds like.

Our students should also know our nation's ideals and aspirations. We believe in liberty and equality, in limited government and the betterment of the human condition. These truths underlie our society, and though they may be self-evident, they are not spontaneously apprehended by the young.

These are things we should want *all* our students to know. We should not hold some students to lesser goals, pushing them into educational backwaters while everyone else is advancing upstream. Albert Shanker once asked a class of average and less than average students: "What should we ask you to read?" After a pause one student raised his hand. "Mr. Shanker," he asked, "what do the smart kids read?"

Not all students have the same abilities, so it is up to our teachers to adapt good material to the level of the student. Good teachers will vary the pedagogy, of course, but they will also retain the substance. Whatever the pedagogy (books, tapes, films, or stories), they must not lose the substance. In certain places in America, there has sometimes been a great zeal to remove certain topics from study. We need to match that zeal for exclusion with a zeal for inclusion.

A second key education reform is providing for much greater accountability. Today, *there are greater, more certain, and more immediate penalties in this country for serving up a single rotten hamburger than for furnishing a thousand schoolchildren with a rotten education.* In fact, there's actually a perverse incentive not to succeed, because if a school district performs poorly, it usually gets more money based on the argument that it's doing poorly because it lacks money.

American education and its educators need good, palpable reasons to avoid failure and good, palpable incentives to strive for success. If we are to improve our schools, we must have ways of identifying and rewarding schools that work, methods that work, and principals and teachers who work. We should give superintendents greater authority to run their districts; give principals greater autonomy to run their schools, and teachers greater authority to run their classrooms; and then hold them all accountable for the results they achieve. We must have ways of identifying and, if necessary, moving out those who fail to do their jobs and of identifying and rewarding those who do their jobs well. As the nation's governors put it in their 1987 report, *Time for Results,* "Someone has to pay a penalty for continued failure, but it should not be the students." To determine results we must have true reliable national standards. Students must be tested to those standards and the results (by state, district, and school) should be made public.

On one of my early visits to Chicago, the union representatives wanted to show me a public school that works. In February 1987, I visited the LaSalle Language Academy, an inner-city "magnet" school that draws students from every ethnic and socioeconomic group in the city because of the force or "pull" of its solid academic curriculum. At LaSalle, foreign language study begins the first day of kindergarten and continues through eighth grade. Students spend forty minutes a day studying French, Spanish, German, or Italian. In the early grades, they develop speaking skills through songs, games, and folktales. In the middle years, they focus on reading, writing, and conversation. And by the time they reach seventh and eighth grade, LaSalle students are engaged in formal study of grammar and literature. On average, test scores of LaSalle students are at least a year above grade level on both the reading and math sections.

In the late 1970s, LaSalle's enrollment had dipped to 175 students and officials were considering closing the school. But a decade after the foreign-language program was established, almost 600 students attended and it received eight applications for every single space available. LaSalle is a school of choice; parents, not bureaucrats, select it for their children.

When I visited LaSalle, I was very impressed by what I saw. It employs fine teachers and it has a terrific principal, Amy Weiss Narea.

When I asked why LaSalle Language Academy performs so well, Narea told me it has a very clear definition of its mission;

high academic standards and expectations; the curriculum is strong; she knows not only the students by name but also the parents and urges them to do their part of the job of educating their children; and the school board allows her to hire her own staff. I then asked why staff hiring autonomy for principals could not be practiced system-wide. The answer I got from a school board executive was that if principals were given the choice, most would not hire many of those working in the Chicago public school system today. (During that same visit, I was told that close to half of Chicago public school teachers choose to enroll *their* children in private schools. That is a telling statistic.)

A third key education reform is parental choice—full, unfettered choice over which schools their children will attend. In a free market economy, those who produce goods and services are ultimately answerable to the consumer; if quality is shoddy, the consumer will buy someone else's product. It doesn't work that way in public education, though. Even when armed with adequate information about school quality (which they rarely have), parents in most places around the country are not permitted to transfer their children from a bad school to a good one.

In a sharp break with my predecessor, Terrel H. Bell, I immediately voiced strong support for vouchers and tuition tax credits when I became Secretary of Education. "The idea of choice is an idea whose time has come," I said at a news conference announcing our proposal. The proposal urged that the federal Chapter I program (compensatory education for the disadvantaged) be administered through vouchers (averaging $600 each) in order to give students from less fortunate environments the chance to choose private schools, too. As I told the National Catholic Educational Association in 1985:

All parents, regardless of income, should be able to choose places where they know their children will learn. And they should be able to choose environments where their own values will be extended instead of lost. It's possible that there are some public schools nobody would choose. They are so bad that they might suddenly find themselves without any students. But I have no idea why we should be interested in protecting schools like that from competition—or any schools from competition. Our worst schools are our non-competitive ones, and that's no coincidence.

The philosophy behind the choice proposal is that we need to break the monopoly currently exercised by state-run schools and allow all schools—including private and religious schools—to compete for public dollars. A full-scale voucher program would promote a healthy rivalry between public and private schools, as well as among public schools. Teachers' unions and the education establishment adamantly and uniformly opposed our voucher proposal, calling it "ridiculous" (Council of Great City Schools), "a Trojan horse" (National School Board Association), "offensive" (National Parent-Teacher Association), "a sham" (NEA), and a proposal that amounted to "cannibalization" (AFT). The education establishment recognized our proposal for what it was: a direct and open challenge to their monopoly control of American education. The teachers' unions knew that if they lost on the issue of choice, their iron lock on power would be loosened. This is why full-scale choice was, and remains, the linchpin of sound education reform.

Critics of full choice for American parents in the selection of schools argue that choice isn't right: public money should go only to public and not religious schools, and so full choice would amount to a violation of the separation of church and state. They have it wrong. Voucher bills have been proposed, including the one we advanced to Congress in 1986, that are fully constitutional. Most of our critics conceded it to be so. Public money goes to Catholic and Jewish hospitals to care for the public, and public money supports fire and police forces that serve religious institutions. Public money should be for the education of the public, and a child in Catholic, Methodist, or Jewish school is every bit as much a member of the public as a child in a state-supported school.

There's another issue associated with choice as well—social justice. At present, our most affluent families do exercise choice, by buying a home in the neighborhood of their choice, or by sending their children to private school. The poor do not now have that kind of choice. In contrast to the dismal report of the Chicago public schools, Chicago's Catholic schools are graduating 85 percent of their children at a cost of about $2,500 a year and with a fraction of the administrators per student (only 32 central-office administrators for more than 160,000 students). Since many Chicago public school teachers, knowing the relative strengths, choose private schools for their children, shouldn't others be given the same choice? It *is* a question of social justice.

The critics of elementary and secondary school choice should also acknowledge the inconsistency and even hypocrisy of their position. The fact is, we already have a system of choice in American higher education and people don't object to it. When we give out billions of dollars every year for students to go to college, with their Pell Grants or their Stafford Loans, they can take them to Indiana University, Notre Dame, Yeshiva, or Liberty Baptist. Indiana University isn't diminished because Notre Dame is a fine school; Liberty Baptist isn't daunted because Notre Dame is a fine school. Broad choice in higher education hasn't hurt public higher education; on the contrary, greater competition has helped it and helped students. Why, then, do we not allow it at the elementary and secondary levels, which are so much more important and formative?

There is an additional benefit to choice. If we invite parents to choose their schools, it can be a good first step in the critical effort of reenfranchising them. Choice among schools is a first involvement in the schools, a critical investment, and it may lead to further involvement, which is something teachers long for. If parents know the results by school of tests with national standards, they will choose more wisely. The more we can do to involve (or reinvolve) parents, the better.

The scholastic success of many Asian-American children has reminded us all of the importance of parental involvement. A few years ago, in the Asian-American community in Riverdale, New York City, teachers and principals were puzzled that their textbooks were being sold at a rate much faster than the number of children registered in classes could account for. They wanted to know why. After doing a little investigating, they discovered that most Asian-American families were buying *two* sets of textbooks. One set was for the child, and a second set was for the mother, who could better coach her child if she worked during the day to keep up with the lessons. These teachers said that Asian-American children entering school in the fall with no English ability finished in the spring at the top of their classes in every subject. At the Department of Education we repeatedly said that the parent is the child's most important teacher, the child's all but indispensable teacher.

Choice advocates have some remarkably convincing success stories to which they can point. One of the best is in the public system in local District 4 in New York's East Harlem. In the early 1970s, District 4 was an educational basket case. It ranked last in reading scores among all the city's thirty-two school districts. Then, under the leadership of superintendent Anthony Alvarado, the district allowed parents to choose for their children from among a wide variety of newly restructured schools, each offering a particular instructional focus. In some instances, several minischools were created within the same building. Before the choice program began, only 15 percent of the students in the district could read at grade level. Recent test scores show 64 percent at or above grade level in reading and 53 percent at or above grade level in math. According to William C. Myers of the Free Congress Foundation, the number of students from the district who qualified for admission to one of New York's prestigious specialized high schools increased from ten to three hundred, and today 96 percent of East Harlem graduates are admitted to college.

Today, East Harlem's teachers are energized and motivated. Lynne Kearney, director of District 4's Manhattan East School, says why: "People are here because they want to be. . . . There's a camaraderie, because this place doesn't have to exist. We can go out of business tomorrow. If it didn't meet needs, it would fold." According to a *New York Times* special report on the East Harlem school district, choice has "helped send test scores, teacher morale, and parent involvement soaring."

At the end of the great Chicago school debate, the *Chicago Tribune* argued for full choice: "The quickest, surest way to explode the bureaucratic blob, escape from the self-seeking union and develop schools that succeed for children is to set up a voucher system. That would bring new people into school management, assure local control, empower parents, squeeze out bad schools and put the forces of competition to work for improving education."

I believe the ideas I have outlined will work. They are the same ideas we put forward to the Congress during my tenure as Secretary of Education, but almost without exception the Congress rejected these far-reaching reform proposals—not on their merits, not because they wouldn't improve American education, but because our proposals were a direct challenge to the power of the education establishment. The political clout of the NEA and its brethren remains considerable. With few exceptions, Congress does the bidding of the education establishment and not of the general public.

This makes the job description for an Education Secretary obvious. In general, the secretaries of domestic Cabinet agencies have much less authority and power than, say, the Secretary of Defense or the Secretary of State. And even more than is the case with most domestic Cabinet posts, there are intrinsic (and I believe wise) limitations on what the Secretary of Education can do. He has very little power or authority to determine the content and course of American education, since education is primarily a state and local matter. That is where 90 percent or more of the spending is done, where the curriculum is set, and where all of the hiring and firing is done.

What the Secretary of Education can try to do is influence the direction of federal programs, reinvigorate a national discussion about education, highlight what works and what doesn't, and set in motion constructive changes.

What we tried to do at the Department of Education was to move the national education debate forward. We kept the debate on educational improvement going, drew attention to what works, and got new ideas and reforms into circulation. In public policy there is often a long delay between the time when new issues are raised, debated, and studied, and when they are finally legislated. Parental choice in education is a good example. "Before the Reagan administration raised the [voucher] issue, it was considered an odd view on the fringes of the public-policy debate," according to Gary Bauer, who was my undersecretary at the Department of Education and is now president of the Family Research Council. "The constant crashing of our heads into the congressional roadblock legitimated the issue and paved the way for developments today."

At the Department of Education I tried to broaden the public discussion on education reform and get the reform movement out of the hands of the educrats and into hands of the public. I tried to bring attention to the right issues: high standards and basics, competency for teachers, educational choice, strong curriculum content, homework, sound moral education, and accountability.

One of the ways I tried to broaden the public discussion was the use of the "bully pulpit." By design, an important part of my bully-pulpit strategy meant utilizing the press. Success in domestic policy in particular depends on articulating a strong public case. Since most education reform will be done—when it is done, if it is done—at the state and local level, it was important for me to advance the ideas others could pick up on. I couldn't advance my ideas to a whole nation without a megaphone. For a government official, the press is often the best megaphone.

As Secretary of Education I wanted to highlight the good in American education. I wanted to draw attention to education heroes, to honor them and encourage others to emulate them. The press played a big role in this effort. The media may not determine what people think, but they can help determine what people think about. What determines what the media choose to write about, which people they choose to profile, and what they choose to think about? A responsible public official does what he can to make visible what needs to be visible.

Some of my critics disagreed. Senator Paul Simon of Illinois said of my high visibility, "There are some pluses to the visibility of the Secretary, but on balance I think the cause is better served by people who are willing to quietly do the solid, substantial things that cause fewer headlines but result in real change."

But for Senator Simon, a man who takes his every cue from the education establishment, those "quiet, solid, substantial things" mean cutting deals that please and help enrich the education establishment. That wasn't my style nor my intent. In any event, "visibility" can aid in the cause of "real change."

When, for example, in Senator Simon's home state of Illinois I called Chicago's public schools the "worst in the nation," it drew enormous attention. It helped lead to the *Chicago Tribune*'s extraordinary seven-month examination that exposed the corruption, greed, and neglect in the Chicago public school system. It helped trigger a new wave of reform measures. This might never have happened without the spotlight and attention. In a 1990 interview Ted Kimbrough, the new superintendent of the Chicago public schools, said, "We owe Bennett a debt of gratitude for shaking people up. That controversial statement helped get people moving toward reform." My predecessor T. H. Bell, who was critical of my "harsh" attacks on educators, said of me: "Maybe he could have been more tactful, but tact doesn't make the impact it should. In retrospect, maybe I was too tactful."

*   *   *

American schools are a long way from where they need to be. Today the battle lines are being drawn over what to do, how to do it, and who gets to decide how to do it. It is a battle over who will control the schools—the educrats who gave us the educational disasters of the sixties and seventies, or parents, taxpayers, and a sizable number of dedicated and able principals and teachers? The fact is, we know what to do; we know what works; we know what we should expect.

The issue, then, is whether we have the political courage and the will to do the job. The future of American education depends on how we answer these questions: Are we willing to reward excellence (merit pay for outstanding teachers and principals)? Are we willing to penalize failure (terminate the contracts of incompetent teachers and bad principals)? Are we going to give parents more say in which schools their children attend (full parental choice)? Are we willing to "deregulate" the teaching profession by making room for men and women of energy, intelligence, and broad backgrounds (alternative teacher certification)? Are we going to insist on high standards (making the receipt of federal student aid or receipt of a high school diploma contingent on passing a qualifying test with real national standards)? Are we willing to get the litter out of the curricula and put the basic subjects back in? Are we going to return to homework? And are we going to stop accepting lame excuses for low performance?

The American people have to answer the tough questions; they have to lead the revolution; they have to take back our schools, for the sake of our children.

2

WHAT WORKS IN AMERICAN EDUCATION, AND WHY

When I was chairman of the National Endowment for the Humanities, I asked several hundred educational and cultural leaders of diverse views and politics to recommend ten books that any high school graduate should have read. Members of the general public were also invited in a newspaper column by George Will to send me their list. Their responses were consistent with the original ones we received; in particular, there was a remarkable *convergence around the first four. They were: the Bible, select plays of Shakespeare, the founding and guiding documents of American political life (such as the Declaration of Independence, the Constitution,* The Federalist Papers, *and the Emancipation Proclamation), and* the *American novel,* The Adventures of Huckleberry Finn. *That's a pretty good curriculum for high school juniors or seniors—or, for that matter, as a yearlong introductory course in the humanities.*

There is probably no field in which the statement of the obvious, of simple truths, is more necessary than in education. It is the bias of the intellectual to value the complex over the simple. The important thing to keep in mind about American education is that *we know what works.* Education reform is not an arcane business; it is not primarily a matter of great complexity, but one of will and political courage. It involves the willingness to hold institutions and individuals accountable, to make a commitment to each child,

71

and the courage when necessary to challenge and change the system.

When you find good schools, you can't help being impressed. The encouraging news is there are hundreds, even thousands, of such schools all across America, along with outstanding teachers and courageous principals. As Secretary of Education I visited elementary and secondary schools all across America, from Seattle to Colorado Springs to Orlando to New York; I met with students, parents, teachers, and principals. My visits to the front lines of American education were the most gratifying and encouraging experience of my professional life. Their success is reason for hope and optimism. And they should be a model and foundation for education reform in America.

The late Ron Edmonds started the "Effective Schools Program" in the 1970s. Edmonds described the characteristics of an effective school: a safe and orderly environment, a clear and focused academic mission, instructional leadership, high expectations, student time-on-task, and frequent monitoring of student progress. My own experiences confirm Edmond's research and findings. In fact, one of the things I noticed in my travels was that when I visited good schools, they were similar to what Tolstoy said of good families: they are all good for the same reasons.

In the late spring of 1985 my wife Elayne, herself a former teacher, urged me to visit schools and teach classes. While we were engaged and I was director of NEH, she had seen me teach high school classes in Portland, Maine. Later, when I became Education Secretary, she told me, "You're a good teacher and people will take you more seriously if they see you doing what you're talking about. In addition to talking about education all the time, why don't you go out and show people you can teach somebody something."

At the time I resisted. "I don't do retail now," I answered. "I do wholesale."

She persisted. "Do some retail," she said, "and you'll do better wholesale."

So I agreed to begin a series of visits to America's elementary and secondary classrooms. At the end of my tenure I had visited and taught in 107 schools. At elementary schools, I usually taught the third grade, at middle schools the seventh grade, and at high schools the eleventh grade.

I don't think that anyone except Elayne could have anticipated the success of these outings. They showed that the classroom is still the heart of education; demonstrated respect for teachers and the teaching profession; and showed that I wasn't going to operate strictly from inside Washington or base my education agenda only on statistical reports and national surveys. My sallies into the classroom helped me to keep some perspective on my job. "It's good for the Secretary of Education to get into a classroom from time to time and be exposed to that irreducible reality," I told reporters. "When you sit in Washington, everything comes through filtered."

Most important, my visits allowed me to find out what was actually going on and discover what works. I wanted to get the "feel" of schools that had distinguished themselves and congratulate them, publicize them, and learn from them. I particularly wanted to visit schools that taught economically disadvantaged students and had succeeded.

These experiences were invaluable in another respect. My critics in the education establishment tended to stay away from America's classrooms. For the most part they elected to stay in Washington among their own; their style of "information gathering" consisted mostly of sharing education reports, newspaper clippings, and hearsay (often over lunch at a ritzy restaurant). But issues look very different at the local level than they do from Washington. Each classroom tells its own story.

Over the years I got to know teachers and principals with whom I regularly kept in contact. They became reliable witnesses who could tell me what problems they faced and how they dealt with them. If our critics said that something we recommended couldn't be done, or some particular problem was found in our schools, here were places we would look to and people we would ask in order to learn the truth.

Over time I gained an empirical and rhetorical advantage over my critics. It was hard to criticize a Secretary of Education as remote and uncaring if he were out in American classrooms almost every week, when most of the critics weren't. My classroom experiences gave to "airy abstraction a local habitation and a name," as Shakespeare said. The particulars—the *stories*, the *places*, the *people*—stay in the memory when the "airy abstraction" is forgotten.

On August 3, 1985, I traveled to Caddo Middle Magnet School in Shreveport, Louisiana. I was scheduled to teach the Declaration of Independence to a class of seventh-graders. This was my first time out of Washington teaching a class as Secretary of Education, and I was apprehensive.

In addition to a class of youngsters, the back of the room was filled with lights, cameras, and reporters. There were more press "visitors" than students, by a ratio of more than two to one. And given my "controversial" start and the largely bad press I had received up to that point, I knew I was on shaky ground. I thought, one false move, one bad or inaccurate lesson, one smart put-down by a twelve-year-old, and I'd be news—and possibly even history. It made the preclass butterflies larger, more color-ful, and more active than usual. But it made it more exciting, too—especially when the fire alarms in my Shreveport motel went off again and again the night before I was to teach. Six or seven times that sleepless night, going over my lesson on the Declaration of Independence, I found myself in the halls with Edward Fiske, who writes on education for *The New York Times*. I confessed that I was nervous about taking on twenty-seven twelve- and thirteen-year-olds. "When you go up to the Hill or hold a press conference, you can usually anticipate the questions," I explained. "Seventh-graders can be off the wall."

During class we discussed the most important words in the Dec-laration: "we" (as in "We hold these truths"), "all," and "equal" (as in "all men are created equal"). We decided these words were important because they symbolized this nation's fundamental act of self-definition. Jefferson's words were the defining, unifying statement of our republic. And they remind us that for all of this nation's diversity, we are finally one people.

The class behaved well and the kids gave me pretty good grades. One student told reporters, "He didn't talk down to you." Another student said, "I didn't expect anyone that impor-tant to have a sense of humor." Walter C. Lee, Shreveport's fine superintendent of schools, said he would even hire me as a per-manent teacher—"assuming that he got an acceptable score on the National Teachers Examination." Lee had reversed "white flight" with this magnet school, and a class of happy and eager thirteen-year-olds, black and white, was eloquent testimony to his success.

On a personal level the school visits were the best part of my job. The children were great, endearing, hilarious. They gave me moments I'll never forget. Some third-graders in Tucson, for example, asked me to ask President Reagan, the next time I saw him, to get more professional wrestling to southern Arizona. (I failed in that assignment.)

Asked "Why did the Pilgrims come to America?" an eight-year-old in New Orleans told me so that teachers could "organize and bargain collectively for wages." (Her teacher was embarrassed.)

Two children in Carol Russo's terrific Garrison Elementary School in the South Bronx told me they went to America's "greatest school" because "there's no messin' around, no foolin' around, and everybody loves you." (That's a pretty good description of what makes for a fine school.)

And although the students at Garden Gate Elementary in Cupertino, California, learn a lot, I discovered that they were not happy with the cafeteria. "The baked chicken is soggy; the roast beef is green; and there's no sausage on the sausage pizza," I was told.

At the Emma Conn Elementary School in Raleigh, North Carolina, I talked about George Washington. One boy raised his hand and said, "Mr. Secretary, when and the other people in the *cupboard* get together . . ." He was of course corrected by a little girl who whispered, "Cabinet, cabinet, cabinet."

The boy, who had heard of President Reagan's penchant for jelly beans, was undaunted. "Do you all really eat jelly bellies?" he asked.

I said, "Well, I just told you about George Washington and I cannot tell you a lie. The President has a bowl of jelly beans in front of him. He takes some, passes them around, and I've had a few."

The little boy, looking at my waistline, said, "Mr. Secretary, you've had more than a few."

At Caddo Middle Magnet School in Shreveport, where I taught the Declaration of Independence, I asked the seventh-grade class for three volunteers. I had them come up to the front of the room with me and I asked the class, "Who's equal?"

The class said, "You're all equal."

I asked, "Who's the biggest?"

The class said, "You are."

I asked, "Who's the strongest?"

The class answered, "You are."

I then asked them, "Who's the smartest?"

And they said, "You are."

"But who's equal?" I asked.

The class answered, "We all are, because we are all created equal." That was of course the right answer, the moral of the story.

If it works in one classroom, I thought, it should work in another. So I tried it in Osburn, Idaho, where I was introduced to the entire student body of Silver Hills Junior High. The principal introduced me as the highest-ranking federal official to visit Osburn "since Theodore Roosevelt was here in 1903." (I reported that fact later to President Reagan at a Cabinet meeting. The President, who often made fun of his own age, said, "Oh yes, I remember that visit." I thought to myself, "Well, that's part of the job of a Cabinet member, being a straight man for the President.")

In Osburn I got Kyle and Jack and Sarah up with me. And I asked the class, "Who's equal?"

The class answered, "You all are."

I asked, "Who's the biggest?"

They answered, "You are."

I asked, "Who's the strongest?"

The class answered, "You are."

I then asked, "Who's the smartest?"

And the class answered, "*Kyle* is the smartest."

I said, "Kyle, sit down. The Secretary of Education didn't travel two thousand miles to be embarrassed by a twelve-year-old."

Kyle then asked me, "Why do we celebrate Independence Day on July 4 instead of July 3, when Adams actually submitted the draft to Jefferson?"

I said, "Kyle, *sit down.*"

Those classroom visits and exchanges gave me the assurance to say that American students can be educated. As the philosopher Immanuel Kant pointed out, the actual proves the possible. If you wonder whether something can be done, and you find an example of it, you've proved it's possible. This may sound remote and arcane, and in some ways I suppose it is, but much of the education establishment fails to appreciate the qualities that make for a good school. It turns out that they have pretty predictable, commonsense features.

The more I visited schools the more I deviated from the Washington/education establishment orthodoxy. Seeing outstanding schools in action makes it clear why they succeed: *local people, leadership, community commitment,* and *shared values,* not federal tutelage.

From time to time we provided the media with lists of schools that work. Those who wished to find out the possibilities of American education, or who thought it couldn't be done, needed only to visit these schools and see for themselves. You can't learn it, you can't know it, simply by the aggregate numbers or the studies. To the doubters, to cynics, to the no-can-doers, you need to repeat what I once heard a parent say to her child about a school: "You go there and then you *will* learn."

In my trips I came across men and women who deserve to be regarded as true American heroes. They are for the most part quiet, unsung heroes. But for the work they do and the lives they change, we can all be grateful. Thankfully, many of their communities already are. There's no exact "blueprint" of what makes for an outstanding teacher; great teaching and great leadership come in all styles. But these teachers and principals are people of good character, committed to academic excellence, and have a genuine regard for the well-being of children.

Ted Yanak, an eighth-grade teacher of American history and government at Miller Junior High in West San Jose, California, had a classroom covered, plastered, and overwhelmed with clippings, posters, and campaign paraphernalia—buttons, hats, and bumper stickers. At a meeting with students, parents, and teachers, he was singled out by the principal to thunderous applause. He frequently appeared at these events dressed in a bright red jacket, blue pants, red-white-and-blue shoes, a flag-print tie, and a tricolor hat. He gives his heart to his students and he works them hard. They learn their history, and they repay him with their affection, appreciation, and achievement born of effort equal to his.

Carolyn Oubray, a self-composed young professional, teaches English the old-fashioned way to young black women at Xavier High School in New Orleans. In her senior class on Edgar Allan Poe, Elayne and I witnessed her stress "disciplined thinking and disciplined analysis" to her students. They responded with thoughtful, disciplined answers. Xavier has a traditional curriculum, heavy on the basic disciplines. Later, Mrs. Oubray and her principal proudly explained to us that the uniformed, well-educated students of Xavier made something good of their lives.

"You won't find many Xavier girls on welfare, and you won't find them having babies as teen-agers because they have nothing else to do," she told us. Elayne was pleased to hear that. She directs a program in Washington, D.C. called "Best Friends," aimed at encouraging young women to remain abstinent while in school. Her program works and so does the regime at Xavier, and with the same effect. "Our girls have plenty to do," Oubray told us, "and they graduate from here and make good lives for themselves. And when they get married and have children, they send their daughters here."

In the end, it is people like this—the individual principal, teacher, superintendent, parent, and citizen—who make all the difference in our schools. "In every case there was someone who took a personal interest in children and their future," I once told a group of business leaders. "Not a government, but a *face*. Such people are like guardian angels we used to hear about in school— close by, watching, helping you and expecting you to do your best."

I told the audience about businessman Eugene Lang, who spoke at the sixth-grade graduation in his old Harlem elementary school and promised each child $2,000 toward college tuition. Most of the children who remained in that district stayed in school to accept the offer, thwarting a 40 percent dropout rate. The $2,000 that each youngster received was roughly the amount of a federal Pell Grant. "But our Pell Grants don't motivate like Eugene Lang motivates," I told them. The difference was personal encouragement and support.

This, then, is the iron law of education: the "system" doesn't educate anyone. Individuals do. Yeats wrote, "All the drop-scenes drop at once/Upon a hundred thousand stages," and it is on those individual stages that the educational dream fails or succeeds. In our time there are a few well-known giants on the school stage. I went to their classrooms to see what all the excitement was about and whether the accolades were merited. They were.

Joe Clark formerly of Eastside High School in Paterson, New Jersey, is probably America's most famous principal. The subject of a movie (*Lean on Me*), and featured on the cover of *Time* magazine a few years ago (with a perfectly cut suit, a bullhorn, and a baseball bat), Joe Clark became a national symbol. Eastside was so bad before his arrival that the district attorney called it "a caldron of violence and terror"; drug use, stabbings, and rapes were rampant. Clark's educational philosophy was not new. In fact, a crucial element of it was spelled out in a teachers' bible from the early twentieth century (unfortunately now out of use), *Classroom Management*: "The first requirement is to get order."

Joe Clark volunteered to take over in 1982. On opening day, three thousand students found him waiting in the hall with a bullhorn in his hand. "I am your new principal," he said. "This is the *new* Eastside High School. What was, exists no more. Get to your classrooms."

Everyone was given a list of rules. If you talked back to a teacher, you were suspended for five days. If you painted on a wall, ten days. Clark announced a dress code. "You've got Calvin Kleins on your behinds and nothing in your minds," he said. The school was cleaned from top to bottom. Security guards were put in the stairwells.

If a teacher was incompetent, Clark told him so to his face. Twenty transferred out. Three hundred juniors and seniors were expelled. "I'm not going to let three hundred hoodlums destroy the lives of three thousand students," Clark told them. As for drugs, he told drug dealers: "If you come here, you just might get hurt."

This firm, clear disciplinarian is the "controversial" Joe Clark with whom many people are familiar. When we first met, I told him, "Joe, you now have the same moniker I do—'controversial.' " But there is another, less well-known side to Joe Clark. To see this side of the man you had to know him, spend time with him, and be in his school. Joe Clark did not carry the baseball bat to wield on his students. He carried it as a warning to drug pushers to stay away from his school and his students. Drug use declined after Clark was put in charge. Why should pushers invite a confrontation with Clark when there were other places where they could do their ugly business with impunity?

Clark showed tremendous affection and regard for his students; I got the sense that I was watching a parent caring for a thousand of his children. In his halls, he directed one student this way, another that way, and asked still another student how his math was going. As you walked through a hall with Clark, there was a handshake here, a gentle pat on the back there, or a quick, firm embrace—and always accompanied by a name. Like other great principals I have come to know, Clark called his students by name. He knew that a correction or an encouragement has far more effect if it is addressed to someone by name. To Joe Clark, each student was a person who deserved personal attention.

As we walked down the hall he said to one young woman, "Carolyn, you're looking splendid today, and today you will master your math." There are plenty of phonies around these days speaking about their "personal interest" in students without ever going to the trouble of learning their names. Clark didn't emote or philosophize or congratulate himself about developing "close personal relations" with students; he just did it. He didn't talk a good game, he played one.

His students knew he cared about them. And they and many of their parents loved him for it. He exercised his authority unambiguously and always with the well-being of his students in mind.

When I visited Eastside on June 3, 1986, I insisted on meeting and talking with parents. I pressed them pretty hard—I wanted to know if there were problems I hadn't heard about. I knew that if the Secretary of Education praised Joe Clark, he would come under even closer scrutiny and suspicion by many in hopes that he (and I) would be brought down a notch. But I didn't hear any substantial objections. What parents spoke about was Joe Clark's record: phone calls home, encouragement to their children, scolding and tongue-lashings for laziness. It was all testimony to thousands of hours of work by this principal. No mere flashy media operator—as some wanted to characterize Clark—could have found the time to have done all these things. Eastside was the real thing.

At an assembly I attended, the likes of which I have never seen before or since, there was singing—spirituals, "The Star-Spangled Banner," the Eastside school song—and a boisterous, emotional, almost deafening outpouring of applause and regard for Clark that would match any testimony given any time, to anyone. Clearly at Eastside discipline was not the enemy of enthusiasm. I asked the students, "Is this a good school?"

They roared, "Yes."

I asked, "Is Joe Clark a good man?" and I thought the roof was going to lift off.

"Is he tough?" a news reporter once asked one of Joe's students.

"Yes," she replied, "he's real tough. But he's good tough. He's tough because he cares about us. And we need him." So they did. Because of Joe Clark, the lives and futures of some of his students were saved, and *that* is education, too.

Jay Jackson's Missouri City Elementary School is a far cry from Paterson's Eastside High School. Located thirty miles from Kansas City, in rural Missouri, Jackson's school is one of the highest-rated schools in Missouri.

When I visited I saw why; it had what all good schools possess: an ethos of community, achievement, and intimacy. In this community, many of the leaders are parents of students. There is a palpable closeness, an identification of school and community that University of Chicago scholar James Coleman has identified as a guarantor of effectiveness. It is an elementary school that has resisted consolidation to a larger system. It doesn't want to be part of a multidistrict, multicounty system. It wants to keep its own distinctive identity. Consolidation would destroy the ethos of Missouri City and the citizens there were right to resist it.

Missouri City is an ideal small American school. When I arrived, the entire community—parents, teachers, and local officials—were assembled in the gymnasium. The nice thing was that you couldn't tell who was "official" and who was "unofficial" simply by looking. They were sitting and talking together and at ease with one another. Normally, I would be introduced to principals and supervisors first, then teachers, then parents, and finally, students.

At Jackson's school there was no hierarchy, no school people as distinct from townspeople. What you had instead was a large community of citizens, young and old, professionals and parents, all mixed together. I got a further dose of school reality when I taught "my" class of second-, third-, and fourth-graders. This was like the one-room school where grades are often combined for certain subjects.

After asking a few questions and getting very satisfactory answers—the right answers to arithmetic problems, locations where I came from on a map, and the proper spelling of "telescope"—I offered the students to turn the table, as was my usual practice. "Do you have any questions for me?" I asked.

An eight-year-old asked me, "Do you carry a gun?"

"No," I assured him.

Then a seven-year-old raised his hand and asked, "What did the first tire say to the second tire after the second tire fell off the car?"

Unlike how the class had been with me, I was unable to answer. Then my questioner told me the answer: "You picked a fine time to leave me, loose wheel" (playing off a well-known Kenny Rogers song, "You picked a fine time to leave me, Lucille").

Here was a young child who had the self-possession to raise his hand and ask the Secretary of Education a riddle and then have the confidence to tell him he missed it. A child's disposition toward strangers reveals much about the school's environment. I have visited schools where, upon my arrival (with the inevitable retinue of security, media and local officials), the student body parted for us like the Red Sea, with students seeking the outer perimeter of the school yard. In some places the visit of a stranger was a fearful thing. But at Missouri City Elementary children learn to trust adults, to trust themselves, and to have confidence in themselves in dealings with others. This is a matter of no small consequence. To teach it is not a matter of a lesson plan; it can only be taught over time by adults nurturing students in a thousand small ways.

Children learned this lesson and many others at Chambers Elementary School in East Cleveland, Ohio, under the direction of one of the most extraordinary educators I have ever met, principal Joe Whelan. Chambers is an urban school. Despite the difficult circumstances that face many of its students at home, Chambers's record was impressive. Of the almost eight hundred students who attended at the time of my visit, almost all were black, three quarters lived in poverty and two-thirds were from single-parent families. Yet it is inconceivable to me that one could find a better inner-city school than this, and there are not many schools its equal in *any* setting. The record is impressive: Test scores keep rising. Sixty-five percent of the students scored at or above grade level in reading, and 75 percent did so in math. They read, read, and read some more. There is no fooling around at Chambers, but there is much joy.

When I arrived, I was met by several small children dressed up in their best, exhibiting the best manners possible and offering presents and souvenirs. They took me on a tour of the school—the Hall of Presidents and the pictures of Cleveland ("Here, Mr. Secretary, is Cleveland Stadium, where our great Cleveland Browns came within forty-five seconds of a Super Bowl trip" [but for the Denver Broncos' miraculous 98-yard drive in 1987]).

I gave some students a quiz, and then they quizzed me on my reputed expertise in rock and roll. In the late morning there was a large school assembly marked by joy and pride and the presence of parents who took part of the day off from work to be there because of their love of the school. Whelan ran his school as a general, father, and cheerleader. He regularly had lunch with small groups of students when their work and attendance records are good, and they work hard for the privilege of having lunch with him. Joe Whelan works the community businesses for his school; he asked local businesses to contribute hats and gloves for the winter season for children who couldn't afford them. No opportunity to help his children is left untried by Whelan. His life is his work, his school, the children of Chambers. And the students remember. Whelan shared with me a letter he received from a former student, who wrote, "When I was a student, the discipline at Chambers was ridiculous; the rules were too strict, so I thought. I thought that we always had so much work as elementary students. Why does Mr. Whelan try to learn all of our names? How dumb, I thought. . . . Now, what I really want to say is thank you. . . . All that schoolwork prepared me to enter high school and leave there as a straight 'A' student. . . . All those rules taught me right from wrong. . . . At Chambers I was special."

And so it is at Edison Elementary in the worst section of Dayton, Ohio. At first look, the day seems to be comprised of equal parts of reading and hugging. In things large and small, principal Brenda Lee's emphasis on achievement was everywhere: a sign in the foyer of Edison states Lee's vision, "Edison Has No Nobodies and Everyone Is Somebody at Edison." Drawing upon the school's name, specially illuminated lights are used throughout the school to symbolize achievement and faith in the children's capacity to learn. The proportion of students performing at or above grade level has risen steadily from 40 percent in 1982–83 to 64 percent in 1985–86 in math, and from 65 percent in 1982–83 to 78 percent in 1985–86 in reading. When I visited Lee's school, student attendance was around 95 percent.

Despite the neighborhood, Lee's school was actively sought out by parents all over Dayton. They were not concerned about sending their children into a poor neighborhood or an old building. Instead, they were excited about a school that works, where children are taught the right habits and learn to read. Here, as at other good schools, the physical environment— equipment and facilities—matters less than the environment of spirit, purpose, and attitude. To achieve this, Lee spent many hours with her staff, and their devotion to children is paramount and obvious.

However, Lee told me over breakfast one day what I have heard before from dedicated principals—that the most time-consuming and frustrating part of her job was working to document the case against an incompetent teacher. "The time I took documenting the case could have been taken with the children," Lee said ruefully.

In every school I have visited where there has been a strong turnaround, the principal has told me that it began by clearing out the individuals who did not want to pull their own weight and that it was a very long and demoralizing bureaucratic process.

In a sound system of school accountability, principals would be given greater autonomy to hire and remove, and teachers would normally be given, as they were given at Lee and Whelan's schools, greater autonomy to teach. Great schools are led by great individuals—but they are not one-man or one-woman shows. Great schools and great principals showcase their great teachers; they let their teachers teach. And the students at Edison Elementary learn. When I asked them why their school was special, the fourth-graders told me they "learn reading, times tables, and spelling." And they said they are taught "no chewing gum" and "keep your hands and feet to yourself." Valuable lessons indeed.

Principal Henry Gradillas at Garfield High School in East Los Angeles let Jaime Escalante teach. And did the students ever learn. Escalante, a Bolivian immigrant, arrived at the school in 1974 to teach math. Now perhaps America's most famous teacher, he wanted to return something to the country that had taken him in and given him opportunity. His plan to teach calculus to disadvantaged Hispanic youngsters was greeted with skepticism and laughter by his colleagues, and he encountered resistance from his students. But he told me that the greatest resistance came not from the students but from others in the profession, other teachers and counselors who urged him not to push so hard. They told him that his plan to teach calculus was a quixotic fantasy. "If you try," some told him, "the students will fail. They can't do it. They will be embarrassed, and their self-esteem will suffer. What you want to do—teach calculus—will be dangerous."

Escalante told me what he told his critics: "If you are fifteen or sixteen years old, in the barrio of East Los Angeles, there are a lot of things that are dangerous. But calculus isn't one of them." His principal, Henry Gradillas, encouraged him to proceed.

Escalante persisted, and in 1982 eighteen of his students took the Advanced Placement (AP) calculus test. By 1991, 160 students from Garfield took the test. According to Jay Mathews, author of *Escalante: The Best Teacher in America,* Escalante has given Garfield the most successful inner-city mathematics program in the United States. In recent years only four or five secondary schools in the country have prepared more students for the AP calculus examination (tests so difficult that fewer than 2 percent of American students even attempt them). Because of Escalante's efforts, about a fourth of all the Mexican-American students in the country who pass AP calculus come from Garfield.

Escalante's methods and approach (celebrated in the movie *Stand and Deliver*) are in marked contrast to the theory and practice of pedagogy as taught in most American schools of education. He consistently violates the canard that a teacher shouldn't "impose his values on students." Indeed, he seeks every opportunity to impose his ethic of achievement, success, and hard work on them. His reason, as expressed to me, is simple: "My values are better than theirs." His way of doing this is direct, manly, no nonsense. In the early days of his career at Garfield, he asked a student whether he wanted to study calculus. "No," said the student, "I want to see my girlfriend."

"Well, then," responded Escalante, "go over to woodworking class on your way out."

"Why?" the student asked.

"So you can learn how to make shoeshine boxes so you can have a career shining the shoes for Anglos as they pass through Los Angeles International Airport on their business trips."

"I don't want to shine Anglos' shoes," protested the student.

"Then study calculus," was Escalante's reply.

Because he genuinely cares about students and because he can see through pedagogical nonsense, Escalante doesn't assume a fake posture of equality with students; he doesn't banter in a pseudo-Socratic method; he doesn't cast about his classroom proffering profound doubts and questions about the dilemmas of the age. He takes his students where he finds them, in a tough barrio of East Los Angeles, and he argues, pulls, cajoles, and exhorts them to the activity of hard work, very hard work, for their own lives, for their own futures.

And Escalante's classroom bulged; seventy students were there the day I visited. This is far above the average class size in Los Angeles or in the nation. But as Escalante said, he will teach whatever number he's given; he will turn away no one who wants to take his class. Despite the fact that parents and teachers alike tend to prefer small classes, research does not show any strong positive correlation between smaller class size and achievement. The critical factor—as common sense and experience testify—is not the size of the class but the quality and command of the teacher. Some teachers, like Escalante, can hold the attention and motivate the work of a hundred students at once. For other teachers, to teach one student would be too hard. In teaching, it is the human qualities of inspiration, competence, and commitment that matter, not a bureaucratic formula. We would be better off letting our classroom sizes follow the abilities, preferences, and gifts of the teacher, than imposing uniform guidelines that often violate or frustrate individual talents.

One story illustrates what manner of man this great teacher Escalante is. Shortly before I left my job as Secretary of Education, I set up a White House luncheon for my "heroes," which President Reagan was gracious enough to host. He was very interested in these educators, who briefly told about their schools, their children, their success stories.

After the luncheon, a White House social secretary came up to me and said, "Mr. Secretary, tomorrow night is a state dinner, and we would like to invite Mr. Escalante to sit at the President's table. The President was very impressed with Mr. Escalante."

I said, "Well, that's a great invitation, and I'm sure Jaime will appreciate it. But with all due respect, I doubt that he'll accept. He's already been away from his kids for two days."

The social secretary persisted. "Mr. Secretary, will you *please* ask him? This is, after all, a state dinner with the President."

I said, "I realize you're talking state dinner. But I'm talking calculus."

I did go to Jaime later that day and told him of the invitation. "That's a great honor, Bill," he told me. "But I'm sorry, I can't go. I've got to get back to my students."

Jaime Escalante's offer to his students is simple and straightforward: He knows calculus; they don't. He has what they need; he will take the time to get them ready, but they must work and they must believe in the watchword of his classroom: *ganas*—desire, effort, perspiration, hard work.

Escalante insists there is no way around this. He will not let his students avoid it or him. He gives the lie to the proposition that the combination of poverty, disadvantaged background, or color are destiny; that the usual rules of good habits, good behavior and hard work don't apply.

Escalante should be the toast of the education establishment for what he has single-handedly accomplished. Instead, he has been undercut for years by the district teachers union, the United Teachers of Los Angeles. Union representatives helped organize a vote by the teachers that ejected him as Garfield's mathematics department chairman in 1990, according to Escalante. Why? Because he is an *embarrassment* to them. Some of them explain away their own lackluster efforts by citing the sociology of their students. The students are poor and unmotivated, they say, so there is little they can do. Escalante proves them wrong. In doing so, he does not earn their emulation or affection.

In the end, the interference by the teachers union was too much for Escalante. In 1991 he moved on to Hiram Johnson High School in Sacramento, which, unlike East Los Angeles, welcomed him with open arms. His efforts are appreciated. Sacramento School Superintendent Rudy Crew said Escalante "represents the kind of teacher a lot of teachers are if they are allowed to pursue their dreams."

Some parts of the education establishment seem to be in a perpetual fever to try *new* ways and approaches that will work with the poor—anything, it seems, except what works, what is right in front of them. Consider what happened to Henry Gradillas, the man who stood beside Escalante. When Gradillas returned to Los Angeles in the fall of 1988 from a year's sabbatical to finish his doctoral dissertation, this impressive man looked forward to a new assignment that would allow him to devote his energies to more than just one school.

Instead, the school district assigned him to scheduling asbestos inspections, "a kind of academic Siberia" according to *The Washington Post*. As Escalante said, Gradillas "cleaned up the school. He eliminated a high percentage of the teachers who were not doing their jobs." But he ran afoul of the system. Joe Lopez, the school's career counselor, observed, "Henry proved [the district] wrong in everything they did." Well, the system struck back. And a great principal was grounded. Whoever said "No good deed goes unpunished" was right, at least about a lot of American education.

In 1987 President Reagan and I visited John Murphy, the outstanding superintendent of the nation's fifteenth-largest school district, Prince Georges County, located on the eastern border of Washington, D.C. We had heard about some remarkable things Murphy had accomplished; we decided to see them for ourselves.

When Murphy took over in 1984, Prince Georges County was ranked twenty-first among Maryland's twenty-four school districts. Test scores were going down, morale was low, vandalism and drug use were rampant, and students were dividing along racial lines. In seven years as superintendent, Murphy turned the school district around. Enrollment went up. Order was restored. Racial tensions eased. And parents were impressed and appreciative. PG County now ranks tenth among Maryland's school districts. The scores of the generally low-to-middle-income students improved from the fiftieth percentile to the seventieth.

Murphy engineered the turnaround by insisting on high expectations and high standards, giving teachers a stronger hand in decision making, emphasizing leadership, a safe and orderly classroom climate, strong school-home relationship, and parental choice. "I'd love to see, in every school system, parents able to pick any school they want. If a school doesn't get picked, it closes up and everybody at that school says goodbye, since they haven't done their job well," he said. Murphy's schools did their job so well that prior to the new school year, parents would camp overnight so they could get in line early in the morning to pick the right school for their children. According to *The Wall Street Journal*, "the magnet schools are so popular about 3,000 students are turned away each year."

"We need more accountability," Murphy told Ken Adelman in an interview that appeared in *Washingtonian* magazine. "We should demand superior performance and be willing to support those schools that achieve it. Once we establish standards and have them accepted across the community, we should work hard to meet those standards." All he asked was that he be judged by his success.

But success wasn't enough. Because Murphy refused to play by the rules of the establishment, it eventually turned on him. Murphy's reform agenda made him a target of the Prince Georges County Education Association, the district's largest teacher union. Murphy advocated more money for the school district, but insisted it be tied to reforms like high standards, accountability, and parental choice. The teacher union wanted more money, a lot more money, and no structural reform. "I am appalled by the level of greed I encountered in dealing with that union," Murphy told *The Wall Street Journal*.

In the end, Murphy was forced out because of politics. The PG school board offered him a new contract. But some Maryland state legislators and community leaders protested, arguing that his hiring would delay the appointment of a black superintendent for the primarily black district. "In 1984, I announced my intention to take a school system 65 percent black and make it competitive with the most affluent white suburban systems in America," Murphy said in the Adelman interview. "That would disprove the myth about race and learning once and for all. We've made tremendous strides in that direction. But, after doing that, to have black political leaders call for my departure in favor of a black superintendent, I found extremely disappointing." A good man was sent packing, and the children of PG County lost. The children of Charlotte, North Carolina, are the winners; Charlotte is where Murphy is now the school superintendent.

There is resistance to the heroes of American education. It is said by some that the Clarks, Whelans, Lees, Escalantes, and Murphys are "exceptions." And so it is said they are too few in number, their success inexplicable, certainly incapable of replication. In

the words of Edward Zigler, a professor at Yale, they are examples of the "Jesus Christ effect."

"The problem," according to Zigler, "is that there just aren't
that many magnificent people in the world."

Well, there are far more than Professor Zigler thinks. There are
the already magnificent, the near-magnificent, and those with
magnificent qualities that a sound system of education should
recruit, discover, encourage, build up, honor, and reward. These
people are not superhuman; they are not gods. Many ordinary
people in our schools already perform magnificently; if schools
were properly organized, and good people were allowed and encouraged to rise to the top, there could be many more magnificent
ones. Ordinary people are capable of extraordinary things.

But there are other reasons why these success stories remain
exceptions today rather than the rule. To many in the education
world, the poor black or Hispanic children of Garfield or Chambers or Edison or Eastside are viewed as aliens, as creatures from
another planet for whom the ordinary rules of affection, aspiration, achievement, and hard work do not apply. For these theo-
rists and practitioners, perhaps, it is due to their own hostility to
"middle-class values"—such as the *ethos* of achievement and success that Escalante espouses—that explains their resistance. Perhaps it is worse; perhaps it is the growth industry of "helping the
poor" that will be endangered if a clear and decisive answer is
actually found—good schools with good principals, teachers, and
curriculum; perhaps it is even envy of people like those profiled
in this chapter.

Whatever the reason, until the education world recognizes that
real achievement against the odds is a fact evident daily in schools
across this country, and that this success depends on committed
and talented individuals working hard, then these shining exceptions will remain exactly that—exceptions. There is no federal
program, no magic bullet, no novel approach or procedure that
will some day be invented to cure the education ills of poor children. It will be done as it has always been done: good schools,
good teachers, good principals, and hard work.

It is a scandal that resistance to these real world facts results in
the loss of equal opportunity every day for hundreds of thousands of children. Schools don't fail or succeed nationally; they
fail or succeed locally. But it is a lot easier to complain about the
low performance of most schools for poor children in the country

than it is to go to one of those schools and make the effort, put in the hours, and make the commitment required to fix it. We can only be grateful that some are willing to do it.

The system does not reward these dedicated men and women for their effort; by and large, it treats its best the same way it treats its worst. Because of the kind of people they are and the kind of commitment they bring to their work, Lee and Whelan, Clark and Escalante would do the same job for a thousand dollars less as well as a thousand dollars more. But they surely deserve a good deal more than a thousand-dollar raise.

Since the time I have visited their schools, some of the people I have described have moved on because of clashes with the establishment powers that be. The fact is, the education establishment doesn't take care of its best and brightest educators. It has often made life more, not less, difficult for them. Great teachers and principals violate the conventional wisdom of the educrats, the "wisdom" that says nothing can be done to improve American education and cites problems, obstacles, and lack of resources. The heroes demonstrate that it can be done. And they do it.

A grateful society should find ways to express its gratitude for people who do nothing less than save children's lives. St. Paul wrote these words to the church at Philippi: "Whatever is true, whatever is honorable, whatever is right, whatever is pure, whatever is lovely, whatever is of good repute, if there is any excellence and anything worthy of praise, let your mind dwell on these things." And in American education, we should do more than think about these virtues. We should reward them.

3

THE AMERICAN NIGHTMARE

I once heard Clare Boothe Luce tell the story of her visit with John F. Kennedy in the White House. She sat down and straightforwardly said, "Mr. President, you must get the Soviets out of this hemisphere." They talked a few minutes. Then the phone rang, and the President went off. He came back rather excited and said, "I got my textile bill passed. What were you saying, Clare?" Replied Mrs. Luce, "Mr. President, there are many great men remembered in our civilization. Of one man, they said He went to a cross and died so that all men's sins may be forgiven. Of another man, they said he went in search of a new route to an old world, and founded a new world. Of another it is said that he took up arms against his mother country and with a motley army of rebels defeated the greatest military power on earth to found a new nation. And of another, it is said that he had to hide in the dark of night as he came into Washington, and grieved for four years that the nation might be half slave and half free. Mr. President, of none of these great men was it said, 'He got his textile bill passed.' "

Political leaders must attend first, and energetically, to the most important things for which they have responsibility.

Harlem Hospital's neonatal intensive care unit is not very big but a very busy place. Too busy. It is a place that treats babies born addicted to cocaine. Neonatal units weren't intended to care for drug addicts. But in large American cities, a lot of them do. In the spring of 1989 the doctors in Harlem Hospital's neonatal intensive care unit told me that the word on the streets was that if you were pregnant and you wanted an easy delivery, cocaine—especially "crack" cocaine—would help. Crack is free-base cocaine; when smoked, it is extremely potent.

What the doctors told me was true: crack would ease the pain of delivery, though the baby would often be born prematurely, at six months or earlier, sometimes weighing a pound or two, with a bulb head and Popsicle limbs. And many times, the baby would be born a cocaine addict. These infants—"cocaine babies" in the modern-day lexicon—are so tiny and vulnerable that they look barely human. And apart from their size, the exposure to cocaine often causes them pain, irritability, anxiety, and constant, uninterrupted crying.

When I had my first look at a cocaine baby in April of 1989, I thought about the child Elayne and I were expecting the following month. In one of the rooms at the hospital I saw tiny babies linked up to elaborate monitoring and support systems. For each baby there was a nurse, doctor, or paramedic nearby, constantly monitoring the baby's well-being. When you see infants like this, the real stakes in the drug war become most evident.

The word on the street was also that the crack high could be sustained if the crack was sprayed with insect repellent. "There are more ways they find to destroy themselves than we can imagine," the head of the pediatric clinic told me. "The street chemists are pretty good in their way. They don't pay any attention to what the long-term consequences are, but they come up with novel ways of giving people bigger 'hits' and higher 'highs.' "

I had returned home to the city of my birth, to one of the greatest cities in the world, to a hospital with some of the best technology in the world, and watched doctors and nurses do their damnedest to keep up with what human beings had done to themselves and to their babies.

A crack house is a small, dark hellhole where people gather to smoke cocaine for a day or two. The typical scene is one of human waste, degradation, and abuse, of people sprawled out on their high, or "crashing" afterward. Food and garbage are littered everywhere. Often human excrement and puddles of urine are found around the room. And, as the police will tell you, there are sometimes children living in the midst of all this. Children do their best to maintain some sense of order in their lives, often leaving crack houses in the morning to seek refuge at school during the day. But they still have to come back home.

A police officer once told a colleague of mine about going into an apartment after receiving a call from a neighbor and finding two young children. They had been there by themselves for three days. When the police entered, the young girl was holding on to the hand of her older brother. The boy said, "This is my sister and my mother told me to take care of her." He was trying manfully to do his best. While the police were there, the mother came in with a roll of money in her hand. She had been out selling her body to get the money to support not her children but her crack habit.

I heard of a six-month-old child who died of an overdose of crack. How does a six-month-old overdose on crack? Because its mother or father, we're not sure which, inhaled crack and then, to quiet the crying baby, blew the crack into its mouth.

And I read about a Detroit woman who owed money to her drug dealer and handed over her thirteen-year-old daughter as payment.

These things have happened, and still happen, in America. Experts on child abuse have told me time and again that dramatic increases in child abuse and neglect are often due to drugs. When people take crack they often become paranoid and violent, frequently taking their rage out on those who are closest and most defenseless—often a child, *in utero* or out. When the drug problem comes home, the children take the hardest blows.

Somewhere along the way, in the late 1960s and 1970s, part of America lost its moral bearings regarding drugs. Drugs were not only seen as a political statement of sorts but were also advertised as a path to self-discovery, self-expression, and liberation. In 1970 Charles A. Reich wrote *The Greening of America,* a best-selling book that was emblematic of the cultural tenor of the times. "The effect of psychedelic drugs does not end when the drug itself wears off," wrote Reich, "it is lasting in the sense that the user finds his awareness and sensitivity has increased, whether he is using drugs at the time or not. In other words, something has been learned."

Even some of those who disagreed with this view often did not know how to challenge it. It didn't help, of course, that drugs were blessed by the highest councils of government and in some quarters of elite opinion. Elaine Shannon, author of *Desperados*

(New York: Viking, 1988), recounts how in 1975 President Ford's Domestic Council Drug Abuse Task Force, chaired by Vice President Nelson Rockefeller, produced a white paper that dismissed marijuana as a minor problem and stated that "cocaine is not physically addictive." The panel recommended that the DEA and U.S. Customs deemphasize investigations of marijuana and cocaine smugglers and give higher priority to heroin trafficking. That finding was acclaimed by a *Washington Post* editorial as "common sense . . . a welcome departure from the heroics of the past." And Dr. Peter Bourne, a psychiatrist who served as President Carter's adviser on drugs, held that "cocaine is probably the most benign of illicit drugs currently in widespread use."

It was the collapse of institutional government authority, essentially giving permission to take drugs, that was largely responsible for the epidemic that eventually hit us. For almost two decades—and with catastrophic consequences—many forgot how to answer the question, "Why not drugs?"

December 18, 1988, was the night of our annual Christmas caroling party. Elayne had invited the neighbors and their children and we went up and down the streets of our Chevy Chase, Maryland, neighborhood. Elayne had distributed the lyrics of the carols and given everyone small candles to hold. It was a good outing, despite a near disaster when I put my arm around her back and torched the bottom of her hair with the candle. I was able to put out the fire with impunity because when it first started Elayne was so engaged with the neighborhood children that she didn't notice it, except to say, a moment later, "Bill, you aren't smoking, are you?"

The next morning I went to my office at the Madison Center, a public policy organization I had founded months earlier. I was restless. In the back of my mind I thought that there was a chance that I might become director of the Office of National Drug Control Policy ("drug czar" as the position became popularly known). As Secretary of Education I had been actively involved in the federal government's anti-drug efforts. I had told friends that the "drug czar" job was the only job in the Bush administration that interested me and I was thinking of expressing that interest to the newly elected President.

My relations with George Bush were good and I had campaigned for him in 1988. During the campaign, while I was Secretary of Education, I caused something of a furor when, on the NBC News show "Meet the Press," I criticized Governor Michael Dukakis for vetoing a bill requiring teachers to start the day with the Pledge of Allegiance. "Let's get into this question of the Pledge," host Chris Wallace said. "What does the Pledge of Allegiance have to do with education?"

"Well, it's the ABCs of civics," I said. "If you have trouble with the Pledge, you're going to have trouble with a lot of things down the road. . . . If you're governor and you're sitting there and someone brings the Pledge before you to sign, do you look for a way to sign it or look for a way to avoid signing it? And with Mike Dukakis it was the latter. I'll tell you what's involved here, because I've said it before. I lived in that Brookline-Cambridge world for eight years. These are people who don't like things like the Pledge. They have disdain for the simple and basic patriotism of most Americans; they think they're smarter than everybody else, and they don't like these kinds of rituals. That bothers me. I think it should bother a lot of people."

Vice President Bush called me immediately after the show. He had seen it, and he told me how much he appreciated my speaking out on the issue, and to be sure and stay in touch after the election.

On the morning of December 19 I picked up the phone and called the President-elect. I congratulated him on his victory and he was, as always, gracious.

I got straight to the point. "Mr. President, I don't know what you are planning to do about this drug job. But if you are really serious about it, and want someone to go after it for you, I'll volunteer."

The newly elected President responded, "That's great to hear, Bill. Listen, I would like to say 'aye' to that right now, but I don't know where things stand. Let me find out what is going on in the personnel process and we'll talk soon." I had no sooner hung up the phone than I got a call from Elayne. She had just spoken to her friend Pat Burch (Pat and her late husband Dean were close friends of George and Barbara Bush). Pat told Elayne that she wanted to recommend me but wanted to check with Elayne first.

We had planned to stay out of government, get some relief from its pressures, and enjoy private life, at least for a while. But then Elayne said to me, "I think you would be the best man for the job. We will soon have two children facing this. If you want the job, you know I'll support you."

A few weeks later—after several calls back and forth—the President-elect, the incoming chief-of-staff (and my good friend) John Sununu, and I met. We discussed what kinds of things could be done to end the drug scourge. I told Mr. Bush that there were definitely some things his administration could do—in fact, a lot more than had been done in the past. I laid out some of my ideas and told him that to be successful I would need some of his time, some of his energy, and some of the budget of Richard Darman, director of the Office of Management and Budget. "This is one issue, Mr. President, where I, a conservative Republican, feel comfortable in advocating a strong federal role."

"Well, Bill, so do I," Mr. Bush said. At the end of the conversation, he offered me the job.

Things got off to a rocky start, at least as far as some outside observers were concerned. I learned I was not going to be a member of the Cabinet (although I retained Cabinet-level status) after I was not invited to the President's first Cabinet meeting. The Office of National Drug Control Policy was a new agency and the President understandably wanted to limit the number of Cabinet members (Thomas R. Pickering, ambassador to the UN, and William H. Webster, director of the CIA, were also not members of the Cabinet). I was not particularly distressed at this turn of events; I had my fill of Cabinet sessions while I was Secretary of Education. A much more important issue as far as I was concerned was whether the President had confidence in me, and whether that confidence would be conveyed to my colleagues. During a January 12 dinner at Blair House, President-elect Bush told his assembled Cabinet members that he wanted them to give me their full cooperation. He had also assured me in two private meetings that I would have easy access to the Oval Office and significant authority in dealing with relevant government agencies. "The fact that I don't have to sit in on Cabinet meetings means I can be more what he wanted me to be: a single-minded person," I told reporters.

Nevertheless, some people, especially in the Congress, interpreted the lack of Cabinet status as a signal that my post was being given short shrift. Senator Joseph Biden (D-Delaware), the influential chairman of the Senate Judiciary Committee, said I was "in for some rough riding. And his not being at that table—I don't care what you say—will at a minimum make the second-level people in each of the departments he has to deal with think he has less clout." Representative Glenn English (D-Oklahoma), one of the authors of the congressional antidrug bill that created the drug-czar post, said, "This kind of symbolism is important. It will weaken the drug czar in his relationship with other members of the Cabinet. . . . It does trouble me." *U.S. News & World Report* magazine declared that "the consensus assessment of Bennett's fate is that he will become a figurehead. The 'czar' will have only the power to cajole federal agencies, not to order them around. Cynics bet Bennett will slowly sink into bureaucratic quicksand and be rendered irrelevant."

Sinking into bureaucratic quicksand and being rendered irrelevant was frankly never much of a concern of mine. At the same time, I was well aware that the director of the Office of National Drug Control Policy was in some ways a unique position. Unlike my job as Secretary of Education, here I had little direct authority, no ability to dispense government grants, a 100-person staff (infinitesimal by Washington standards), and no precedent on how the job was to be done. In many ways, then, it was a make-it-up-as-you-go situation. There were some inherent, potentially debilitating, institutional weaknesses that I had to overcome. I felt that in order to be effective, I needed to mount the "bully pulpit." At the Education Department I had seen how effective it could be in terms of raising issues, setting the terms of debate, and laying the groundwork for future legislation. But if the bully pulpit was useful at the Education Department, it was indispensable at drug policy.

I also had to sharpen my skills at the "bureaucratic inside game," as one political reporter called it. Unlike my post as Education Secretary (where I was given pretty wide latitude in performing my job), my effectiveness as drug czar depended to a large degree on how much support I was able to muster within the White House and how well my office was able to work with other federal agencies. My power in that sense was derivative.

In the long run the "Cabinet short shrift" probably worked to my advantage because the President bent over backward to make it clear that I had his support. At every critical juncture during my tenure, President Bush backed me up, whether publicly or internally, within the administration. He more than kept his end of the deal.

I already had some experience with the drug issue long before I was appointed drug czar. Though I never used drugs, I had spent almost all of 1965 through 1975 on or around a college campus, so I had certainly been around some of the stuff.

As a proctor while I was a Harvard law student, I once came back from spring vacation to find one of my freshmen waiting for me outside my door. "Please go into my room," he said, "because you have to see what is going on there."

"I can't go in by myself," I told him. "You know the rules, so you'll have to take me in with you." (The rules prohibited a proctor from entering student rooms unless a student took or invited him in.)

When we walked into the room, two other freshmen were on the floor on their knees, bending over suitcases from which they were selling pills to kids no more than thirteen years old.

"What in the hell is going on?" I yelled.

Everybody scattered, the two freshmen boys and the junior high students all out the window and down the fire escape. These two freshmen later turned themselves in to Harvard's assistant dean of freshmen. They actually went to him for refuge because they were afraid that I was going to do physical harm to them.

I filed a written complaint to the authorities at Harvard, but I regretted doing so because the university took a scandalously long time to act. When it did, it suspended the two students for one year each. I should have complained instead to Cambridge Criminal Court where charges would have been brought against these students. (That's what would have happened if they had not been enrolled at Harvard.)

That experience and others made me well aware of how inimical illegal drugs were to a good education. During a segment of the "Today" show, while Secretary of Education, I was asked, "Do you see drugs as the biggest problem as kids head back to school in the next few weeks?"

I responded that drugs were "the biggest outside impediment to learning in the schools. All the reform efforts that we're talking about . . . will just come to nothing if kids are stoned or high. It's one of those things which, if we don't attack, all the other things we're doing won't make much sense."

I believed that there was no issue that demanded more immediate and sustained attention than drug use and it was an issue I would return to again and again as Education Secretary. Early in my tenure I contacted the heads of the National Education Association and the American Federation of Teachers, urging them to adopt a policy requiring teachers using drugs to resign (I never heard back from either). My reasoning was pretty straightforward: teachers are a group that obviously ought to be drug-free. In a 1986 speech in Nashville before the International Association of Chiefs of Police, I renewed my call. "There could be a pledge everyone takes as part of signing a contract, to promise they would give up their jobs if they were caught using drugs," I said. "I think teachers should be four-square in their opposition to drugs. They should be drug-free, not for reasons of national security, but for reasons of setting an example."

The president of the Metro Nashville Education Association said I was being "unrealistic."

"Teachers should be careful of their actions in front of the students, but teachers are still part of society," the MNEA president said. "It's unrealistic for teachers to be so different. Substance abuse is an illness and should be treated as such. No group is going to be 100 percent clean, be it chiefs of police, ministers or teachers." Here again was an example of the teacher unions getting in the way of sound reform, this time because of a startling lack of moral clarity or moral courage.

In response to what I saw and heard from many school superintendents, principals, teachers, and parents, the Department of Education released in 1987 a comprehensive book entitled *Schools Without Drugs*. It profiled successful antidrug programs and discussed what practical steps educators, parents, and communities should take to prevent drug use. We wrote about the signs parents should look for, and about the psychological and physical effects of various drugs. As we had tried to be with all of our publications, the book was straightforward in its language, commonsensical in its approach, and tough-minded in its policy recommendations. The book was very well received by the general public. Our office distributed over three million copies.

As is sometimes the case, the Congress was not so enthusiastic about common sense and tough-mindedness. In 1986 I appeared before a hearing presided over by New York congressman Charles Rangel. We butted heads over this issue.

"What we want at the Department of Education is to get drugs out of schools," I said. "Right now, no ifs, ands, or buts. We strongly support drug education programs, [but] almost every school in this country has a drug education program, [and] we are still awash in drugs. We need to get tough, we need to get tough as hell, and we need to do it right now."

Citing a number of programs that we could learn from, I said the first step to an effective school drug prevention program is "sending a clear message to all kids that if you're using drugs, you're out of that school."

"To kick them out is an easy thing to do," Rangel responded. "Now that they're kicked out, what do we do? Where's the education?"

I told Rangel that when principal Bill Rudolph acted in this way at Northside High School in Atlanta, he got rid of drugs at his school. "That is a real achievement," I said.

I then cited principal Joe Clark of Eastside High School. At that point Representative Benjamin Gilman jumped in. "Joe Clark may be getting [drug users] out of school," he said, "but he's putting them out on the street, he's not really solving the problem. I hope we can find a better solution, Mr. Secretary."

"Mr. Gilman, are you suggesting that kids who are using or abusing drugs should be kept in school?" I asked.

"No," he replied, but added that kicking kids out of school is "not educating kids, that's just scaring the hell out of them and hoping that some of them are not going to use drugs."

"I'm sorry," I said, "I believe that *is* education. I think it's a very effective form of education."

Rangel then asked, "Are you suggesting that a junkie kicked out of school no longer is a junkie?"

"No," I responded, "but you have taught a profoundly important lesson to the other children in that school, which is that this school does not tolerate junkies, and we're not going to have someone around this school to try to destroy you. That's a good educational lesson, Mr. Chairman; we ought to have more teaching of it more regularly."

I think what Rangel hoped for from us was something less severe: a course of instruction, a drug education program, lectures, slides, and tapes—in short, a magic bullet that would inoculate the young from ever using drugs. There is no such solution, nor can there be. An education program by itself is not enough.

Of course we want to teach children not to play with matches. But if a house is burning, we've got to put out the fire—and we've got to grab matches out of some hands before they start any more fires.

I saw this principle in action while I was drug czar. In 1989 I visited W. R. Thomas Junior High School in West Miami. The school is situated in a middle-class Latino neighborhood that had been labeled "Cocaine Alley" by a local newspaper. It had been a very busy cocaine-trafficking area, but the school, thanks to the leadership of former principal Jeff Miller, was essentially drug free. Principal Miller told me so, the teachers told me so, the kids told me so, and the cops told me so (you should always check these claims with the police). When I asked the kids why the school was drug-free, they told me, "We were 'indoctrinated' against drugs." The message is clear and unambiguous: if you use drugs, there will be a price to pay. The first time a student is caught using drugs, he must enroll in a drug intervention or private rehabilitation program or, depending on the severity of the infraction, he may face suspension. Subsequent infractions lead to suspension and possible expulsion from school. If a student is caught dealing drugs, he is turned over to a police agency and faces either suspension or expulsion from school. When students know that adults are serious about stopping drug use, they adjust their behavior accordingly. It's a sound program that's worked very well.

As Secretary of Education, I had also been an active member of the Drug Enforcement Policy Board, President Reagan's intergovernmental commission, chaired by Attorney General Edwin Meese III. I was outspoken at the meetings and soon became known as a "hawk" on the drug issue. At one meeting I asked whether our efforts to help the Bolivian government by using American military planes to bomb cocaine-processing plants were successful. The answer was yes.

I asked how many planes were used.

About nine, came the answer.

I then asked how many planes we needed to totally wipe out the processing plants for a year.

About fifteen, was the answer.

I asked how many planes we had for such purposes.

At that point an official from the Defense Department said that was classified information.

"Hell," I said, "I'm a member of the Cabinet."

I was then told that we shouldn't send in any additional military aircraft or helicopters into Bolivia because a prominent U.S.A., painted in red, white, and blue, would stir up already existing anti-American sentiments in Latin America.

"Then paint the face of Daniel Ortega [the head of the communist government in Nicaragua] on them," I said.

Toward the close of my tenure as Secretary of Education, in a speech before the White House Conference on a Drug-Free America, I called for "a transformation of government policy to match, and build on, the transformation of public sentiment."

"We cannot win simply by doing more of the same," I said. "We must consider a qualitative change in how we conduct our war against drugs." Among other things, I called for heightened inspections of international cargo and mail, more prisons, higher fines, and, for parolees, longer probationary periods and regular drug tests.

But the real stir came when I argued for an expanded military role in the war on drugs: "As the greatest military and economic power in the world," I said, "we can do more to prevent criminals in foreign nations from growing and processing illegal drugs. It is to be hoped we can do this in collaboration with foreign governments, but if need be we must consider doing this by ourselves. And we should consider broader use of military force against both the production and shipment of drugs."

My remarks were the lead story that evening on NBC News. Correspondent Fred Francis reported that "the suggestion that the military be used to stop drug smuggling is based on the government's private admission that the war on drugs is lost; that only firepower and men in uniform can stop shipments. Secretary Bennett became the first senior official to indicate that if Latin American nations refuse to cooperate, then military intervention by the United States could be used to end cocaine smuggling."

As I sometimes did, I was free-lancing. I hadn't received White House clearance for my remarks, and I heard through back channels that my remarks caused heartburn among some members of the Domestic Policy Council, and especially at the Pentagon. But I was not troubled. We were at stalemate on this issue, and I felt that the most important thing was to move the debate (and, I hoped, policy) in a new and more aggressive direction. In the weeks following my remarks, the idea of the use of military force gained more and more adherents, both in the administration and on Capitol Hill. It didn't hurt that a few days before my speech, the public had already stated its support of greater use of the military, by a ratio of better than four to one.

This episode revealed a tactic I frequently used. I believed in what I said. But I would also try to throw out an idea with the intent of sparking a debate, to get the national conversation going in a new direction. The reason this is necessary is that there is an enormous inertia in government; thinking on policy matters is rutted, and if you hope to effect real change, you have to overcome the inertia. Sometimes this approach worked. This time it did.

In this particular case, I was speaking out of a good deal of frustration. Kids were dying on the street, neighborhoods were being torn apart, and the federal government was not taking an aggressive enough posture. We were reacting to events instead of initiating them. And there were administrative problems with the Drug Enforcement Policy Board, problems Attorney General Meese was working hard to correct.

In a long memo to Meese, I laid out what I thought were the deficiencies of our efforts. "The effectiveness of almost every action taken against a part of the [drug] problem (production, shipment, sale, and use) depends upon effective pressure simultaneously and continuously being applied, and maintained, on the other parts," I wrote. "I'm afraid our current structure isn't suited as well as it might be to the mounting of such comprehensive, sustained, and effective pressure." I offered specific suggestions for strengthening our fight against drugs in the areas of production and shipping, sanctions against drug pushers and users, education and treatment. I later heard that the memo was taken up with President Reagan, but no final decisions were made. I didn't know at the time that I would later have the opportunity to put some of these ideas into action.

While waiting for confirmation as director of the Office of National Drug Control Policy, I thought I would get a jump on the job and do a little homework. I had scheduled a speech at a school in a Detroit suburb in February 1989, and through a friend arranged a tour of the drug zone.

I flew out early Sunday morning and spent three hours with the police in downtown Detroit. I thought it important to see what happens when drugs take control of an area, so I had the police take me to neighborhoods where the police said drug abuse involved more than a third of the residents. I went to housing projects that had deteriorated badly after becoming havens for crack dealers. We drove around corners and the police captain told me to look at a window to spot a "lookout" before he ducked his head down. We saw crack houses and small groups of young men on the corners quickly disperse as we came near them. The officers were giving me what became the standard police tour, standard in what was said as well as what I saw.

"We have a deadly serious issue on our hands," I said, following the tour. "It's compelling. This was fact-finding for me, very preliminary, to find out what people on the ground are facing. [The police] emphasized what I was looking at was the heart of the problem. Downtown Detroit is as bad as it gets anywhere."

The scene was familiar to almost every American who watches television: parts of an inner city resembling what the philosopher Thomas Hobbes described as "the state of nature," where life is "solitary, poor, nasty, brutish and short."

During the tour of downtown, one of the police officers accompanying me asked, "Why should a kid earn four bucks an hour at McDonald's when he can make two or three hundred dollars a night working drugs?"

"For a lot of reasons," I said on that first tour, as I was to say a hundred times after. The police officer had picked up this line of reasoning from the media. It became increasingly fashionable in some circles to wonder how we can expect *any* inner city child not to succumb to the lure of peddling drugs. After all, the argument goes, jobs paying the minimum wage don't hold much appeal when youngsters have the opportunity to make $100 or $500 or $1,000 a day. Drugs are so pervasive, their allure so strong, the money so easily obtained, the draw of evil so powerful—and the power to resist evil so feeble—that we should simply face reality and surrender any quaint notion we continue to harbor about children resisting drugs. Not surprisingly, a lot of youngsters picked up on this argument.

On June 22, 1989, when President Bush visited residents of New York's Covenant House (a home for children involved with drugs, prostitution, and crime), a teen-age boy made the same argument to the President. "I'm not working for a hundred twenty-five dollars, a hundred and ten dollars, there's no way," he

said. "For a whole week and sitting over a hot oven flipping ham-
burgers? One hundred dollars a week, that ain't no money. I can
make a hundred dollars in fifteen minutes by dealing drugs."

Following his trip, the President called me. He was moved and
deeply bothered by what he had seen and heard, as anyone would
be. We talked for twenty-five minutes and discussed what the
proper response should be.

It violates everything a civilized society stands for simply to
throw in the towel and say, "Okay, we give up. It's not right that
children use drugs, but we adults can't seem to do anything about
it." Of course the lure of drug money can exert a tremendous
pull. But responsible adults are supposed to pull back—to be better, and do better, and point to a better way. Inner-city parents
who are trying to do right by their children, who are trying to
shape their children's character, need allies. Those faraway commentators who excuse these children trample on the parents who
are trying to teach good lessons. And when this "what can we do?"
attitude trickles down to mayors and police captains and social
workers, the situation gets much worse.

At the very time we need to affirm belief in things like individual responsibility, civic duty, and obedience to the law, too many
segments of society are equivocating and sending mixed messages. This sort of moral enervation must be challenged. If people
think poor black children aren't capable of moral responsibility,
they should say so. I think otherwise. I *know* they are capable of it.
I have seen that they are. The inner-city children who obey their
parents and obey the law give witness to the lie. Most inner-city
kids—including those living in or near drug markets—refuse to
serve as drug runners. We should honor, support, and reinforce
those youngsters.

We are witnessing the emergence of a new "invisible man" (the
title of Ralph Ellison's classic novel) in American society. This new
"invisible man" is the black inner-city citizen who doesn't "do"
drugs. In fact, significant numbers of inner-city residents do *not*
commit themselves to the drug world. Most blacks in our inner
cities are law-abiding citizens who lead decent lives and disdain
drugs; they are victims, not perpetrators, of drug crimes. Americans need to see that because, unfortunately, these citizens are
almost invisible so far as much of public opinion is concerned.

In the place of the law-abiding black man and woman we have
seen the emergence of a new, all too "visible man"—the black

predator, the young, inner-city black male who terrorizes communities, preys on innocent victims, or is arrested in drug busts. The image of the "visible man" is given wide currency through the camera lens. Film report after film report sears images in our sensibilities: drugs, violence, the inner city, and blacks. These images and associations perpetuate a racial stereotype. We need to confront it immediately, directly, before this myth and these images harden into dogma.

Moral surrender needs to be challenged for another very important reason: when adults don't teach children how to live responsible lives, they will become cynical and go astray. It's not surprising to discover that, left to their own devices, children will want everything, and they will want it all at once. One of the tasks of adults is to tell children, "You can't have everything all at once," and explain why. That used to be part of education; it still needs to be.

Drug dealers are teachers—malevolent teachers. They are teaching our children the terrible lesson that you can get it all at once—money, cars, gold chains, fancy clothes, and all the rest—and it doesn't matter how. That is one more compelling reason we need to remove drug dealers from our children's lives. They are teachers of a wicked lesson. This kind of wickedness will flourish if good men do nothing, or if they throw up their arms in despair, or (worse yet) if they give credence to the lie of hopelessness and fruitlessness.

I made this point while I was Secretary of Education in a debate I had on the "MacNeil/Lehrer Newshour" with Jesse Jackson. In discussing the causes of the drug problem, Jackson referred several times to the Gramm-Rudman Deficit Reduction Act on federal spending.

The program ended with a vigorous exchange between us.

"For those who are escaping pain, the pain of unemployment and lack of job training, the pain of family farm foreclosures, the pain of the threat of nuclear war, that's one level that we must grapple with," Jackson said.

"Let's keep politics out of it, Reverend Jackson," I said. "You know as well as I do . . . that this problem crosses sex lines, race lines, class lines, community lines. This is a problem throughout society, and I don't think we're going to get very far by suggesting this is . . . due to some kind of governmental policy. That just won't fly."

"Oh, I submit to you that when I talk with some of the farm children out in Omaha," Jackson said, "their sense of impotence, their sense of alienation is that the future is not very bright for them . . . and their lives are quite tied up with what they see as their future."

"Reverend Jackson," I began to interject.

"I've been with these inner-city youth who make a buck this way or get high to escape their pain," he went on. "And we would make a sad mistake to just deal with the fruit of alienation and not deal with the root of this problem."

"Well, Mr. Jackson," I replied, "as a Christian minister you know that you have to be very careful about indulging people when they want to put responsibility onto somebody else, and if sixteen- or seventeen- or eighteen-year-olds in possession of their faculties are blaming their addiction to drugs or their use of drugs on somebody else, I hope you're correcting them on the grounds of individual moral responsibility."

"Well, there's a valid balance," Jackson conceded.

If adult leadership doesn't stand for individual responsibility, how can we expect children to learn it?

Some debunking of the myth of the drug trade is also needed. The reported earnings and the number of children involved are exaggerated. Some kids do make big money, but they are rare. And the risks are high. Young people are often injured in the course of doing "business" (one frequent means that major drug dealers use to inflict pain on low-level dealers is to break their kneecaps).

The New York Times, in a special report entitled "Selling Crack: The Myth of Wealth," said "the crack business, it turns out, is a modern, brutalized version of a 19th-century sweatshop. . . . Social scientists, ethnographers and others who have studied the workings of the crack trade describe lives built around a kind of shimmering lure, built on myth and self-deception; and on a reality that all too often ends in prison, violent injury or death." According to Dr. Ansley Hamid, an anthropologist at John Jay College of Criminal Justice, "[crack dealers] always say they will get rich, but they don't get rich. They just get farther and farther away from a job." But that's not the story most people have heard over and over.

*   *   *

A few weeks after I visited Detroit, I witnessed a reverse buy bust in Liberty City, Florida. This is a standard operation in which an undercover police officer stands on an inner-city street corner posing as a drug dealer. An assistant from the Office of National Drug Control Policy and I were in the basement of an abandoned building across the street, observing the scene for two hours. I remember thinking about how different this job was from my previous jobs. When I was chairman of the National Endowment for the Humanities, I would spend a typical evening at the National Gallery of Art listening to speeches about Degas's contribution to Western art. I would be wearing a black tie, looking at flowers on the table, and fidgeting, wondering how long it would be before it ended. Now here I was, two jobs later, in the basement of an abandoned building in Liberty City, standing in the dark, watching drug buys go down while fleas crawled up my legs.

I was struck by how many people who drove into that almost exclusively black neighborhood were white (probably from the suburbs), and by how many local people were watching the activity. This was their evening's "entertainment." There was a convenience store on the corner and the customers were taking in everything that was going on. At the end of the evening, when the police announced that they had made their last arrest for the evening, the citizens on the corner applauded them. Despite reports that inner-city residents are unhappy with the police because of the drug war, my experience is that they are unhappy only when there aren't enough police, when the police are not aggressive enough against drug dealers.

As we got into our police car for the ride back to the hotel, two boys, about eleven or twelve, stared at us. One turned to the other, pointed to me, and asked his friend, "Who's that, the mayor?"

"No," the other boy said, "you're crazy. That's Ronald Reagan."

When I took the job of director of the Office of National Drug Control Policy, there were many people (including a lot of my friends) who said that I was on a fool's errand. Even though the task was clear and the stakes high, they were convinced the war on drugs was a hopeless undertaking. Every which way I turned, I

heard dire predictions. "Bennett has a daunting, some say hopeless, assignment," said one report. Another said, "This is a drug
epidemic that seems beyond the reach of any government." *The
New York Times* wondered whether I had taken on a "mission impossible." In 1989, a nationwide poll showed that an astonishing
64 percent of those interviewed identified drugs as the nation's
leading problem—far ahead of the threat of nuclear war, pollu-
tion, or crime. The general climate of opinion, then, was that
there was not much we could do, that we were done and damned
before we even started. And the scenes most often seen on American television and most often talked about resembled what I saw
in Detroit and Liberty City.

Clearly one of my central tasks was to change the psychology
that gripped much of the media and, in turn, much of the American people. I had to reassure people that the war on drugs was
not a lost cause. There were huge hurdles that we faced; few
people had a better sense of the terrible problems we faced than
I. But despair clearly was not an option. America had prevailed
against monarchy, bigotry, a civil war, a great depression, Nazism,
and the Cold War; it could certainly prevail against the drug
epidemic, too. I hit the issue head-on: "It's way too soon to say
[the drug war] is over, we lost, because we haven't really waged it
yet," I said. "Public opinion at this time, at this hour, gives us
perhaps the most valuable weapon we can have in this campaign
to end the scourge of drugs."

"Mr. Bennett is in for the fight of his life, but more important,
he is in for the fight of our children's lives," said Senator Alfonse
D'Amato (R-New York). I girded myself for a tough battle. A few
congressmen even encouraged me. "The thing that made [Ben-
nett] troublesome at Education may make him very valuable in
this position," said Senator Joe Biden. "He's never been afraid to
pick a fight."

"Do you think you can restrain yourself?" asked Senator Howard Metzenbaum (D-Ohio), a longtime liberal critic of mine.
"You've been a real loose cannon at times," he said.

"That's fair enough," I conceded. But I bristled at what I described as the notion that "I ought to disassemble my bully pulpit,
put on my green eyeshades, and run numbers for a couple of
years."

I went to work fast. I worked on the job twenty months, but
it was probably the hardest, most intense twenty months of my

life. (As Elayne put it, I went from the American dream, education, to the American nightmare, drugs.) As with each job I took, I started by doing my homework, reading, talking to experts, and taking inventory. And one of the great things about a high-profile government job is that when you ask people for advice, they give it to you.

In room 180 of the Old Executive Office Building situated next to the White House, I held about a dozen meetings, lasting two to three hours each. Each meeting included ten to fifteen experts from a single field: law enforcement, treatment, education, religious leaders, community leaders, parents, and so on. My questions were the same to each group: What do we do? How should we wage a drug war? And how do we win one?

I chose the best-known and most respected people in their fields, without any regard to politics or ideology. I was struck by the high degree of agreement among those gathered. The operative words were "more" and "smarter": more and smarter efforts are needed, they said, in law enforcement, interdiction, treatment, prevention, and education.

One very good piece of advice came from Jack Mendelson, professor of psychiatry at the Harvard Medical School. On leaving the conference room, with his hat and coat on, he turned to me and said, "Remember the most important thing."

"What's that, Dr. Mendelson?" I asked.

"Remember," he said, "don't just do something—stand there." What he meant was something very subtle, but very important: Don't just put forward a good antidrug plan. In addition, make sure you stand up for the right things and, if necessary, be a lightning rod for criticism. Don't worry if the critics beat up on you. Most antidrug efforts will be made locally. But what the federal government can do that the localities cannot is to serve as a kind of national reference point. By standing up for certain things, you will encourage others to act. This fit in well with my own view that an essential part of governing consists of standing for the right things, giving voice to the right sentiments, praising the right actions of others and condemning the wrong ones.

During my swearing-in ceremony, President Bush had the entire Cabinet stand behind me to symbolize that they would be behind me in this effort. One of the problems that had marked earlier efforts was that the Drug Enforcement Policy Board had become widely known in the press for its "turf battles": Customs encroaching on the Coast Guard, the Coast Guard encroaching on the Drug Enforcement Administration, both in turn encroaching on Defense, and so on. One of my major responsibilities—and one of my major problems—was drastically reducing the turf battles. Kart Besteman, executive director of the Alcohol and Drug Problems Association, summarized the concern: "It's like he's got eight teams of horses out in front of his wagon; one wants to go right, some want to go left, and some don't want to go at all. He must get that all in motion and in step."

The President's efforts in this area helped a great deal. Again, my non-Cabinet status probably helped in the long run, because the President bent over backward to make sure I was listened to. During his first State of the Union address, he said, "Bill Bennett and I will be shoulder to shoulder in the executive branch, leading the charge." In New York he declared, "The scourge will end. I will lead the fight. Bill Bennett, our nation's first drug czar, is going to be right there at my side." These kind of public pronouncements meant a great deal.

Still, we needed to send the right message internally, inside the complicated, arcane, government apparatus. In Washington, one needs from time to time to make it clear how one is going to act in the future, to "send a signal." I did not develop a comprehensive plan to resolve turf problems; instead, I waited for a major issue to present itself. It didn't take long.

I wanted to have greater expertise in drug interdiction, the use of the military to monitor and detect drug-trafficking patterns. And I found a military officer who I was told knew something about this. I wanted to hire him. But then I got a phone call indicating that the Pentagon wanted to block his appointment to my office. At the time there was no Secretary of Defense, because John Tower had been rejected by the Senate. And two or three phone conversations made it clear that the Pentagon and I saw this issue differently. The Pentagon said, in effect, "No, you can't have him." And they thought that was that.

It wasn't. I called the President and told him I needed his help. I asked him to call the Pentagon, and he never hesitated. This was a crucial early test, and it would send a vital signal.

A second test case involved my right to coordinate the Administration's supply-side drug policy. Some people argued that the supply-side was a law-enforcement problem that belonged under the jurisdiction of another Cabinet agency. I saw the issue as nonnegotiable. If I gave up my role as chief coordinator of the Administration's war on drugs, I would have been effectively neutered. Again, I went directly to the President. Again, he came through.

Aristotle describes power as the ability to be and to make things be, and on these particular decisions I needed to make things be. Word of the outcome of these turf battles got around (as it inevitably does in government). From then on, we didn't have to issue proclamations of our influence to various agencies. People knew. And while some disputes simmered, it was increasingly clear that the President was firmly behind us and committed to a serious war on drugs. We experienced many fewer major turf conflicts.

In the early days of my tenure, I spent a lot of time at the Pentagon. Public-opinion polls showed the American people wanted the military to become more involved in the drug war, to help stem the flow of drugs into the country. They were right to want to enlist the military, and the Commander-in-Chief agreed. In a speech in Florida, the President said the "war" on drugs was no metaphor. But getting the Pentagon on board was no easy task; it meant a sharp break from recent history. As *Newsweek* magazine put it:

> The Pentagon, ironically, is the one agency that hasn't wanted a piece of the action. Vietnam taught it to avoid wars it was destined to lose. At [drug] policy meetings "everybody at the table is trying to protect his turf and take somebody else's," says a congressional aide. "The DOD guy is sitting there with this little piece of turf, saying 'Anybody want mine?'"

I stressed repeatedly to the Pentagon brass (and later to my colleague Dick Cheney), that what we wanted was "their eyes, ears and brains." They could see the sky, the land, and the sea. They could hear traffickers talking to each other and could track the flow of drugs out of South and Central America. Soon they wanted a piece of the action, and in a big way. I was thrilled with their change of mind; it meant we were bringing in the heavy artillery. But as Jack Lawn, the former head of the Drug Enforcement Administration, told me one day at lunch, "Bill, now that you've got them interested, you're going to have a problem."

"What do you mean, Jack?" I asked.

"Well," Lawn said, "you're now going to find out what it means when an eight-hundred-pound gorilla falls in love with you."

His point was well taken. The military is so big and so effective it tends to dominate almost every situation in which it enters. But overall I was very pleased at the Pentagon's enthusiasm, its interest, and its contributions. And the eight-hundred-pound gorilla did in time learn to step quite carefully and cooperatively.

The Pentagon's efforts in interdiction made a big difference. We wanted to stop the flow or at least slow it, though most of our critics said we could never succeed. Early on, a well-known analysis by Peter Reuter of the Rand Corporation, a prominent public policy research organization, was widely reprinted, arguing that there was little the federal government could do to stem the flow of cocaine into America. But we did slow it significantly. To Reuter's credit, he later acknowledged the success. With our interdiction effort, the efforts of the Colombians, and better law enforcement, the price of cocaine doubled and even tripled in 1990 in some major American cities, while the purity fell. Recent reports of increased production in South America implicitly concede that the U.S. has made it tougher to import drugs here, since more and more of the production is going elsewhere. Because of our huge borders, it is of course impossible to halt the flow of cocaine into America. But we have made it more difficult and have raised the price of doing cocaine business.

Of course, the press was ever skeptical—but it *was* paying attention. There were members of Congress who wanted to carp and criticize, but early conversations with Senator Biden and with Senator Strom Thurmond, the ranking minority member, suggested that although there might be some politics involved, we would be able to work together. Biden said to me privately and later publicly, "I want you to succeed." And he meant it. For the most part, over twenty months, Senators Biden and Thurmond were valuable allies in our effort.

Nevertheless, residual pessimism remained—in the reports about the turf battles in front of us, the high number of drug users, and the nightly news pictures of violence in the streets. Instead of pressing us to step up our efforts, the pessimists urged surrender in the form of drug legalization. The issue trailed me almost everywhere I went. "Why not legalize drugs?" became the familiar refrain. Given what I had seen after only three months on the job—given what drugs were doing to our cities, to our communities, and to our children—I thought it was an astoundingly naive and ridiculous question. How could anybody be in favor of making drugs *more* accessible, cheaper, and morally permissible? Here again was this incredible gap between a select but influential group in favor of legalization—and the great body of the American people. A foreigner visiting this country, listening to television newscasts and reading press reports, editorials, and columns, would think that the American people were about evenly divided between those who favored legalization and those who did not. In fact, the overwhelming majority (88 percent) of the American people reject drug legalization. Nevertheless, a tremendous amount of ink was spilled, commentary offered, and talk show discussions held on the merits of legalization. Some of the more prominent voices in favor of (or leaning toward) legalization included Ethan A. Nadelmann, a professor at Princeton University; Kurt Schmoke, mayor of Baltimore; U.S. District Judge Robert Sweet; Representative George Crockett (D-Michigan); *New York Times* columnist Anthony Lewis; *The Nation; The Economist;* and some writers and editors of *National Review.*

The legalization debate presented me with a somewhat unusual situation. Throughout my public life, most of my battles had been against leading liberal voices. But on this issue, I drew criticism from the political right flank, including a number of prominent conservatives: William F. Buckley, free-market economist Milton Friedman, former Secretary of State George Shultz, and others. So legalization seemed respectable at both ends of the political spectrum.

At first, I resisted getting heavily involved in this debate. As I told a congressional committee, I was hired to wage the war, not to discuss whether it was worth fighting. That issue had already been resolved.

Some members of my staff and a few friends told me that the argument was impossible to ignore and that the more we engaged the debate, the more arguments we advanced against legalization, the more support we would get from the public. So I began to more directly and more publicly take on the issue of legalization, in interviews, speeches, public forums, and even on national television.

Appearing on CNN's "Larry King Live," I found legalization getting a very sympathetic hearing. But after three or four phone calls in favor of legalization, a man in Villa Park, California, asked,

"Why build prisons? Get tough like [Saudi] Arabia. Behead the damned drug dealers. We're just too damned soft." I sensed that King thought the guy was a bit of a crank.

In response I said, "One of the things that I think is a problem is that we are not doing enough that is morally proportional to the nature of the offense. I mean, what the caller suggests is morally plausible. Legally, it's difficult."

I could see King's eyes light up. He asked for a clarification. "Behead?"

"Yeah. Morally I don't have any problem with it," I said.

"You would behead . . ." King began again.

"Somebody selling drugs to a kid?" I said. "Morally I don't have any problem with that at all. I mean, ask most Americans if they saw somebody out on the streets selling drugs to their kid what they would feel morally justified in doing—tear them limb from limb."

King then asked what we should do.

"What we need to do is find some constitutional and legally permissible way to do what this caller suggests, not literally to behead, but to make the punishment fit the crime. And the crime is horrible." During the program I strongly rejected the calls for drug legalization and endorsed capital punishment for major drug sellers.

The next morning *The Washington Post* ran extended excerpts from the show. Newspapers from around the country ran headlines saying "Drug Czar Bennett: Beheading Fitting." The political cartoonists had a field day. Massachusetts Governor Michael Dukakis ripped my "beheading" comments. Many newspaper editorial writers and columnists were critical. Even Dick Darman got into the act, sending me a "decision memo" comparing French technology (the guillotine) with Saudi Arabian/British technology (the scimitar or broadax).

The reaction was illustrative. Many of the elites ridiculed my opinion. But it resonated with the American people because they knew what drugs were doing, and they wanted a morally proportionate response. The late Lee Atwater, then chairman of the Republican National Committee, had been traveling in South Carolina when the story hit the wires. An assistant of mine asked Lee what the reaction beyond the Beltway was. "Hell, Bill," Lee told us, "the people are saying, 'We've finally got somebody in Washington who understands what's at stake.'"

I later used the incident in speeches to gauge the moral sentiments of my audiences. I would ask, "If you saw a drug dealer selling drugs to your children, what would your impulse be?" Most audiences responded that their impulse would be to do violence to the drug dealer. And that impulse is right; it is simply a matter of channeling that impulse into law, of civilizing our retribution into a proper sense of justice. "This war [on drugs] is not for delicate sensibilities," I said in a speech at the National Press Club. "This is tough stuff. We need to get tough, we need to get tough as hell, we need to do it right now." But many of the critics didn't agree, and they couldn't quite figure out why I wasn't brought down, or even harmed, by my "intemperate" comments to Larry King. What they didn't recognize is that the moral sense of the American people is sound. They had had it with drugs. They had seen the devastation. And they wanted us to fight.

In Alaska—where personal possession of marijuana was legal— Senator Murkowski and others implored me to weigh in on behalf of a new initiative seeking to recriminalize possession of marijuana. Not surprisingly, the percentage of high school students using dope in Alaska was much higher than in the rest of the nation.

When I accepted the invitation, the prolegalization forces went into action. The "pothead lobby," as I called it, distributed fliers in Anchorage and Fairbanks saying "Confront the Drug Bizarre." But when I arrived, there was very little opposition. A few bedraggled sixties types (including one woman who introduced herself as "the Dragon Lady") asked me mostly incomprehensible questions at an assembly in Anchorage. But there was no major confrontation. It later became apparent why. When the "pothead lobby" passed out fliers announcing my visit, they had put the wrong date on them. I had been saying for a long time that marijuana makes people inattentive and stupid. I rested my case.

The legalization debate is for all intent and purposes over. But even to call it a "debate" suggests that the arguments in favor of drug legalization are rigorous, substantial and serious. At first glance some of the arguments sound appealing. But on further inspection one finds that at bottom they are nothing more than a series of unpersuasive and even disingenuous ideas that more sober minds recognize as a recipe for a public policy disaster.

Legalization removes the incentive to stay away from a life of drugs. Some people are going to smoke crack whether it's legal or illegal. But by keeping it illegal, we maintain the criminal sanctions that persuade most people that the good life cannot be reached by dealing drugs. And that's exactly why we have drug laws—to make drug use a wholly unattractive choice.

One of the clear lessons of Prohibition is that when we had laws against alcohol, there *was* less consumption of alcohol, less alcohol-related disease, fewer drunken brawls, and a lot less public drunkenness. And contrary to myth, there is no evidence that Prohibition caused big increases in crime.

I am not suggesting that we go back to Prohibition. Alcohol has a long, complicated history in this country, and unlike drugs, the American people accept alcohol. They have no interest in going back to Prohibition. But at least advocates of legalization should admit that legalized alcohol, which is responsible for some 100,000 deaths a year, is hardly a model for drug policy. As the columnist Charles Krauthammer has pointed out, the question is not which is worse, alcohol or drugs. The question is, should we accept both legalized alcohol *and* legalized drugs? The answer is no.

If drugs were legalized, use would surely soar. In fact, we have just undergone a kind of cruel national experiment in which drugs became cheap and widely available: that experiment is called the crack epidemic. It was only when cocaine was dumped into the country, and a three-dollar vial of crack could be bought on street corners, that we saw cocaine use skyrocket—mostly among the poor and disadvantaged.

The price that American society would have to pay for legalized drugs would be intolerably high: more drug-related accidents at work, on the highway, and in the airways; bigger losses in worker productivity; hospitals filled with drug emergencies; more students on drugs, meaning more dropouts; more pregnant women buying legal cocaine, meaning more abused babies *in utero*. Add to this the added cost of treatment, social welfare, and insurance, and welcome to the Brave New World of drug legalization.

To listen to legalization advocates, one might think that street crime would disappear with the repeal of our drug laws. But our best research indicates that most drug criminals were into crime well *before* they got into drugs. Making drugs legal would subsidize their habit. They would continue to rob and steal to pay for food, for clothes, for entertainment. And they would carry on with their drug trafficking by undercutting the legalized price of drugs and catering to teenagers who (I assume) would be nominally restricted from buying drugs at the corner drugstore.

In my travels around the country I have seen nothing to support the legalizers' argument that lower drug prices would reduce crime. Virtually everywhere I have gone, police and DEA agents have told me that crime rates are highest where crack is cheapest.

If we did legalize drugs, we would no doubt have to reverse the policy, like those countries that had experimented with broad legalization and decided it was a failure. In 1975 Italy liberalized its drug law and now has one of the highest heroin-related death rates in Western Europe. One Italian government official told me that the citizens of Italy are eager to recriminalize the use of drugs. They had seen enough casualties.

And what about our children? If we make drugs more accessible, there will be more harm to children, direct and indirect. There will be more cocaine babies and more child abuse. Children after all are among the most frequent victims of violent, drug-related crimes—crimes that have nothing to do with the cost of acquiring the drugs. In Philadelphia in 1987 more than half the child-abuse fatalities involved at least one parent who was a heavy drug user. Seventy-three percent of the child-abuse cases in New York City in 1987 involved parental drug use.

And it would be disastrous suddenly to switch signals on our children in school, whom we have been teaching, with great effect, that drug use is wrong. Why, they will ask, have we changed our minds?

The whole legalization argument is based on the premise that progress is impossible. But there is now incontrovertible, unmistakable evidence of progress in the war on drugs (more about that in the next chapter). Now would be exactly the wrong time to surrender and legalize.

The legalization argument also revealed something troubling about some intellectuals. I elaborated on this point at Harvard's John F. Kennedy School on December 11, 1989:

America's intellectuals—and here I think particularly of liberal intellectuals—have spent much of the last nine years decrying the social programs of two Republican administrations in the name of the defenseless poor. But today, on the one outstanding issue that disproportionately hurts the poor—that is wiping out many of the poor—where are the liberal intellectuals to be found? They are on the editorial and op-ed pages, and in magazines, telling us with a sneer that our drug policy won't work. . . . One would think that a little more concern and serious thought would come from those who claim to care deeply about America's problems.

John Jacob, president of the Urban League, has said, "Drugs kill more blacks than the Klan ever did. They're destroying more children and more families than poverty ever did." But many of the same intellectuals who strongly supported a "war on poverty" were AWOL in the war on drugs. I talked about this the next day on "Good Morning America."

> The intellectuals are way out of sync with the American people. The American people have seen the drug problem. They've seen it up close, unfortunately, and don't have any tolerance for the idea of legalization. The problem with intellectuals—the reason that it's worth making a speech and making a point—is that they do form a lot of opinion. What they say affects what gets said on the editorial pages, what's regarded as respectable and reliable views on this. And right now, by their objections or their intransigence or their disagreement, they're keeping us from moving ahead. And again, the thing I don't understand is why those who say they speak for those worse off in society aren't just full-fledged in this effort. Nothing is destroying poor communities in this country so effectively as drugs and yet we have people balking at the idea of waging a full-scale effort.

Legalization is a fine position for those who wish to stand out from the crowd and who have the luxury of speaking from a safe distance. But instead of sophistication, advocates for legalization should seek out a clearer connection with reality. They should take a close look at the devastating effects of drugs.

James Q. Wilson, Collins Professor of Management and Political Science at UCLA, has written:

> . . . even now, when the dangers of drug abuse are well understood, many educated people still discuss the drug problem in almost every way except the right way. They talk about the "costs" of drug use and the "socioeconomic factors" that shape that use. They rarely speak plainly—drug use is wrong because it is immoral and it is immoral because it enslaves the mind and destroys the soul. It is as if it were a mark of

sophistication for us to shun the language of morality in discussing the problems of mankind.

In the end drug use is wrong because of what it does to human character. It degrades. It makes people less than they should be by burning away a sense of responsibility, subverting productivity, and making a mockery of virtue.

Using drugs is wrong not simply because drugs create medical problems; it is wrong because drugs destroy one's moral sense. People addicted to drugs neglect their duties. The lure can become so strong that soon people will do nothing else but take drugs. They will neglect God, family, children, friends, and jobs—everything in life that is important, noble, and worthwhile—for the sake of drugs. This is why from the very beginning we posed the drug problem as a moral issue. And it was the failure to recognize the moral consequences of drug use that led us into the drug epidemic in the first place. In the late 1960s, many people rejected the language of morality, of right and wrong. Since then we have paid dearly for the belief that drug use was harmless and even an enlightening, positive thing.

Drugs undermine the necessary virtues of a free society—autonomy, self-reliance, and individual responsibility. The inherent purpose of using drugs is secession from reality, from society, and from the moral obligations individuals owe their family, their friends, and their fellow citizens. Drugs destroy the natural sentiments and duties that constitute our human nature and make our social life possible. As our founders would surely recognize, for a citizenry to be perpetually in a drug-induced haze doesn't bode well for the future of self-government.

When all is said and done, the most compelling case that can be made against drug use rests on moral grounds. No civilized society—especially a self-governing one—can be neutral regarding human character and personal responsibility.

4

FIGHTING BACK

"Our children need our best example and encouragement right now," I told an audience at the National Press Club. "If you want to be a conscientious objector in the war on drugs, I guess it's your constitutional right to be so. But don't get in the way of people who are fighting—people all over this country."

In late July 1989, I was in North Carolina with my family when my chief of staff called me with news that the government's National Institute on Drug Abuse (NIDA) was soon going to release the results of its ninth National Household Survey on Drug Abuse—the first comprehensive national study of drug-use patterns since 1985. The estimated number of Americans using *any* illegal drug on a "current" basis (at least once in the thirty-day period preceding the survey) had *dropped* 37 percent: from 23 million in 1985 to 14.5 million in 1988. And a survey of high school seniors recorded record significant drops in their overall use and tolerance of drugs. Drug use was down everywhere: in inner cities, in rural and suburban areas, among blacks and whites, rich and poor.

This substantial falloff in the overall number of drug users was great news and gave a great lift. Clearly the drug problem was not hopeless. Although the addiction rates were at an all-time high (they would not begin to fall until a year or so later), the American people in the aggregate were turning away from drugs in record numbers. Why, then, the perception that the problem was getting worse? "One word explains much of it," I wrote in the first National Drug Control Strategy. "That word is *crack*." Unlike heroin (which sedates people), crack cocaine produces dangerous behav-

ioral side effects—including paranoia, irritability, and quick resort
to violence on minimal provocation. Crack was responsible for the
fact that vast patches of the American urban landscape were rap-
idly deteriorating beyond effective control by civil authorities.

I said at the time that we were fighting two drug wars, not just
one. The first and easier was against "casual" use of drugs by
many Americans. That war we were winning. The other, much
more difficult, was against addiction to cocaine. And on that second front we were losing—badly.

These two wars, however, are not wholly unrelated. People
don't start as drug addicts; they start as *casual* users. If you drain
the pool of casual users, sooner or later the addiction rates will
fall. So the dramatic drop in the number of casual users was
encouraging and augured well for the future. The myth that
drugs were stylish and chic, and a means to self-realization, was
being shattered by the enormous human cost they had exacted—
especially on inner-city residents and children. Drug-using flower
children of the late 1960s set the stage for the drug gangs of the
late 1980s. Americans saw our social fabric ripping and the children dying. And they were reacting against it.

A problem that had been "spiraling out of control" was now
receding on the main front, at the point of entry. As early as the
late summer of 1989, it was clear not only that we were *not* in a
no-win situation, but that the situation was improving. As I developed the President's National Drug Control Strategy—for pre-
sentation to the nation in September—I planned to build on these
good trends and on the American people's capacity for self-
renewal. The President had agreed to make drugs the topic of his
first prime-time address, delivered on September 5. "All of us
agree," he said that evening, "that the gravest domestic threat
facing our nation today is drugs."

There were very few people who took issue with that statement.
The next day we released the National Drug Control Strategy to
an eager but skeptical press. It was a sharp break from previous
policy. In the past, there had been action on a number of separate
fronts, with some isolated success. But there had also been cross
purposes, incoherence, and waste. We sought to bring these to an
end. What was crucial to the strategy, and what set it apart from
past efforts, was the integrated relationship among the various
pieces: interdiction, treatment, education, prevention, and law
enforcement. Each is necessary, but none is sufficient. For exam-

ple, I stressed that treatment is not effective without law enforcement. Why? Because many people do not go into treatment until they are arrested. Studies indicate that those under legal pressure to undergo treatment do as well or better than those who seek treatment on their own, in part because legal pressure keeps an addict in treatment for a longer period of time. The mayor of Washington, D.C., is a very good example of the link between drug treatment and law enforcement. Marion Barry did not see the light until he saw the law.

Once our strategy was released, we had to meet a fiscal-credibility test. In this instance, that meant we had to come up with the money to implement the strategy. I knew that the critics would argue it was fine to have the President speak on prime-time television and it was all well and good to have a well thought-out national strategy. But if the Administration agreed that there was a substantial role for the federal government to play in the war on drugs, didn't we need to put up or shut up? The answer was yes. And we put up in record numbers.

In our strategy we called for a significant increase (70 percent overall) in spending on every relevant drug-related program: law enforcement, treatment, prevention, education, interdiction, and in the international arena. The country—and the critics—had never seen this kind of federal money before. Not only was it a record federal increase, from just over $6 billion to over $10 billion, but we were determined to get the money out in record time.

My reputation was not that of a big spender. As Secretary of Education I never fought for raising the federal education budget. I was convinced that the problem with American education was not that it is underfunded, but that it was underaccountable and underproductive. Over a twenty-five-year period, we were spending more and more money, and getting fewer and fewer results. In many cases, we were throwing good money after bad. The main action in education is, and should be, at the state and local level. Often in education the greater the federal involvement, the less state and local involvement there is. The federal role in education, then, should be modest; the dollars—and accountability—should come locally.

But in the drug effort I thought there was an important federal role and I argued for a larger federal budget. Because, unlike education, there are some areas in the war on drugs that *only* the federal government can provide for—interdiction and international affairs, for example. I met several times with Richard Darman. He agreed there should be an increase—but not the kind of increase I wanted.

I understood that Darman had to oversee the entire federal budget, and I absolutely agreed that he had to operate within constraints. But I had been in government long enough to know that there were hundreds of programs, costing billions of dollars, that weren't effective (beginning with the arts and parts of education). Drug control was one area in which we needed to pony up the money. The money to pay for the war on drugs is "Dick Darman's worry," I argued. "This is one you just have to pay for. . . . If you have to pay for it out of something else, then pay for it out of something else."

Darman was not in principle opposed to an increase, but he did want to shave the drug budget more than I felt was necessary. We went back and forth on the issue, and had a widely reported, very heated shouting match. Finally we met with the President to resolve our differences. We both presented our cases, and the President made the final decision. The drug budget ended up between my figure and Darman's; I thought it was a very reasonable and defensible number, and I was satisfied. Despite the sometimes intemperate confrontations Darman and I have had, my relations with him remained good. I didn't pout or hold a grudge and neither did he. I always thought one of the great virtues of the Bush administration was that Cabinet secretaries and agency heads had to make their cases to Dick Darman and John Sununu, two of the smartest people in (or out of) government. After going head-to-head with them, making your case to Congress was a breeze.

The strategy was generally well received, even on Capitol Hill. This was a bit of a shock to me, since there had hardly ever been a policy statement of mine at the Department of Education that wasn't immediately attacked by our opponents in Congress, and elsewhere, as being philosophically awry, ideologically driven, and intellectually bankrupt.

The morning after the President's speech to the nation, many Democrats were tying themselves closely to our plan. I joked that "Joe Biden said he was going to be more like me than I was." We didn't realize it at the time, but the "intellectual" debate over drug policy was basically over that day. Following the release of the

President's second national drug control strategy (which essentially built on the foundation we had laid in the first), *The New York Times* editorialized that there has been a "victory over confusion." A majority of the public—and our two political parties—agreed on our *fundamental* approach to fighting drugs. There were of course differences of emphasis, differences sometimes rooted in partisan politics. But most of the key players on both sides of the aisle agreed on the essentials.

We agreed on the need to work with source and transit countries, on tough law enforcement, on expanding treatment and making it more accountable, and on improved and focused efforts at prevention and education. We agreed on expanded use of the military, expanded drug intelligence, and more research. In short, we agreed on the nature of the problem and how to attack it.

It was clear that discouraging drug use (particularly casual drug use) was at the heart of the solution. Through sanctions, persuasion, education, and treatment, we would in time reduce drug addiction and its awful consequences. But this strategy had its detractors, especially among elite opinion. *The New Republic,* an influential liberal magazine, wrote, "Ivy League college students and suburban stockbrokers who smoke marijuana or snort cocaine on weekends do not represent a national emergency." The editorial went on to argue that "tracking down and punishing people who have managed to reconcile recreational drug use with fairly productive life" constitutes a "waste" of public resources.

Answered syndicated columnist Christopher Matthews (the former chief spokesman for House Speaker Thomas P. "Tip" O'Neil, Jr.), "What burns the elite about the Bush-Bennett drug plan is not that it's poverty-stricken, not that it's too tough, but that it fails to honor the age-old distinction between rich and poor. The plan is aimed directly at the long-protected culprits in the nation's drug holocaust." Matthews went on to write:

> The American cultural elite has formally demanded separate treatment. If the police catch some illiterate street pusher, they should nail the dude. But if they should happen upon some Ivy League type, some "swell" with the right academic and social credentials consuming exactly the same substance that the low-life was selling, they should pat him on the back. Better yet, they should congratulate the fine fellow on being

able to balance two careers: bond selling, lawyering or whatever on the one hand, lawbreaking on the other.

Matthews had it exactly right. But another reason we went after
the casual user was it made sense as public policy. Very few people
buy drugs for the first time from a stranger. It's usually a "friend"
who gives that person drugs for the first time. Casual users like
company in what they're doing.

Sanctions against the casual user are consequently the best kind
of hardheaded prevention that we could think of. A young person
may see a cocaine user who has a nice job, a nice car, and a nice
family, and think, you can have all this and drugs, too. That casual
drug user is a carrier. And he needs to be stopped from spreading
the problem. Nobody wakes up one day and thinks, "I want to
become an addict. I want to end up on the street, in the gutter, as
a burnt-out case." A big part of our job was to keep people from
ever starting or, once they started, get them off before they found
themselves addicted.

Once we released the strategy and had secured the President's
blessing, I hit the road. I've never liked being desk- or Washington-
bound; as in the education job, I could find out more by going to
where the action was and talking to the people. Also, given all the
reports, I needed to sell our strategy. I needed to see *with my own
eyes* what was happening. I needed to gauge the sentiment of the
American people. Was there despair and surrender out there? Or
was there encouragement, hope and a determination to fight
back? Finally, I needed to sell it to the American people and to
state legislatures, where many of the efforts (particularly against
casual users) were actually going to be implemented. If I was
wrong, if the strategy didn't make sense, I wanted to hear it from
the people in the trenches, and not simply from congressional
committees. If some critics didn't like our approach, that was fine
by me, provided we could make our case to the majority of the
American people.

By the time my tenure had ended, I had been to more than one
hundred cities across the country. I was reassured by what I saw
and what I heard. In fact, nothing I saw or heard caused me to
fundamentally reassess the strategy. I believe we got it right the
first time.

Because drugs were such a prominent issue in the American
consciousness, my visits often would attract a lot of attention—not

just locally, but from the representatives and senators in Washington. They didn't want to be far from the action in what polls identified over and over again as the nation's number one problem. In an October 1989 trip to Wisconsin, Senators Robert Kasten and Herbert Kohl were present at a Milwaukee school where I talked to students about the problems of drug use.

Following the school visit, we toured the Penfield Children's Center, which treats children from birth to age three who have disabilities. About one in five of the children were born to mothers who used cocaine or other drugs. This trip, like my trip to Harlem Hospital, was moving and even heart-wrenching. We saw adults working one-on-one with children, trying to develop their ability to think, to reason, to get up to a level of performance for their age. But the children were struggling against something over which they had no control, in which they had no responsibility, and from which many would never fully recover: their parents' abuse of drugs.

When we left the center I was asked a few questions (as usual) about legalization. I invited the reporters asking the questions to go inside and look at the children. I reminded them that the effect of these drugs had nothing to do with whether they were legal or illegal. Those who believe in drugs and the "do your own thing" philosophy need to see the result of drugs.

During the Wisconsin visit I was interviewed by a local TV station. The lead-in to my interview included taped excerpts of State Senator Gary George, a Democrat from Milwaukee, criticizing me for allegedly putting money into prisons at the expense of treatment and education. Then George appeared live, arguing that "building prisons will not solve the problem."

I never argued that prisons *alone* would solve the problem. But they are an important part of the solution. I pointed out to Mr. George that he needed to do his homework: we were putting record amounts of federal money into education and treatment programs, as well as for the construction of prisons. "What I don't understand," I said, "is when we concede the importance of treatment and education, others will not concede the importance of building jails and prisons. Now I don't know where the critics think these [drug dealers] should go. Maybe they're willing to volunteer to have these guys live in *their* houses. But they certainly should not be left free to prey on innocent people."

I then pointed out the link between law enforcement and education. "Your education programs aren't going to do much good if, when you say to the children, 'Crime does not pay,' the lesson to the children . . . is 'Crime does pay.' The only way you teach that lesson is to put the criminal behind bars. Some people think everybody can be rehabilitated. . . . There are some people out there who cannot be rehabilitated. They need to be behind bars. Period."

From Milwaukee I went on to Madison where I addressed a joint session of the state legislature. I wanted to lend my support to Governor Tommy Thompson's plan for the state's war on drugs, which included tougher criminal penalties, mandatory suspension of driver's license for those convicted of drug use, and expansion of prison facilities.

"We have a choice," I told the legislature. "Do we want to see drug dealers down the road in the prisons or do we want to see them down the streets in the shadows? We had better make up our mind about that, because if we don't solve this bottom-line issue by building more prisons, we will not win the war on drugs."

Following the speech, State Senator George lost no time in criticizing me for espousing a "hard-line" law enforcement solution to the drug problem. "That strategy is bankrupt," he told the *Milwaukee Sentinel*. "But like a snake oil salesman, Bennett packs his bag and tells us lock 'em up and things will be better."

George's senate colleague, William P. Te Winkle, also criticized me again for focusing on law-enforcement crackdowns and incarceration. He invoked the by now familiar liberal mantra: "Merely warehousing more addicted people is not going to solve the problem," he said. These guys still couldn't get it.

They don't get it because of a certain cast of mind. The critics don't appreciate the utility of punishment and they don't appreciate the compelling moral case for punishment. I do *not* subscribe to the belief that the first purpose of punishment is to rehabilitate. The first purpose is moral, to exact a price for transgressing the rights of others. Stanley C. Brubaker of Colgate University has put it well (*The Public Interest*, Fall 1989):

We should understand punishment as a kind of mirror image of praise. If praise expresses gratitude and approbation, punishment expresses resentment and reprobation. If praise expresses what the political community admires and what unites it, punishment expresses what the community condemns and what threatens it. Punishment, like praise, publicly expresses our determination of what people deserve.

A civil society that is reluctant to protect innocent people by punishing criminals, administering justice, and expressing moral outrage is not going to last.

Much of the criticism that politicians make against law enforcement draws on the intellectual arguments advanced by academics. Charles Trueheart of *The Washington Post* asked me in an interview about the criticisms I received from many academics because of my emphasis on law enforcement. "What has the academy given us?" I asked. "An attack on the nuclear family. *That* was helpful. An attack on the school curriculum. *That* was helpful. Now we have an attack on law enforcement."

"One disagreement I have with the American people," I told Trueheart, "is that they have an undue degree of deference to the opinions of people with degrees. I worked there. I know how little those people know."

I had been a visiting assistant professor of philosophy at the University of Wisconsin (Madison) fourteen years earlier, so I had a pretty good idea what to expect on my Wisconsin trip. Demonstrators appeared with bags over their heads calling for a marijuana smoke-out and generally ridiculing the war on drugs. During a Madison press conference, I was asked about the annual "Great Marijuana Harvest Festival," a pro-dope rally held at the capital prior to my arrival, which drew about 7,000 people. "Marijuana causes people to lose their memory and lose their energy, and it makes them stupid," I said. "It's the last thing one would want to see happen on or around a university or a state capital. . . . And people who are casual about drugs ought to realize that a lot of people are dying in America."

Some people saw clearly what was at stake. All around the country, I was heartened by the common sense and clarity of most Americans. Even the very young could see what the very sophisticated sometimes could not.

For some time, Senator Edward Kennedy of Massachusetts had been wanting me to visit Boston so he could take me on a media "tour." On December 11, 1989, I arrived at the modest Joseph Lee Elementary School early in the morning, with Senator Kennedy, Senator John Kerry (D-Mass.), Governor Dukakis, and

a large media contingent (who were expecting some real fire-
works).

We went into the classroom and I started talking with the fifth-
grade students. We had a good discussion about why drugs are
bad. Then Senators Kerry and Kennedy got into the act. "What
do you children think we should do about the drug problem?"
Senator Kerry asked. "Fry the dealers," the first student said.
"Lock them all up," the second child said. "Do something awful to
them," a third child said. This was not the response two liberal
senators from Massachusetts wanted to hear. But the students
were candid. Senator Kennedy then tried to shift the conversation
in a direction he is much more comfortable with. He went into a
long oration about job conditions and asked the children whether
it was true that the real problem was that people didn't have jobs.

The kids looked at the senator with puzzled expressions and
didn't respond. Then Senator Kennedy asked whether many of
the children didn't have enough heat in their homes because of
the cost of heating oil.

Again, no hands went up.

It was awkward to see Senator Kennedy embarrassed in front of
a class of fifth-graders. Despite the clear effort to have the kids
make the case for his agenda, the kids from Massachusetts resisted. This particular classroom of lower-middle-class children
did not complain about the absence of heating oil or jobs. What
they complained about was the absence of tough sanctions for
people who seek to do them harm. It was a telling conversation
and, as in many places, I was grateful for the wisdom of children.
The kids, blessedly, were not sociologists. They were moralists.
Their education at Joseph Lee looked pretty good to me.

Some trips were important enough to merit the President's attention. He had promised me he would travel to the front lines of the
drug war, and he did. We visited a neighborhood in southwest
Los Angeles, a community that had been in the forefront of efforts to fight against drugs. Two months earlier, I had visited a
neighborhood where the Los Angeles Police Department had
launched an interesting counterattack: Operation Cul-de-Sac.

It was a Hispanic neighborhood in south-central Los Angeles,
one of the most drug-ridden areas in the city. It had been home
to a violent drug gang, and the residents had seen their share of

drug dealing and drive-by shootings. So the police tried something unusual. They barricaded parts of the neighborhood and operated street patrols in cooperation with Neighborhood Watch groups. Overall, crime within the barricaded area was down 12 percent over the previous year; drive-by shootings were down 85 percent. And overall crime figures *outside* the zones were also down, suggesting that Operation Cul-de-Sac hadn't simply pushed crime beyond the wall. Neighborhood residents were enthusiastic supporters of the police operation. The Los Angeles Police Department canvassed 563 people *before* erecting the barricades; 558 of them approved of police intervention.

Something else happened, too—something that surprised the neighborhood itself: school attendance in the neighborhood went up—way up. According to Phil Saldivar, principal of Jefferson High School, 150 to 200 more students were back in school once a police presence was established. The police had made it safe to go to school. When I was told this I thought if this isn't drug prevention, I don't know what is.

Here was my answer to critics who said that education by itself was the answer. Here was proof that without law enforcement, there would have been no education for many students. The police provided the basic security so that parents felt safer about sending their children to school and the children felt safer in going. Without restoring community order, going to school was just too risky.

President Bush and I visited another neighborhood where similar efforts had been made. While he was speaking on the front porch of a house, a demonstration began off to our left. The Secret Service got nervous and started to move. But it was clear that the demonstration was against neither the President nor his drug policy. The demonstrators were chanting for *more* police patrols.

Here, again, was evidence of a great cultural divide: the incredible discrepancy between those criticizing law enforcement from a safe distance and the opinion of besieged communities, asking, literally *demonstrating*, for more police. In my visits back and forth and up and down America, I made a point of speaking to people in the most victimized, vulnerable, and drug-infested parts of those cities. I almost never heard residents complain about too many police, or too much law enforcement, or too much safety and protection.

If more of the critics of tougher law enforcement had spent more time on the firing line, in public housing projects and on inner city streets, they might hesitate to voice their arguments; at the very least, they would know they were doing so in bad faith.

In my maiden speech on May 3, 1989, I said that we needed "confrontation and consequences" in our effort against drugs. "The drug user, the drug dealer, and the drug trafficker alike believe that the laws forbidding their activities no longer have teeth, and they consequently feel free to violate those laws with impunity. Those guilty of drug offenses must believe that punishment is inevitable." I knew that using such unequivocal language would upset some of my critics, particularly since I spoke of the drug crisis as fundamentally a crisis of social and moral authority.

I expected that some of our biggest allies in our law-enforcement efforts would be the police and national leaders in law enforcement. And most street-level police and many police chiefs did support our strategy from the very beginning. But unfortunately, some police chiefs have become little better than obfuscating bureaucrats, unable to see and to understand the important role they should take. Increasingly I found that talking to some police chiefs was like talking to some of the school superintendents I had encountered while Secretary of Education. They knew all the problems and cited them to me. They spoke of deep social problems, alienation, and illiteracy. They sounded as they wished to sound, like contemporary social scientists. But they had little sense of how to provide solutions, and they told me that, too. They didn't want the responsibility for solving the drug problem. They, too, had become theoreticians of society's woes.

Nobody, least of all me, wanted to dump all of the responsibility on the police. But some law enforcement officials were unwilling even to step up to their own self-evident, mandated responsibilities. I got the sense from more than one that we couldn't (and shouldn't) expect them to do anything. Afraid of failure and being held accountable, some police chiefs and law-enforcement representatives were throwing up their hands in despair.

I emphasized to them that the drug problem provided a tremendous opportunity for the police to make an important contribution to communities, win the praise of the American people, and at the same time do their job. I told a national meeting of chiefs that many people had become disenchanted with the police in the sixties and seventies. Police look back to those days as the bad days, when they weren't trusted, when people called them "pigs," when they were regarded as an occupying army in many communities. But now communities looked to them, even begged them, to help solve the drug problem. And still some chiefs pointed instead to "prevention and education" as the only answers.

Prevention and education are of course parts of the answer. In the long run the drug problem will be solved by prevention and education—meaning education in the broad sense, a change of heart and mind. In many places, fortunately, that is occurring. Virtually everyone knows that in the long run the solution to drugs (and to many other social problems) rests with stronger families, stronger churches, and stronger schools. If we had those things, we could reduce the drug problem by 80 percent or more. But reinvigorating those institutions is not the primary business of the police. Something is wrong when law-enforcement officers start sounding like sociologists and when their leaders want to spend more time psychoanalyzing a drug dealer's behavior than getting their men to arrest him. While it is of major importance to strengthen the institutions of family, church, and school, a first priority, certainly law enforcement's first priority, must be to restore order to the streets and ensure domestic tranquillity. The most immediate need is not to teach fire prevention, but to put out the fire. When drug dealers own the streets and are shooting innocent people, what's called for is not a lecture on the need to change attitudes, or a seminar on the "root causes" of drugs, but strong, rapid law enforcement. Yet even to this day some police chiefs continue to talk about their inability to deal with the problem. According to an article in *The Wall Street Journal*:

> The emphasis on beefed-up law enforcement at the expense of treatment, prevention and education "has done more harm than good," contends Patrick Murphy, director of the U.S. Conference of Mayors' police policy board. Lee Brown, the police commissioner of New York City, says, "We're being forced to shoulder the greatest part of the drug problem, and we can't do it by ourselves." . . . The sentiment among chiefs at a recent gathering, says Yale University drug historian David Musto, was, "Yes, I'll carry out your orders, but if you knew more you wouldn't give out those orders."

Happily, however, there are exceptions to this attitude of inertia and fecklessness born of overtheorizing. Reuben Greenberg, the black Orthodox Jewish police chief of Charleston, South Carolina, is the best, most dramatic example I know.

Chief Greenberg has been out on the street, teaching by example what he wanted the men and women of his force to do. On my tour of Charleston with him, it was clear that he knew the city like the back of his hand. He called many residents by name as we walked the streets and visited public housing projects. "You have got to disrupt the drug dealers," he told me, "and make life miserable for them. You arrest some, but others you just disrupt, make life unpleasant, and they will move along somewhere else."

The tactics Greenberg developed in Charleston include posting uniformed police officers on corners where drug sales are common. There they confront suspicious-looking people. He reestablished foot patrols in the ghetto and set up "flying squads" to chase down street-corner crack dealers. And strict enforcement of laws authorizing eviction of public housing residents involved in illegal activities has been a major factor in reducing crime in public housing. "You don't have to have a place where drug dealers can make a living," Greenberg told me. He and his men meet regularly with tenants to gather information.

He equips all his officers with cameras so they can take pictures of people wandering around neighborhoods where they don't belong. Drug dealers do not like their pictures taken by cops. Greenberg also announced that he would have police at all of the drug "hot spots" in Charleston, wherever there were suspected drug dealers. He knew that the American Civil Liberties Union (ACLU) would react. They insisted that ACLU observers watch the police watching the suspects. Then the media announced that they too would be out on the street observing. Greenberg's plan was for all of this to happen. The result was that when a drug dealer took to the streets in Charleston he was liable to find himself tailed by a police officer, an ACLU observer, the local media, and, attracted by the fuss, residents of the neighborhood as well.

This was not what drug dealers wanted, so they moved. When Greenberg was asked where they moved, he said, "I don't know where they are, maybe in North Charleston, maybe in Columbia. But they are not in Charleston anymore. They are not Greenberg's problem anymore. They are now Bennett's problem." He was right. As the criminologists will tell you, displacement is never

100 percent; if you force drug dealers to move, some will drop out of the business, others will lose customers, and even for those who stay in business, you are at least complicating their life.

Greenberg's aggressive, no-nonsense, "let's get to it" approach had encouraging results. Since he took over as police chief in 1982, he has succeeded in cutting total crime by 35 percent. The crime rate in 1989 was the lowest in twenty-five years. In 1989, there were only eighteen arrests for drug trafficking, and it had been five years since anyone was murdered in the projects. "The drug dealers either go out of business or they move elsewhere," he says. "We don't tolerate drugs here." Greenberg has shown it can be done. Other chiefs—Bill Moulder in Des Moines, Reuben Ortega in Phoenix, Bob Smith in Tampa, and Drew Diamond in Tulsa—have done likewise, and they, too, have gotten results.

"This is what America looks like when it works," I said after touring the Gadsden Green housing project in Charleston. "This is a country which works when people get together, when they throw their hands in on a common effort and that seems to be working." Because drug use is down in Charleston, it is harder to find drugs on the street. And so the streets are safer. The community has a sense that things are being done because things *are* being done. It's harder to get drugs in public housing in Charleston, Greenberg told me, than it is on most college campuses. I believe he's right. So evident was Greenberg's success that even the lieutenant governor of North Carolina (I say "even" because the two Carolinas are rivals in so many ways) conceded that Charleston had done a superb job and he went to observe first-hand.

Greenberg and Charleston are not unique. Wherever we have seen similar kinds of aggressive community policing efforts undertaken in conjunction with the community, we have seen positive results.

Some days I felt as if I had seen almost as many public housing projects as my good friend and colleague Jack Kemp saw as Secretary of Housing and Urban Development. There is a sameness about these communities that sends a clear message. They are often vulnerable communities, so drug dealers go there to prey.

Many occupants of public housing are unprotected. Often, shamefully, there is less police protection. And there aren't many men around to confront. In visits to some thirty public housing projects, I saw very, very few men as tenant representatives. In the meetings I went to, the tenant councils were made up almost exclusively of women. For the most part, public housing projects in the United States today are inhabited by women and children. Sometimes the only men around are bad ones.

Men would be there when I visited, of course. There would be some local authorities, people seeking to get on television, and people wanting a government grant. But often when the television cameras were gone, so too were the men. And the women and children were left to fend for themselves.

Nevertheless, action is possible in the projects. In Tulsa, a small police unit was established in the public housing project. When I went there to celebrate the removal from the project of two ruthless drug gangs—the Bloods and the Crips—the residents decided to hold a big ceremony. It began with many of the residents of the project, all black and almost all women and children, hugging the police officers who were assigned to the substation of the public housing project. The officers were all white. Here was another example of what the police could do, what human difference they could make, when they took their jobs seriously and were there on the spot, and what a possibility of community it suggested.

In Raleigh, North Carolina, I saw a similar situation. But in addition to the police substation and a jobs center, the city fathers had added a Marine recruiting station. And so two uniformed Marines walked on the property of this public housing project every day. I have no doubt that this by itself discouraged some drug dealers from operating in the project. And it gave a striking counterexample to the bad example of the drug dealers. Young people could look up and see two role models, one black, one Hispanic.

These steps taken in Tulsa and Raleigh are not difficult to think up or implement. They simply require breaking out of bureaucratic inertia, not buying into overly complicated theories of policing and human behavior, and remembering the basics: what communities need first is order and safety, what children need above all is love and order and good examples. Simple, direct efforts can make an astonishing difference.

Yet critics attacked our efforts (made in conjunction with Secretary Kemp) to secure public housing from drugs by building fences and other security apparatuses around public housing and giving residents official identification cards. Some critics charged that we wanted to turn public housing projects into virtual concentration camps. The American Civil Liberties Union attacked our proposals as repressive. I responded:

> I don't know why, when public housing projects begin to resemble exclusive Connecticut Avenue apartments, where you have security systems and checks, why the ACLU gets more upset. I would think that in the interest of social equality that is a *good* thing, not a bad thing. That's what rich people have: security. That's why they charge so much rent at these places. It's a good thing for poor people to have security like rich people have. And when you go to these projects and talk to the people, you'll find an occasional person saying, "It's a hassle," and "I lost my card and they wouldn't let me in. . . ." But by and large, I think the results and the return, by way of the sentiments of the residents of public housing, are very much in favor of this kind of effort.

As Kemp has tirelessly argued, before HUD goes into the business of fixing up, refurbishing, and improving public housing, it should make sure it's doing this for families, for mothers and fathers and their children who live there and are obeying the law, rather than for drug dealers. Why put in new light fixtures for drug dealers? So they can see better? First let's get them out of the projects.

One of the most striking and encouraging examples of civic action against drugs was provided in Kansas City, Missouri. I wanted President Bush to see a man I had met in one of my early travels: Al Brooks, the former police officer, and his group of men who walk the once drug-ridden streets of Kansas City.

In 1977 Brooks founded the Ad Hoc Group Against Crime, a grass-roots antidrug and anticrime organization. In 1987, he helped start Black Men Together, an auxiliary to Ad Hoc, intended primarily to offer role models for young black children, which was one of the most extraordinary sights I saw. Black Men Together—forty or fifty black men walking the streets of Kansas City—had an impact on the Kansas City community that I'm not sure any federal or state program could ever have.

In coordination with the police, these men walk down the street with bullhorns, chanting to the drug dealers to get off the street: "You better run, dope dealer, you better run," and, "Hey, you dope dealer, Black Men out here are watching you." This sends a very clear message. There's nothing subtle or nuanced about this message. It's clear; it works.

It's not just that dealers avoid them, but that young black children see grown men who are strong, righteous, decent, and worth emulating. I suspect their effect on the *education* of the young men in that community is probably more profound than anything that can happen in a school. Brooks told me, "Just our presence causes drug pushers to leave the area. We stand like men, act like men and we're respected like men."

Our strategy was not limited to the United States. We wanted to have an agreement with the Andean nations (Peru, Bolivia, and Colombia) providing economic assistance in exchange for a serious crackdown against drug production and drug cartels. So, again, we went to the President and asked him to make a high-profile visit to Colombia. Although there were wide differences at the Cabinet level on whether this was a good idea, he agreed. Before he could go, however, on December 15, 1989, an official at the Drug Enforcement Agency called to inform me that Gonzalo Rodriguez Gacha, one of the key leaders of the Medellín cartel, had been killed in a shoot-out with the Colombian police. I called President Barco in Colombia to get the details. As I later told the press, here was the first indication of the frailty, the fallibility, and the finitude of the cartel leaders. It also showed the resolute attitude of the Colombians. It was a great victory for them and a great victory for us. The myth of the cartel leaders' invulnerability and invincibility had been smashed. Of the men who once ran the world's largest drug empire, four (Carlos Lehder, Jorge Luis Ochoa, Fabio Ochoa, and Pablo Escobar) are in jail, and Rodriguez Gacha is dead. Despite criticism of the Colombian effort (and criticism is deserved because of the negotiated surrender agreed to with Escobar), no one can say that the Colombian people have not made serious efforts and paid a heavy price. Colombia's efforts against narcoterrorism have involved a long, bloody struggle.

We needed to show real American support in order to give the Andean nations a better chance, and to give them more reasons to fight. The question they had of us was, were we committed? Apart from our own efforts at home, we thought there was no better way to show deep American commitment than to ask the President to meet with the presidents of the Andean nations and sign what became the Document of Cartagena. No trip the President has made before or since has had so many people worried. Public opinion polls showed a majority of Americans opposed to the trip. Many of the President's own advisers, family members, and friends urged him not to go. But he had said he would go, and go he did.

Early in the morning on February 15, 1990, we left Andrews Air Force Base on Air Force One. Four hours later we were in a Marine Blackhawk helicopter skimming not more than a hundred feet above the Atlantic Ocean. We were flying from Barranquilla (where Air Force One had landed) to the site of the meeting at Cartagena. Jammed into the helicopter were the President, his physician, a Secret Service agent, Secretary of State James Baker, John Sununu, and I. I peered out the window, trying to see behind us, when Secretary Baker asked, "Czar, what are you doing? What are you looking for?"

I told him I was looking for the fighter jets that Dick Cheney had promised would accompany us. "Oh," was Baker's reply. A minute or so later, he started to look out the window. Then Sununu peered out the window. President Bush stared steadily at the water, not turning his head to see if the F-14s were there. Finally I turned to him and asked, "You're not curious about the planes, sir?"

President Bush said, "I'm sure they are there. I'm just wondering what the fishing is like down in that water."

I was struck by his equanimity, then and throughout the day. The meeting went smoothly and the document was signed. Unfortunately, the efforts Peru, a party to the Document of Cartagena, have been a major disappointment ever since Alberto Fujimori was inaugurated president. The jury is still out on Fujimori. He has so far talked a far better game than he's walked. If he doesn't step up to the drug issue in a serious way, a lot will be lost, including United States support and assistance. Thankfully the Colombians have maintained their effort, and the Bolivians have increased theirs, especially in their attempts to take down indigenous drug organizations. Overall in this country, cocaine seizures are way up. Some progress overseas has been achieved and our assistance has helped bolster the Andean nations' ability to fight back. Though much remains to be done, I believe the Andean Initiative was a necessary and wise one to undertake.

* * *

When I took over as drug czar, I was basically agnostic on the issue of drug treatment. It was an area I simply didn't know very much about. That's why I brought Dr. Herb Kleber on as my deputy director for demand reduction. Dr. Kleber was on leave from Yale University, where he was professor of psychiatry at the School of Medicine and director of the Substance Abuse Treatment Unit at the Connecticut Mental Health Center. Although many of my critics argued that I didn't "believe" in drug treatment, it is the area that I learned the most about and was in some ways most impressed by. By the end of my tenure I had visited some twenty-five treatment centers. I met with drug addicts whose lives had been reformed and improved, and learned how important and effective good drug treatment can be. But I also learned that drug treatment is not a panacea. According to Dr. Kleber, "only half, at best, of cocaine addicts are drug-free one to two years after treatment; the rate for crack addicts appears to be lower still." Those "compassionate" critics who insisted we focus almost all our attention and money on drug treatment were putting their hopes on something that often cannot deliver. For many, drug treatment works only partially or not at all.

Good treatment programs have many of the same features and they are not what you might imagine. The common tendency is to think of drug treatment as a soft, coddling, easy route away from drugs. The reality is far different. To the drug addict, drug treatment programs that work are often demanding, difficult, and physically and emotionally exhausting. An ethos of personal accountability and adherence to rules is a part of effective drug treatment. The marks of good, effective treatment programs are an insistence on a code of conduct, individual responsibility, personal sacrifice, and sanctions for misbehavior.

In Detroit I visited the Self Help Addiction and Rehabilitation (SHAR) program. SHAR, Inc., is a therapeutic community treatment program which serves the indigent population of Detroit and emphasizes behavior modification. When I sat down in the summer of 1990 with Allan Bray, the program's director, he said, "Mr. Bennett, meet the bottom of the barrel." His "clientele" may have been at the bottom of the barrel before they met Allan Bray and enrolled in SHAR, but because of Bray and his fine program, the SHAR residents I spoke with were getting better.

I saw that Bray was doing a lot to help his patients recover from their drug addiction. But I also saw him do something else. He was rebuilding—or in many cases building for the first time—the moral life of addicts. He told me that he models his drug-addiction program after two institutions: the military for teaching discipline and the church for nourishing the soul.

What I saw at SHAR, Inc., was true of the best drug-treatment centers I visited around the country. Basic lessons are taught— lessons about individual responsibility, commitment, and caring. They offer a sense of community and, even better, a sense of family.

One of the most impressive treatment programs I visited was in Maricopa County (Phoenix), where possession of any illegal drug, including marijuana, is a felony. Under the "Do Drugs, Do Time" program, people convicted of drug possession pay stiff fines and can then choose either jail or treatment. Almost 90 percent opt for drug treatment, and all but the very poor pay for the program out of their own pockets. If a person successfully completes treatment, his conviction is erased from his record.

Everybody wins in this program. Drug users are penalized, but not by overloading the criminal justice system. The drug user usually pays for the program, thereby saving the taxpayers' money. And a person who has a severe drug problem has the opportunity to enter a first-rate program. The "Do Drugs, Do Time" program also demonstrates the crucial and often over- looked link between law enforcement and treatment. During my visit every one of the people enrolled there had been forced to choose between incarceration and treatment. It was the coercive power of the law that was responsible for getting those people the kind of help they needed.

One of the most dramatic examples of this that I saw was dur- ing a trip to Alabama. On May 9, 1990, following an early- morning speech to more than two hundred of Birmingham's civic and government leaders, I arrived at the St. Clair Correctional Facility to talk with sixty inmates in cell block G4-A. The *Birming- ham Post-Herald* captured the setting well:

Around the common area of the cell block, which has been designated a therapeutic community for the New Outlook drug rehabilitation program, hung dozens of signs. "Drugs or Faith. You Can't Have Both," one sign read. . . . A series of simpler signs bore one word: "Sacrifice," "Courage" and "Commitment."

The inmates and supervisors recited the New Outlook Philosophy, written when the program started in July 1988. "To grow requires honesty and accepting personal responsibility for our actions. . . . Our past ways of doing things did not work, and we are now committed to listening, learning and applying new principles that we know will work," they read in unison.

Bob Kennington, one of the group's two supervisors, told me that there was a lot of anger from prisoners outside the program toward the ones who had gone straight. "A lot of the drug supply has dried up because some of the major dealers are sitting right here," he said.

As I sat on a chair facing the inmates, I asked them some questions. "I know that all of you were bad, otherwise you wouldn't have gone to prison. But how many of you were *really* bad?"

Every man in the room raised his hand.

"How many of you are in here for life without parole?" I asked.

A bunch of hands shot up.

"Why do this, then? What difference does it make whether you're off drugs or not?"

The inmates told me about the moral lessons they had learned for the first time. "I was miserable until I got into the group," one inmate told me. "I'd feel like a new person even if I never got out of here."

"What we're talking about here is learning things that should have been learned early in life," I told the press later, outside the prison. "Basic things, like caring and responsibility. More than what they said is how they said it. They stood up straight, and they looked me in the eye as they spoke. Heck, two-thirds of Congress won't look me in the eye."

We heard them talk about how they had become better, in their own words, by becoming born-again Christians, feeling their own sense of personal responsibility, and recognizing what they were doing was wrong. We asked their advice, and they told us that kids should be taught the difference between right and wrong, that adults needed to exercise more responsibility, that society was in bad shape because it wasn't living up to its own messages. Here were statements from people who had no reason to say anything but the truth. This was a very different message from what we got

from the protestors in Madison. This one was far more persua-
sive; it encapsulated a lot of what had been reinforced in me
during my decade in public life.

The liberals in Congress who were on their high horse over our
alleged "neglect" of treatment turned out to be hypocrites. During the debate on the final budget I oversaw for fiscal year 1991,
after eighteen months of accusations that we were underfunding
treatment and education programs, the Democratically controlled
House Appropriations Committee slashed more than $230 mil-
lion from President Bush's proposed increases for drug treatment, prevention, and education. As many as 100,000 people
would have lost access to drug treatment if the committee's cuts
held up.

I was angry, and I went public. "I'm mad as hell," I said. "Bill
Bennett is not going to take more Democratic garbage about the
need for more treatment, education, and prevention. . . . This is
cheap, dishonest and sneaky. I will not be flogged by these
clowns."

One member took to the House floor and attacked me for my
"reckless" remarks. The late Silvio Conte, then the committee's
senior Republican, said that I "acted like a bear awakened from
his winter's sleep." Representative Charles Rangel, chairman of
the House Select Committee on Narcotics, announced that "Bill
Bennett has lost his effectiveness on the Hill." He said that after
the House of Representatives, responding to my criticism, voted
to restore $230 million to our antidrug efforts. That was the
kind of "ineffectiveness" I could live with. The amount of
money that we put into treatment was extraordinary compared
to what Congress had previously authorized. The drug-
treatment budget we submitted to Congress in fiscal year 1991
was $1.5 billion, a 68 percent increase from the time George
Bush took office. We also insisted on spending the money more
wisely than we had in the past. As with education, we insisted on
accountability.

This game played by some members of Congress on the drug
issue was not wholly unexpected. When President Bush took office, we picked up word that some Democrats were out to embarrass him politically on the issue. They thought that progress
against the drug epidemic was impossible to achieve and they
could hang failure around the President's neck. After two years,
however, there was very little political ground on which the Dem-

ocrats could attack him. The issue actually worked in his favor; we were making progress on an issue President Bush took on squarely at considerable political risk (and against the advice of some of his political advisers). He provided leadership, record levels of federal effort and funding, and with the major effort supplied by the American people, the "impossible" task was getting done.

In fact, the Democrats were on the defensive on the issue, and some of them wanted to change the subject. One of their tactics was to talk about "the root causes" of drug use, the "deeper and more profound problems," as they put it, of homelessness, poverty, helplessness, and the like. The elites liked this shift in emphasis, too. It took the discussion away from moral considerations to the (for them) more comfortable ground of social theory. They wanted to talk about "hopelessness" as a condition caused by lack of government involvement. We talked about hopelessness, too, but talked about it as a condition caused by social decomposition and the breakdown of the family and a lack of law and order in these communities. We also argued that one solution was a greater police presence on the streets in order to restore order, the first condition of civil society and the first promise made by government to its citizens. I found it shocking and disappointing that when we argued for more police, jails, courts, and prisons because of the exploding crime epidemic in some of America's inner cities, some people responded by saying, "But what are the root causes of this?"

That's an interesting debate which should go on at an elite university. But if there are drug dealers going around shooting people in the affluent suburbs, the citizenry will not call for a seminar on root causes. They will raise hell and demand that the dealers be arrested. And they are right to do so.

"When we have a drug dealer where I live, in Chevy Chase, Maryland," I pointed out, "we don't sit around and talk about root causes of drugs. We call the police and get the drug dealer off the street. But when a drug dealer is running free in the inner cities of southeast Washington, or Watts, or Newark, we have people calling for a seminar on root causes and hopelessness. Hold the seminar later. Right now get the cops, get order, get back control of the streets. The law demands it."

There's a fundamental issue involved here: equal protection of the law. It's a promise made to every citizen. Inner city residents deserve the same police protection as residents of affluent suburbs. When Americans finally got angry about racism and decided it was wrong, the country didn't wait to eliminate the "root causes" before going after it aggressively, in law and through social stigma. And it was right not to wait.

I sometimes infuriated our law-enforcement critics by posing this analogy: Imagine that you own a beachhouse and discover a school of great white sharks in the water just off your property. They don't leave. As the people continue to swim, the casualties mount. What do you do? You certainly should provide for hospitals, health care, emergency services, rehabilitation, therapy, and artificial limbs. And you certainly should teach people not to go into the water, and take particular care to tell the children that they should not go near the water.

But is there something else you should do, perhaps something else you should do before anything else? Of course there is. *You need to get the damn sharks out of the water.* Drive them out, surround them, net them, spear them, you do whatever it takes, but you get rid of them.

It was the last part of the message that seemed to resonate most with the American public— especially among the underclass, residents of public housing who were (to remain true to the analogy) most often ripped apart by the sharks. But it was the part of the message that almost always shocked the conscience of some of the elite. Why? *Because it involved the language of law and order, of right and wrong.* The problem for some of my critics was not that we weren't putting money into treatment (we were, in record amounts), but that I was not talking about the drug problem exclusively as a "medical" problem.

Jim Vance, the well-known news anchor of Washington, D.C.'s WRC-TV, said in a commentary that one cause for celebration for black Americans in 1990 was "we finally got rid of William Bennett with his terminally myopic inability to distinguish between bad people and sick people." My insistence on the moral dimensions of the problem apparently irked Vance (a man who had his own well-publicized battles with cocaine use), and I can understand why. But I took this approach on purpose. I began many of my congressional hearings by saying that the premise of the National Drug Control Strategy was that drug use was morally wrong. Unlike the late 1960s and 1970s, I could express these sentiments without creating a stir and without fear of contradiction by even one member of Congress. The country and the Congress had come a long way.

In the campaign for character, Charles Eliot, a former president of Harvard, once said, no auxiliaries are to be refused. Though the National Drug Control Strategy had the look of a neat, rational, analytic tool—and it was—it could also be translated as saying we were throwing almost everything we had at the problem. If a burglar is coming in your back door, you use everything to stop him: toasters, rolling pins, chairs, and tables. That was analogous to the National Drug Control Strategy: taking careful aim and throwing everything civilized society has at this form of barbarism.

I am no McLuhanite; I do not believe the medium is the message. But I knew that the news media could be important allies in our efforts. The news media helped simply by giving intense coverage to the devastation wrought by drugs. People sitting in their living rooms were watching children die and neighborhoods ripped apart. And they began to pay attention.

We also got a good assist from the Partnership for a Drug Free America, headed by Jim Burke, which came up with riveting, hard-hitting TV ads about drug use (which showed everything from eggs frying in a pan—a metaphor for a brain on drugs—to a young woman jumping off a diving board into an empty swimming pool).

One of the most encouraging signs of a strong cultural shift away from drug use occurred when I visited Los Angeles in October 1989. I accepted an invitation from Richard Frank, president of Disney Studios and a valuable ally in our efforts, to address the American Academy of Television Arts and Sciences. Members of the Academy told me that there was a new "sobriety chic" in Hollywood. Drug use was no longer "in."

I told the Academy that the deglamorization of drugs was a very good thing indeed. I then used the earthquake that shook California in 1989 to make an often overlooked point. Few people knew that the earthquake that hit the Bay area was more powerful than the one that hit Mexico City a few years earlier, because in Mexico City the casualties were much higher and the overall damage much worse. The reason is that when the earth shakes, the devastation often depends less on the magnitude of the quake than on the stability of the structure on which you stand.

In some ways, Hollywood is stable and well situated. Its residents have resources of which they can take advantage. Many can afford expensive drug-treatment programs like the Betty Ford Clinic. But Watts is an altogether different story. "For every Hollywood and Beverly Hills, there is a Watts," I told the members of the Academy. "For every Chevy Chase, Maryland, there is an Anacostia [part of the inner city of Washington, D.C.]. For every Scarsdale, there is a Harlem. . . . There are some communities in America today that are literally getting the hell pounded out of them from [the] aftershocks."

My warning was that the affluent should not become indifferent to the struggles of the underclass. Hollywood after all bears some responsibility for getting us into this mess by glorifying drug use in the 1970s. It seemed to me that they should bear some responsibility for helping us to get out of this mess today.

I'm glad to say that Hollywood is responding. Very few movies glorify drug use. Some movies even make strong antidrug statements. Richard Frank helped put together a half-hour animated antidrug cartoon that simultaneously aired on more than 750 television stations in early 1990. These are the kind of steps that help shape the culture.

Early in my tenure I was returning from a visit to one of America's inner-city communities. Seeing a community unite and fight back against drugs always bucked up my spirits. And although I was being cautioned by experts against placing too much hope on the pace of recovery, my instincts (and my eyes) told me that things were getting better and getting better faster than we had been led to believe. There was a palpably different spirit in the nation. We had undergone the great American change of mind about drugs.

When crack hit this country the American people were stunned. We were like a boxer knocked back against the ropes. We lost our balance. Our legs buckled. But we got our balance back. Our legs were stronger. Our vision was clearing. And we were starting to fight back. I knew then, in a way I had not known before, that America was on the road to recovery.

When the twenty-fourth annual survey of college freshmen was released in the early part of 1990, I knew things were turning our way. The survey director said, "When it comes to matters of crime and drugs, college freshmen are more conservative than they have ever been."

As a former college professor, I know that college freshmen aren't known for their tough-minded, hard-nosed approach to "life-style" issues. Being a college freshman is one of those periods in your life when you consider all sorts of options and you are most likely to take a more latitudinarian attitude about things in general. So when I heard that college freshmen were becoming more conservative on the issue of drugs, I knew that a sea change in attitudes was taking place.

Where do we stand today in the war on drugs? According to Dr. Mark Gold, a leading authority on drug use and author of *The Good News About Drugs and Alcohol,* "the good news is, we're winning." Dr. Gold cites the following evidence:

· The number of current drug users *fell* from 23 million to 12.9 million—a drop of 44 percent—between 1985 and 1990.
· In 1985 there were 5.8 million current users of cocaine: five years later, that number was cut down to 1.6 million.
· From 1988 to 1990 there was a 26 percent decrease in the number of cocaine-related emergency room visits.
· Marijuana use is at its lowest points since 1972.
· Drug rehabilitation centers are half-full and many are closing.

In 1989, the Office of National Drug Control Policy laid out detailed two-year and ten-year goals and objectives, all with specific numerical and proportional targets, and almost all of which directly address the most urgent drug use problems. In 1991, the ONDCP issued the following two-year assessment:

· The goal for current overall drug use was a decrease of 10 percent; the actual decrease was 11 percent.
· The goal for current adolescent drug use was a decrease of 10 percent; the actual decrease was 13 percent.
· The goal for occasional cocaine use was a decrease of 10 percent; the actual results were a decrease of 29 percent.
· The goal for frequent cocaine use was a 50 percent reduction in the rate of increase; the actual result was a 23 percent decline overall.
· The goal for current adolescent cocaine use was a decrease of 20 percent; the actual result was a decrease of 49 percent.
· The goal for drug-related medical emergencies was 10 percent; the actual result was a decrease of 18 percent.

• The goal for student attitudes toward drug use was a 10 percent decrease; the actual result was a 28 percent decrease.

In other words, the national goals were exceeded in every category. The healing process has begun.

If you live in a crack-infested, violence-ridden neighborhood, the numbers are of little comfort; they are mere abstractions. It's hard to feel encouraged about the overall state of the war. The sober, hard reality is that there are casualties—real casualties, lots of casualties—in this war every day. There are lots of inner-city and rural communities that are still getting the hell beat out of them, and they need assistance and support.

But in the aggregate, we are winning the war on drugs. The number of drug users continues to go down, and the news is generally good. Almost all the trends point in the right direction. We will prevail, but not without having paid a heavy price—a financial price, of course, but a much higher cost in terms of lives lost and damaged, communities destroyed, and children abused, beaten, and poisoned. A million addicts or more will do nothing to help themselves; for many of them, nothing can be done. They will not accept the regimen of treatment or be rehabilitated in prison. Despite our best efforts, they will die.

In the near term, the number of heroin users will probably rise, mainly because people coming off a cocaine "high" will seek the narcotic "down" of heroin. That is the normal pattern of drug epidemics. In addition, we're seeing an increased supply of heroin from Southeast Asia. But the rise in heroin is not likely to be anywhere near the fall in the number of cocaine users.

Communities that have not intelligently focused their efforts at law enforcement, treatment, prevention, and education will not prevail against drugs for some time, while others like Charleston, Mobile, Tulsa, Raleigh, Phoenix, Minneapolis, and Miami, will. Effort and intelligence matter. But there is nothing inevitable about either victory or defeat. It depends on the hearts and hands of individual citizens and on the clarity and energy of local leadership.

Overall, most cities in America are getting better. A few, because of the sheer magnitude of the problem and because some local leaders are unable to attack drug use effectively and intelligently, will take more time. And of course there will always be some drug problem of unpleasant size in this large, free, and affluent society. But if efforts continue apace, in 1995 the country will have half or even less than half the size of the drug problem of 1990. The great American change of mind on drugs has occurred. Government needs to build on it and put resources behind it. The job of government today is to continue to coordinate national policy, say why drugs are wrong, show how to attack the problem, provide the necessary resources, and point to what works. If the leadership does that, the American people will do most of the rest of the work themselves. The American people never fully bought the notion of some counterculture elites that drugs were nothing more than harmless fun. We let our immune system down for a while, and we paid a price. But we are recovering.

As I said at the National Press Club in January 1990:

If there is credit to be given [for progress made], that credit goes to the American people—to everyone and anyone who has done anything about this problem in a positive way—to those people who did not say, "Let's surrender," or "Let's legalize," or "There's nothing we can do." Credit belongs to all those people who said, "This is a terrible problem, let's do something about it" . . . to local cops, to federal cops, to treatment heroes, to spouses and employers and advertising executives and teachers who stood against drugs in 1979 and stand against drugs today, and who have helped change many American minds, because we need to be clear what's happening now is not historic inevitability or fate. It's people doing something; it's people acting; it's organized effort; it's public attitudes hardening; it's communities in all parts of America rising up and saying, "We're not going to take it anymore."

5

THE GREAT UNIVERSITY DEBATES

When I arrived as a freshman at Williams College in 1961, I had definite ideas about how I wanted to use my four years of higher education. I wanted to major in English and become "sophisticated." I wanted to become sophisticated because I wanted to land a good job in advertising with a big salary. Because of my college's course requirements, however, I found myself in an introductory philosophy class, confronted by Plato's Republic *and a remarkable professor, Laszlo Versenyi. He knew how to make the text come alive. Before we knew it, my classmates and I were ensnared by the power of a 2,000-year-old dialogue.*

In the posture of youthful cynicism and arrogance, I resisted at first the idea that the question of justice should really occupy my time. But something happened to me that semester as I fought my way through The Republic, *arguing about notions of right and wrong. Along the way, without quite knowing it, I committed myself to the serious enterprise of raising and wrestling with questions. And once I was caught up in that enterprise, there was no turning back. After Versenyi and* The Republic, *everything changed: my undergraduate major, postgraduate plans, and my thinking about a lot of what was important. A college course had altered my life.*

Every student is entitled to that kind of experience in college. He should discover great works that tell us how men and women through the ages have grappled with life's relentless questions: What should be loved? What deserves to be defended? What is noble and what is base? College should animate a conscious examination of life's enduring questions. Know thyself, Socrates said.

*Higher education worthy of the name aspires to nothing less than
the wisdom of that dictum.*

In an interview during my first week as Secretary of Education, I
told *The New York Times:* "there are good grounds for suspicion
that some students are not getting their money's worth. Some
people are getting ripped off." Poor management and ill-
conceived curriculums made it reasonable to ask whether so many
young people should go to college. I then added:

> The institutional identity crisis has been encountered. Insti-
> tutions have to decide about their means, their definition and
> their purpose. Do they believe what they say in their cata-
> logues, that the purpose of this education is to help an indi-
> vidual become better intellectually and morally? Or do they
> really believe in something else? Sometimes you get incoher-
> ence and disarray because you've lost your bearings. . . . The
> fact that we have 3,200 institutions of higher education is a
> wonder of the world. It would be an even greater wonder if
> they all lived up to their promises.

This interview came on the heels of my opening press conference as Education Secretary, in which I responded to a question by CBS correspondent Phil Jones on the effects of the
Reagan administration's proposed reduction in student aid. I
pointed out that many students—particularly low-income
students—would not be affected. The better off would be affected by our proposed cuts (for example, some grants would
become loans). And other students would have to borrow more
money or find additional work during the summer or the school
year. But that's not what caught the press's attention. Instead,
they focused on the comments I made about the well-to-do:
"For some it may require divestiture of certain sorts—stereo divestiture, automobile divestiture, three-weeks-at-the-beach divestiture," I said. "Tightening the belt can have the function of
focusing the mind," and the cuts in student aid might cause parents and teens to choose a college "with the same sort of care we
do in buying a car."
A Harris poll that year found that despite general support for

student aid, 77 percent of the American people felt too many well-off families had received loans and 62 percent felt that student loans had to be included in budget cuts.

Student reaction to my comments showed that they not only are not the least intimidated by their government but they also have a great sense of humor. I received dozens of postcards from students spending spring break on the beach at Fort Lauderdale, Florida. One read: "Dear Mr. Secretary Bennett: Wish you were here. The sun is great. Send money, preferably not one of those things that takes six months from your department. Stereo broke; would appreciate your sending bureaucrat down with a Walkman."

Another postcard read: "Dear Secretary Bennett: Having fun in the sun. Wish you were here. Thanks for the loans." It was signed by Jim, Larry, Dean, Cindy and "a $17,000 debtor." Their postcard also bore postscripts: "P.S. Could use a stereo. P.P.S. Thank Uncle Ronnie, too." The flip side showed a girl in a skimpy bikini and read, "It's Twice as Nice in Florida."

But the reaction to my remarks among the representatives of higher education and their defenders in Congress was animus and fury. (I was later told that I was the *first* Cabinet officer in memory to criticize colleges and universities.) Senator Robert Stafford, a Republican member of the Senate education subcommittee, said, "If I knew he would make these kinds of statements, he would not be the Secretary of Education."

John Brademas, president of New York University, said the proposed cutbacks "threaten an entire generation of scholars. This is a war," he declared, "and we need everybody in the ranks."

Albert Shanker, president of the American Federation of Teachers (who had earlier said I had the qualities to make an "outstanding" Education Secretary), said, "We need an Education Secretary who will be a forceful spokesman for quality in education. We don't need a Secretary who sees his job as being a hatchet man for the President."

Leon Botstein, president of Bard College, wrote in *The New York Times* that "Mr. Bennett reveals a mistrust of the young, a disregard for the fact that it is hard to pay for college. . . . we also need a Secretary who does not bludgeon educators and offers caricatures of education."

The Washington Post's influential columnist David Broder wrote that I had all "the earmarks of being a disaster" and suggested that I would prove to be "a terrible political burden to the Republican Party."

My comments immediately made me persona non grata on many university campuses. Shortly after coming into office I had been invited to give the commencement address at California's University of the Pacific. But its president, Stanley E. McCaffrey, withdrew the invitation, saying, "I am very disappointed—indeed, shocked—at your statements. I find it hard to comprehend that one in your vitally important position could be so insensitive. I find your views to be directly contrary to those held by me and our University of the Pacific. We simply cannot honor a person holding [your] views."

In response the columnist George Will wrote, "The hysterical condemnation of Bennett illustrates the moral exhibitionism of people like McCaffrey. It also reveals that the academic lobby—like, say, the tobacco lobby, but with more moral pretenses—has become an organized appetite. Bennett has interrupted its concentration on the social pork barrel by raising disturbing questions about academic purposes and competence."

I had been in office all of three weeks.

A few months after my divestiture comment, I was talking with a high-ranking education official from Holland. He had understood me to be a harsh critic of American higher education, so he asked what I took to be the system's worst faults.

Excuse me, I told him, but you misunderstand. What you overheard were the words of a man speaking candidly to those whom he proudly considers his own. "Proudly" because he knows that the flaws he sees at close quarters are significant flaws, but that they are nevertheless flaws in a great structure. No system of higher education, I stressed, has traditionally afforded greater intellectual freedom to students or their teachers. No system can boast nearly as much public and private support, or half the variety and diversity. We have the world's best research and teaching. We offer more second chances, more choices, more ability to tailor one's actual educational experiences to one's changing goals and circumstances throughout life. Well over half of our high school graduates go on to some form of higher education (although considerably fewer finish). Few countries in the world approach those numbers.

Although I began many higher-education speeches by noting these achievements, my reputation in the higher-education community became that of its fiercest critic, perhaps because I was one of its first very vocal critics.

Criticisms *were* merited. Since the late 1960s, there has been a collective loss of nerve and faith on the part of many faculty and academic administrators. The academy has hurt itself, even disgraced itself, in many ways. Course requirements were thrown out; intellectual authority was relinquished; standards were swept aside; scholarship increasingly became an extension of political activism; and many colleges and universities lost a clear sense of their educational mission and their conception of what a graduate of their institutions ought to know or be.

Today the problems are manifold and manifest, including the imposition in some places of a radical left-wing political orthodoxy; an all-out assault on the great works and ideas of Western civilization; exploding tuition costs that have outpaced inflation every year for over a decade; a drop in the quality of teaching as professors flee the classroom for their research projects; and a loss of moral and intellectual purpose. While colleges and universities are battered from within, too many feckless administrators, trustees, and alumni stand idly by.

The traditional mission of the university ("to enlarge and illuminate your life," in the words of Robertson Davies) is far too important to abandon without a fight, and this was a fight in which I was a willing participant. When I spoke as a critic—a "loving critic" in the words of Madison—I spoke as a member of the family. I am a product of the academy and found intellectual nourishment there. I taught and administered there. So I believed myself entitled, even obligated, to speak freely to my colleagues.

Any enterprise as strong, wealthy, and self-confident as American higher education should be able to take criticism from one of its own. Over the course of three years, however, the higher-education establishment reacted to my words as if I were hurling rocks through the stained-glass windows of a cathedral. The response among the academic community ranged from hurt feelings, surprise, and dismay to ferocious indignation and personal vituperation. And the usual response to my criticisms was not "Prove it" or "You're wrong for the following reasons"; it was more in the vein of "How dare you attack the high priests of culture?" or more simply, "Who do you think you are?"

The modern university bears some resemblance to the medieval church. In tone and posture it often acts like a direct descendant of the old church: assured of its own authority and purity and ready to censure philistines who would speak against it. With the church, however, most divines at least paid attention to the injunction "Heal thyself"; they knew they had to attend to their own souls before they preached to the outside world. The inhabitants of the modern university are quick to proclaim their duty to address all sorts of things that are wrong in the world, to speak truth to power, to debate the most complex social and moral issues beyond their walls, and to instruct political business, military, and religious leaders on the proper path to follow. They often do so in a tone that reveals a sense of moral superiority, and yet they also do so without even a cursory acknowledgment that they ought first attend to healing themselves.

There is another analogy that can be drawn between the contemporary university and the medieval church. The old church fell into some disrepute because its exhortations to poverty and holiness were too often belied by the worldliness and sumptuousness of its clerics. Similarly, American higher education simply refuses to acknowledge the fact— often obscured, sometimes denied—that it is, in general, rich. I know of no other group in America that is more cocksure of its right to full entitlement to the United States Treasury than the leadership of higher education. Despite complaints about its financial condition, the American people have been very generous in this regard. Gross national spending on higher education in this nation has gone, in constant 1991 dollars, from $15.1 billion in 1950 to $65.6 billion in 1965 to $155.4 billion in 1991. The wealth, the endowments, of our institutions of higher education have also continued to increase, especially in the last few years. And the number of institutions of higher education in the United States has increased from 1,852 in 1950 to 2,230 in 1965 to 3,231 in 1980 to 3,535 in 1990. The representatives of higher education should not pretend this is a shrinking enterprise, in a perilous state, on the edge of the abyss.

Despite the sensitivity of higher education on the subject of quality and cost, the public trust dictated candor and truth-telling by the Education Secretary. A $155-billion-a-year enterprise is a proper object for close scrutiny, straight talk, and consumer advocacy. Unfortunately, there's a tendency among the American people to resist scrutinizing colleges and universities. The feeling is, "Colleges and universities are filled with better and smarter people. They know what they're doing. Who are we to raise questions?" The university often encourages such deference. But one of the prices of deference is that it reduces the incentive for self-examination and self-improvement.

Now it might not be surprising that few representatives of higher education wanted to be held accountable. After all, General Motors would probably prefer not to be held accountable either— except that car buyers give them no choice. But the university chieftains resisted any idea that they were similarly responsible for their own product. At one meeting, the president of an Ivy League college said to me, "Why don't you stop bashing us and just go back and bash the elementary and secondary schools? Nobody objects to that."

They were missing the point. Education is a continuum, and we need to look at what happens after secondary school. Jonathan Yardley, a columnist for *The Washington Post,* put it this way:

> [Bennett] is trying to engage the community of higher education in a serious conversation about its mission, but that community simply refuses to talk seriously about the issues he raises—and in so doing demonstrates precisely the narrow-mindedness that he laments. Bennett is the best friend higher education now has in public life, because he cares so deeply about educational standards and is in a position to do something about them, but because he works for Ronald Reagan he is not given a chance. Bennett, like Reagan, is a buzzword: If Reagan does it, it must be wrong, and if Bennett says it, it must be wrong.

The irritant was not so much that I was a former academic myself—not even that I was Secretary of Education. The real irritation, as Yardley noted, stemmed from the fact that I was Secretary of Education in the *Reagan* administration. "It's not just that you work for Ronald Reagan that bothers the university types; they might eventually forgive you that," said a friend of mine, a former colleague and one of the handful of conservative academic philosophers in America today. "What bothers them about you is that you have your Ph.D., you're a scholar, and you really, actually, honestly like Ronald Reagan, agree with him, and defend him without winking or crossing your fingers."

Those who have not spent time in the elite institutions of American higher education cannot comprehend the depth of this animus toward Ronald Reagan, the Reagan presidency, and therefore against Reagan's Education Secretary. Werner Dannhauser, professor of government at Cornell University, summed it up this way: "Show me a college professor and I'll show you someone who mocks Ronald Reagan." Or, as *The Harvard Salient* student newspaper put it, "Harvard hates Bennett because he is a Reagan man, because he goes along with the Reagan policy . . . and perhaps because he hit so close to home with his crack about stereo divestiture."

My concern with the condition of higher education in America did not begin with my stint as Secretary of Education. While I was chairman of the National Endowment for the Humanities, I said that when students demanded a greater role in setting their own educational agendas, higher education eagerly (and unwisely) responded by abandoning course requirements of any kind and with them the intellectual authority to say to students what the outcome of a college education ought to be. With intellectual authority relinquished, we found that we did not need to worry about what was worth knowing, worth defending, and worth believing.

This cave-in had its most devastating impact in the humanities. I made a vigorous case for the place of liberal arts in American higher education in the report *To Reclaim a Legacy*, issued at the end of my three-year term at the National Endowment for the Humanities. I argued that in many of our colleges, curricula had become diluted, diffuse, and directionless; that many of our colleges and universities had lost sight of their fundamental role in conveying our common culture; and that young Americans had become increasingly removed from the taproots of their society:

> Few of [America's college graduates] can be said to receive an adequate education in the culture and civilization of which they are members. Most . . . remain shortchanged in the humanities—history, literature, philosophy, and the ideals and practices of the past that have shaped the society they enter.

I suggested several reforms to help remedy the problems. These included: having senior faculty teach introductory courses

in the humanities; distributing humanities requirements throughout the four years of college to "complement and add perspective
to courses in the major field"; familiarity with at least one non-
Western culture along with knowledge of history, science and
technology; demonstrable proficiency in a foreign language; a
careful reading of several masterworks of English, American, and
European literature; a basic understanding of the most significant
ideas and debates in the history of philosophy; and an understanding of the development of Western civilization.

My critics, however, contended that the prescription of more
classics and masterworks was at best inadequate and at worst a
polemical attack on twentieth century scholarship. "Bill is an evan-
gelist for certain forms of scholarship," said Joseph Duffey. "His
approach of 'more Aristotle' represents a rather provincial idea of
the humanities. . . . It seems he's not aware that the time is past
when black studies can be regarded as a passing fad of the 1960s.
His is a rather tight canon. It's a religious rather than an intellectual position. . . ."

Mary Beth Norton, a Cornell historian and former member of
the NEH advisory council, said, "It strikes me that Bill doesn't
believe it's legitimate humanistic inquiry unless you're studying
ideas of great white men who are dead." And in a 1986 sym-
posium at Yale University prompted by *To Reclaim a Legacy,* a
panel of professors from some of the nation's leading campuses
reached general agreement that the view of Western culture em-
bodied in my report was variously sexist, elitist, imperialist,
bourgeois, ethnocentric, racist, selfish, and solipsistic. One
speaker exclaimed, to great applause, that diminishing the study
of the West is one important step toward freeing the world from
"the final fruits of bourgeois humanism: North Atlantic ethnocentrism."

The battle lines, then, were drawn while I was at NEH. But
there was more, much more to come. It came, dramatically
enough, in visits to two of the citadels of American higher education: Harvard and Stanford.

Harvard

As Secretary of Education I was determined to begin a candid,
constructive conversation on the purpose and quality of American
higher education in the hope that it would lead to closer scrutiny

and, eventually, to the much-needed reform of the American academy. And the most appropriate place to offer a serious, substantive critique of American higher education was to go to the brightest star in its constellation.

On October 10, 1986, I traveled to Cambridge, Massachusetts. My visit was part of the week-long celebration of Harvard's 350th birthday, so the forum was ideal. People were paying attention. Almost without exception, every speaker at that event came to pay homage. My task was different; I came to offer constructive criticism as well as praise.

I began by thanking Harvard for my education at its Law School, which I attended from 1968 to 1971 and from which I earned my J.D. I praised Harvard's resources, its faculty, its high-quality student body, its distinguished, indeed its world-class, reputation. And I fondly recalled my years as a proctor in Harvard Yard. But I did not then sit down to polite applause.

Out of these various Harvard experiences, and especially from the intense experience and illuminating vantage point of a proctor, I formed some notions both about Harvard and about American higher education in general. My subsequent experiences at other colleges and universities have served to strengthen these notions into convictions. There is an extraordinary gap between the rhetoric and the reality of American higher education. The gap is so wide, in fact, that we face the real possibility—not today, perhaps not tomorrow, but someday—of an erosion of public support for the enterprise.

The gap, I explained, is between expectations of parents and students and the quality and performance of colleges and universities. Too often our institutions of higher learning are not providing the kind of education their students are promised and that they deserve. At a minimum, I said, a real education embraces the classical and Judeo-Christian heritage, the facts of American and European history, the political organizations of Western societies, the great works of Western art and literature, the major achievements of the scientific disciplines—in short, the basic body of knowledge which universities once took it upon themselves as their obligation to transmit.

I took Harvard as an example. Neither the vast sums that parents pay for the privilege of sending their children to such col-

leges as Harvard, nor a $3.1 billion endowment, nor a faculty
justly renowned for its scholarship and intellectual brilliance, nor
even, for that matter, a brainy and resourceful student body was
evidence that Harvard or any other university is really fulfilling its
obligation to its own students of seeing to it that they graduate as
educated men and women.

"That Harvard is a place where one can get a good education,
no one can doubt," I went on. "But under the justification of
deferring to individual decisions and choices, much is left to
chance. Sometimes a proctor, a professor, a dean, steps in and
takes a real interest in a student's education—but that's often the
luck of the draw."

American colleges and universities had given up on what was once
a central task: the study of a core curriculum, a set of fundamental courses, ordered, purposive, and coherent, that should constitute the central, foundational part of a liberal education.
Dropping the core curriculum had terrible consequences. This
view was not idiosyncratic to me. The distinguished historian
James H. Billington had characterized the typical undergraduate
curriculum as a "smorgasbord." The 1985 Association of American Colleges report, *Integrity in the College Curriculum,* said:

> As for what passes for a college curriculum, almost anything
> goes. We have reached a point at which we are more confi-
> dent about the length of a college education than its content
> and purposes. . . . [T]he major in most colleges is little more
> than a gathering of courses taken in one department, lacking
> depth and structure. . . . The absence of a rationale for the
> major becomes transparent in college catalogues where the
> essential message embedded in all the fancy prose is: pick
> eight of the following. And "the following" might literally be
> over a hundred courses, all served up as equals.

Harvard had achieved quite a reputation for its Core Curriculum. But I had studied the Harvard catalog carefully, and what in
fact Harvard offered under the heading "Core Curriculum" was
an agglomeration of unrelated courses, on a wide variety of subjects. What they had is "a symbolic nod, a head feint, in the di-

rection of a core curriculum," I said, "but I cannot discern . . . a [real] core curriculum here."

I then raised the issue of the obligation of higher education to foster moral discernment in its students. Colleges and universities should go to greater pains to care for the development of sound values, good character and behavior in their students. To cultivate a student's intellect alone is not enough. Students need the institution's attention to their moral well-being as well. Yet where do many of our colleges and universities stand on the issue of their responsibility to protect their students? With a few honorable exceptions, higher education is silent. Many colleges freely dispense guidance to those who live beyond their walls, but when faced by a real problem, such as drug use on campus, they throw up their hands. "This unaccustomed modesty from higher education is puzzling," I said.

The final issue I addressed at Harvard was the topic of tolerance, the university as a home for the free exchange of ideas. At that time there were well-publicized incidents of speakers, almost all conservative, being denied the opportunity to speak on college campuses. I spoke out against the silencing of unpopular speakers (unpopular at least among administrators and faculty), but warned that we should also be careful not to allow a more subtle and pervasive kind of conformism and intolerance to permeate the institutions of higher education. "Let me put it simply," I said. "Prestigious, selective, leading universities— whatever modifier you wish—have a tendency in our time to show a liberal bias. . . . This need not be a great problem, as long as we are very careful that a generally shared political viewpoint does not lead to the explicit or implicit censorship of unpopular ideas."

The reaction to my Harvard speech was anger, even defensiveness. President Derek Bok was on the podium as I spoke. Afterward, he responded:

Mr. Bennett must also live by the intellectual standards of the academy. Meticulousness in the respect for available evidence, care in stating conclusions, perceptiveness in exploring issues beyond the level of superficiality and cant. By these standards, I fear that he has fallen short of what higher education needs and expects from a public servant of his status.

Bok took particular umbrage at my criticism of the putative jewel in Harvard's pedagogical crown, its Core Curriculum. My characterization of Harvard's Core Curriculum as an artificial construct of courses arbitrarily plucked from departmental offerings was simply incorrect, he insisted. "It may well be that our criteria and purposes are not those of Mr. Bennett," he said. "But it is one thing to discuss differences between two established curricular philosophies and quite another to insist that curricula that depart from one's own preferences are merely sham and rhetoric."

"I just don't think you can call it core curriculum," I responded. "You can call it a sort-of-core curriculum, an imitation of a core curriculum, a core 'lite,' but it just isn't a core." (A throng of Harvard students showed their good humor by presenting me with a six-pack of Coors Lite beer at a post speech reception for me, in mock tribute to my remark.)

Shortly after my speech I received unexpected support from the *Harvard Crimson,* a student newspaper, whose course guide, "The Confidential Guide," said:

[Bennett's] right ... the core is designed not to teach any select body of knowledge, but to introduce presumably eager undergraduates to different "modes of inquiry." ... Thus after four years you will hopefully be able to flip a mental switch and think like a historian, or an economist or a scientist. And you better be able to, because the Core won't give you a coherent picture about Western history, scientific advances, or philosophical thought.

The Core courses also rely heavily on graduate students to teach the sections. "Even the process reflects the inattention of the faculty," according to Charles J. Sykes's book *Prof Scam.* Citing the *Crimson,* he wrote, " 'At the beginning of each semester, there is a desperate scramble for graduate students to lead sections in oversubscribed core courses with course advertisements for [Teaching Fellows] on departmental bulletin boards. Yet these last-ditch section leaders provide the only personal instruction students get in large lecture classes.' " According to Sykes, "Harvard professors continue to regard the Core as a great success."

*   *   *

On the issue of moral discernment that I raised in my speech, President Bok responded that Harvard was quite concerned with ethics. As evidence he cited a dozen or so courses on ethics in the undergraduate curriculum, an increasing interest in ethics at the business school, courses on ethical responsibilities at the law and medical schools and so on. But this, I said that day, misses the point.

"I wasn't talking about courses in moral philosophy or in casuistry and sophistry," I told him. "I was talking about getting drugs off campus."

As a former professor of philosophy with an interest in theoretical and applied ethics, I have seen this confusion made hundreds of times over the last fifteen years. Usually it's made by academics and journalists. Ever since Watergate, we have had an outpouring of courses in ethics designed to stem a rising tide of bad behavior. The speed with which the study of ethics has become institutionalized is remarkable. Suddenly a whole new breed of moral experts—made up primarily of professors and psychologists—has emerged in American life; they are equipped with a vocabulary and methodology all their own and are perpetually on call. They are like an ethicist fire brigade, ready to minister to one or another moral dilemma of contemporary life.

The study of ethics is a good and laudable thing, especially at a university. But the academic study of ethics is not the answer to bad behavior. Taking courses on ethics may actually be a bad thing if the real lesson is one of hypocrisy. If the life of the campus, its ethos, is indifferent toward drug use—a serious and fundamental ethical and legal matter—then the lesson transmitted is that ethics are to be talked about, but not lived.

The way to improve behavior is to provide rules, teach precepts, offer good examples, and enforce the law. The answer to bad behavior is to hold people accountable, and if necessary to punish them. Simply offering a course on theories of responsibility isn't sufficient. You don't change a scofflaw's or a drug pusher's behavior by making him take an ethics course. You change it the old-fashioned way, by telling him to stop and why; and if he doesn't stop, you force him to stop by the power of the law, if necessary. It's not complicated, but it requires resolute action and tough-mindedness. In many of our leading universities, these are precisely the qualities often in short supply.

My experience as a former member of several philosophy departments has taught me that the prolonged study of ethics does not by itself make you a better person. If it did, philosophy professors would in general be better people than average. But they aren't. Yes, a few are better than average, but many others are worse. And the latter, thanks to their study, are more clever at achieving their ends. Being clever at ethics doesn't make you a good, decent, or responsible human being. It only makes you clever. Richard C. Cabot of Harvard put it well when he wrote in the early part of this century, "If there is not education of men's purpose, if there is no ethical basis at the foundation of education, then the more we know, the smarter villains and livelier crooks we may be. Knowledge is ethically neutral."

While I was teaching at the University of Wisconsin in the mid-seventies I saw the members of a seminar on advanced ethics, led by the professor, raid a broken soft-drink machine during a break and steal twenty cans of soda. I told them that what they were doing was wrong and that the delivery man might be forced to pay for the shortfall out of his own pocket. The professor of advanced ethics was unmoved; he reconvened the seminar for further elaborations of ethical dilemmas. Talking a good game is not the same as playing one; or if one prefers the more familiar proverb, actions speak louder than words.

As a Harvard resident adviser to freshmen for two years and as a tutor to undergraduates I had observed too many casualties. Many students were left unguided and unwatched; they were unable to handle the freedom they were given. What was glibly called "exploration" and "self-discovery" sometimes turned out to be a dead end, a waste of time, or even self-destruction. There are more than enough people in Harvard Yard and places like it on campuses across the country eager to take advantage of kids who lack street smarts or who do not wish to appear naive to their classmates.

One freshman I knew at Harvard took in a "runaway" girl and kept her in his room; she turned out to be a young but experienced prostitute. Many freshmen told me they were turned on to drugs in a "serious way" in college because it seemed everybody was doing drugs and they did not want to appear to be "unsophisticated."

*   *   *

These experiences stayed with me. When I was Secretary of Education I urged college presidents to write the following statement to students at the beginning of each school year, "Welcome back for your studies in September. But no drugs on campus. None. Period. This policy will be enforced—by deans and administrators and resident advisers and faculty—strictly but fairly." When parents send their children to college they have a right to expect the colleges to take measures to protect their sons and daughters from drugs. Colleges and universities have basic responsibility to care for the moral and, indeed, the physical well-being of their charges. Parents do not expect colleges to be neutral between morality and decadence.

While I did not advocate mass drug testing unless there was evidence of widespread abuse on campus, I said I would welcome getting the authority from Congress to withold federal funds from institutions that do not pledge to rid their campuses of drugs. I advised parents to write the universities and ask: "What is your policy on drugs? Why am I spending $11,000 a year for tuition while I cannot be assured that my son or daughter will not be proferred drugs at a basketball game or after class or in the student union?"

"That's a perfectly reasonable request to make for that kind of money," I said. "I am tired of hearing spokesman after spokesman say, 'We have a terrible problem here, but it's everywhere; the problem on our campus is no worse than it is on anyone else's campus.' "

On another occasion I said, "I don't know why colleges and universities can't get their act together and declare themselves drug-free learning zones. They'll get the biggest cheer from the American people, and I'll be leading that cheer." In response I was criticized by some in the academy as sounding like "a small-town PTA president."

In 1986 I again called on Harvard to lead the way, this time by taking a tough, visible stand against drug use on campus. (Harold Rosenberg's phrase "a herd of independent minds" applies to higher education. Where Harvard goes, much of the rest of the herd will follow.) "It's a violation, an offense to everything that higher education stands for," I said. College administrators still pay "insufficient attention to the problem." John Shattuck, Harvard's vice president for Government and Public Affairs, replied: "I think Mr. Bennett is once again engaged in an effort to grab the headlines on a complicated issue, and he's using the Harvard name to do it."

Here again was a university administrator invoking the specter of awful complexity. What are the facts? According to an October 1987 *Harvard Salient* poll of upperclassmen, 57 percent of Harvard seniors had taken an illegal drug. In response to the question "How easy do you think it is to get drugs at Harvard?" 77 percent answered it was either "easy" or "very easy."

According to a series in the *Harvard Crimson,* "the big money is in cocaine, and to a lesser extent, Ecstacy, dealers say. But because of the recent popularity of Ecstacy, much of Harvard's drug trading centers on the little white pills and tablets." The *Crimson* interviewed students who used and dealt drugs, as well as administrators. Students generally said they were not afraid of being caught. When asked if they thought Harvard might make their business more difficult in the future, a dealer of the designer drug Ecstacy and another who sold large amounts of marijuana said that it depended on administrative reaction to the *Crimson* articles. The Ecstacy dealer said he wasn't alarmed by the new attention in high places to drug dealing at Harvard, adding, "By this point, Harvard administrators probably don't take Bennett very seriously."

During the years I was at Harvard, and since, it was generally the policy of the university to look the other way on the drug problem. Surely Harvard could hold standards at least as high as those found in a good high school. *Minimal* moral standards, *minimal* standards of responsible behavior, *minimal* adherence to law—these were not asking too much. At the very least, the university should not teach by its actions (or by its inactions) that it is a sanctuary from the law. Indeed, once universities have assured the public and their own communities that they can handle a straightforward, obvious, and simple ethical matter such as drug use in their own environs, they will then be in a much better position to address complex ethical issues like divestment of stocks in South Africa.

When I was drug czar, I was asked by Lisa Myers of NBC News whether, in general, colleges and universities were taking a sufficiently aggressive stand against drugs. "The fact is," I replied, "a lot of universities just don't have the courage to do it;

they don't have the will to do it; and many of them, frankly, I don't think really made up their minds that this is a very bad thing." I was sick and tired of hearing university spokesmen say that they wanted to combat sexism, racism, and ethnocentrism, but when it came to drugs, in effect they would throw up their hands and say, "That's a society-wide problem, and we can't do anything about it."

"Bill Bennett . . . came to Harvard University the other day as part of Harvard's 350th anniversary celebration. He rained all over the birthday party." So wrote the nationally syndicated columnist James J. Kilpatrick. Despite the criticism I received following my Harvard address, I considered it to be a success. The point of the speech, after all, was to provoke and engage American higher education into a serious discussion about its purpose and direction. Following my speech, Robin Wilson of the *Chronicles of Higher Education* wrote, "Mr. Bennett's critics acknowledge that he has successfully drawn public attention to the problems of higher education and forced college officials to address them." If the price for accomplishing this is to be criticized and to no longer be invited to give commencement addresses . . . well, it's not really much of a choice.

The issues I raised at Harvard—about quality, the core curriculum, moral discernment, and academic intolerance—are now the subject of a vigorous, ongoing national debate. "[Bennett] stirred up the academic animals," Kilpatrick wrote, "and at Harvard or anywhere else, that's a fine way to spend an afternoon."

Stanford

In the spring of 1986, a small but very vocal group of students called on Stanford University to abolish a freshman course called Western Culture, by all accounts one of the most popular courses offered on the campus. In its place, they proposed a course that would emphasize the "contributions of cultures disregarded and/or distorted by the present program." This marked the beginning of a steady stream of charges against the Western Culture program, its supporters, and the Western tradition that sustained the program— charges of racism, sexism, imperialism, elitism, and ethnocentrism.

Two years later the Stanford faculty senate met to discuss replacing the Western Culture program with a new course called "Cultures, Ideas, and Values" (CIV). The familiar core reading list of fifteen significant works in Western philosophy and literature was to be thrown out. Instead, CIV instructors would decide year by year what the content of the course would be. And the instructors would have to include works by "women, minorities, and persons of color," and at least one work per quarter that explicitly addresses issues of race, gender, or class.

Throughout the two-year debate, tactics of intimidation were employed by CIV supporters. Free and open discussion was discouraged; opponents were publicly taken to task by the Stanford administration while a pro-CIV student group that occupied President Donald Kennedy's office for five hours and released a set of ten demands was not disciplined or even censured for the occupation. In the end, the adoption of CIV was a political, not an educational, decision.

After Stanford decided to alter its Western Culture program in 1988, a group of student organizations invited me to deliver an address and, they hoped, engage in a debate with President Kennedy. I was anxious to make a strong case as I had done as chairman of the National Endowment for the Humanities for the study of Western culture. I accepted the invitation, knowing full well that the central question underlying the Stanford debate was under debate on other campuses across the country. Stanford, sometimes referred to as the "Harvard of the West," is a flagship university. What it does matters.

My office offered a handful of debate dates to President Kennedy, but we were told that he was not going to be on campus for any of them. Finally, suspecting that I might never find a date when the president of the university would be on campus and ready to publicly discuss the issue, I accepted the invitation to speak and left ample time for discussion with faculty and students afterward. On April 18, I traveled to Palo Alto to offer my judgment on what had taken place at Stanford:

> Stanford's decision . . . to alter its Western Culture program was not a product of enlightened debate, but rather an unfortunate capitulation of pressure politics and intimidation. Does anyone doubt that selecting works based on the ethnicity or gender of their authors trivializes the academic enter-

prise? Does anyone really doubt the political agenda underlying these provisions? The events . . . at Stanford serve as a striking example of what Allan Bloom has called "The Closing of the American Mind." In the name of "opening minds" and "promoting diversity," we have seen in this instance the closing of the Stanford mind.

The events at Stanford had taught a terrible lesson: the tactics of intimidation work. The loudest voices won, not through force of argument, but through bullying, threatening, and name-calling. "A great university was brought low by the very forces which modern universities came into being to oppose—ignorance, irrationality, and intimidation," I said.

I had been led to believe that I would face an overwhelmingly hostile student audience. Judging from the response both to my speech and the question-and-answer period, however, I would guess as many students agreed with me as disagreed. More surprising was that during the long question-and-answer session, not a single faculty member rose up to challenge either my account or interpretation of events. My hopes for a candid exchange with the principal figures involved was thus frustrated. On the one great opportunity the faculty had to show me the error of my ways, they passed. The Stanford faculty and administration wanted to avoid the debate. They couldn't. It was moving ahead without them. That's why President Kennedy, who could not find the time to debate me while I was there, found time after it. He *had* to respond.

On the day after my speech at Stanford, I flew back to Washington where, ironically, Stanford's President Kennedy was visiting. I appeared on "The MacNeil/Lehrer Newshour" to debate him. Co-host Robert MacNeil asked me how Stanford's decision trivialized the academic enterprise, and what the harm was. "Dropping Homer and dropping Dante and dropping Freud, and dropping Darwin and Luther and Thomas More, I think is pretty significant," I said.

I argued that students at Stanford should study non-Western cultures, and study them more seriously and in greater depth than they do now (ironically, while I was chairman, the National Endowment for the Humanities gave Stanford a grant to develop a course in non-Western culture). But "you don't make the case for studying non-Western culture by trashing Western culture," I told Kennedy. "And you don't know non-Western culture any better by knowing Western culture less."

"I promise everybody that we didn't trash Western culture," President Kennedy said.

"Check the record," I insisted.

When Kennedy claimed that I "mischaracterized" the climate that surrounded the CIV debate, I told him, "You may want to turn this frog into a prince, but you can't. A frog is a frog. All one has to do is go back and examine the record."

The record was grim. Despite attempts to lend an air of intellectual respectability to their efforts with talk about "diversity," "self-understanding," and "the common intellectual experience," the target of Stanford's "enlightened political reformers" was from the outset Western culture itself. The frustrating feature of the recent debates at Stanford and elsewhere, the philosopher John Searle wrote in *The New York Review of Books* (December 1990), is that "the underlying issues seldom come out in the open." According to Searle, the real issues underlying the debate are

> Unless you accept . . . that the Western tradition is oppressive, and that the main purpose of teaching the humanities is political transformation, the explicit arguments given against the canon will seem weak.

In 1987, for example, the birthday of Dr. Martin Luther King, Jr., was marked by Jesse Jackson leading a group of Stanford students in the cry: "Hey, hey, ho, ho, Western culture's got to go." During the CIV debate there was a spate of editorials in the Stanford newspaper accusing Western culture of being sexist, racist, and imperialistic. One of the editorials caught the prevailing mood on campus: "We're tired of reading books by dead white guys," it said. The problem with that sentiment, of course, is that a lot of dead white guys wrote very important books that all college students should study. The fact that they were white is irrelevant as is the fact that they're dead. If the books are important, they should be read.

*   *   *

The core issue under debate at Stanford was not a new one to me. But even after all the years of being either at the center or the periphery of the debate, it's still hard to know exactly what accounts for the contempt many academics bear toward the West in general and America in particular. I suspect it involves a complicated set of reasons, including a commitment to a radical left-wing party line, intellectual trendiness, the belief that many Western values are inherently oppressive, and a general disaffection from a society that, ironically, treats the universities so well. The attacks on the West come from those so riven with relativism that they doubt the preferability of civilization to savagery, of democracy to totalitarianism. Theirs is not an America that has served as a beacon to the world; instead, theirs is an America corrupt with a host of unholy "isms," such as racism, elitism, sexism, and imperialism. Their ideology keeps them from seeing a number of important (and what should be self-evident) arguments on why we must study, nurture, and defend the West.

First, we are a part and a product of Western civilization. That our society was founded upon such principles as justice, liberty, government with the consent of the governed, and equality under the law is the result of ideas descended directly from Western civilization—Enlightenment England and France, Renaissance Florence, and Periclean Athens. These ideas are the glue that binds together our pluralistic nation. We all know intuitively that we cannot understand ourselves as individuals without understanding the ideas, the Western ideas, that constitute us as a people. The fact that we as Americans—whether black or white, Asian or Hispanic, rich or poor—share these beliefs aligns us with other cultures of the Western tradition. It is not ethnocentric or chauvinistic to acknowledge this.

Second, the West is the source of the most powerful and pervasive influences on America and its people. It is simply not possible for students to understand their society without studying its intellectual legacy. If their past is hidden from them, they will become aliens in their own culture, strangers in their own land.

Third, for a person who seeks serious answers to great questions, there is no better place to look for guidance than the great books of the Western tradition. The classics of Western philosophy and literature amount to a great debate on the perennial questions. In the end, the study of the seminal works of Western civilization is not a case for ideology; it is a case for philosophy and for thoughtfulness. To deprive students of this debate is to condemn them to improvise their ways of living in ignorance of their real options and the best arguments for each.

The West is the most self-critical of cultures. Reason is exalted, and reason leads to a look, a second look, and, where necessary, readjustment, redefinition, and change. It is one of the distinguishing features of Western civilization, in fact, that it has engaged in this dialogue, self-examination, and correction over the centuries. The Western tradition is one of discussion and dissent as much as one of affirmation and agreement.

Finally, and probably most difficult for the critics of Western culture to acknowledge, the West is good. The West is not all good, to be sure. There are great blots on its record, volumes of injustices, sins, omissions, and errors. Still, the West has produced the world's most just and effective system of government: representative democracy. As Professor Lino Graglia has written, in the story of inhumanity and misery that is history, in the totality of its acts, the Western achievement stands high. It has set the moral, political, economic, and social standards for the rest of the world and has led the rest of the world toward an appreciation of individual liberty, equality, human rights, and the inviolability of conscience. Since the collapse of communism and the end of the Cold War, one wonders if the only people who cannot clearly see the virtues of Western civilization today are some of our professors at our leading universities.

Today the debate rages on, though the context has changed somewhat. To the pernicious effects of economic determinism, logical positivism, structuralism, psychologism, and deconstructionism (all intellectual movements that have found a welcome home on university campuses), we can now add the phenomenon of "politically correct" thinking. "Politically correct" thinking is the term given to the political orthodoxy that is pervasive on many college campuses. It insists that students be "politically correct" —meaning left wing—in speech and opinion, particularly on issues having to do with homosexuality, feminism, race, "Eurocentrism," "colonialism," and the like. In reality, it is an academic thought police, the new McCarthyism of the left. Here are some widely reported recent examples of "political correctness" run amok:

- A proclamation banning "inappropriately directed laughter" and "conspicuous exclusion of students from conversations" was issued at the University of Connecticut.

- A controversy erupted at Harvard Law School when Ian Mac-Neil, a visiting professor, quoted Lord Byron: "And whispering, 'I will ne'er consent'—consented." The Harvard Women's Law Association was offended and denounced it as a "sexist insult."
- Professor Stephan Thernstrom, a distinguished professor of history at Harvard, was forced to drop an undergraduate course after he was harassed because he used the term "Indian" instead of "Native American."
- During the Persian Gulf war, officials at the University of Maryland asked students not to hang American flags and pro-war banners from their dorm windows. "This is a very diverse community, and what may be innocent to one person may be insulting to another," according to Jan Davidson, a University of Maryland official.

The "politically correct" mentality would be laughable if it weren't so serious and so pervasive. If you can no longer hold or express or argue for an unorthodox view, or even for common sense or love of country, at a university without risk of penalty, either explicit penalty or social disdain, the university will collapse like a deck of cards, falling of its own weight. If we cannot protect the basic principle of academic freedom, then we cannot even begin to hope that our colleges and universities will evolve into a recognizable imitation of what they claim to be.

If the university continues to capitulate to political pressure and becomes not a place for the disinterested pursuit of truth and knowledge but an institution dedicated to the pursuit of a radical political agenda, it will lose its *raison d'être;* the whole justification for its support will evaporate. And colleges and universities will become increasingly irrelevant to the intellectual life of the nation.

The good news is that many liberal arts faculty members of our elite universities may have overstepped the threshold of common sense once too often. The largely untold and, I think, encouraging story about "politically correct" thinking is that once the movement became public, the advocates of "PC" suffered a blistering attack from almost all quarters—the popular press, influential commentators and columnists, some liberal intellectual journals, and many others. Left-wing academics have so publicly offended common sense that the American people now react to them not only with outrage, but also with ridicule. This reaction is healthy, particularly if we can benefit from it to reform some of the administrative practices that have contributed to the crisis.

Some of the reform legislation I proposed as Secretary of Education included new student aid programs, cutting default rates on student loans (through regulatory attempts to exclude schools where more than 20 percent of students had defaulted), reform of student aid requiring accrediting agencies to base their accreditation on whether institutions assess and document student learning, and taking measures to contain college costs. Unfortunately I faced a Congress seemingly enraptured by the pieties, pontifications, and poor-mouthings of American higher education. There was virtually no interest in any kind of serious reform, whether it had to do with academic purpose, quality, accountability, or cost containment.

I wanted to do with higher education what I tried to do with elementary and secondary education: engage in some truth telling, set the stage for a full-scale effort at much needed reform, force Congress to go on record, and keep the pressure on. Perhaps we did succeed in demystifying American higher education. Given the political climate of the times, I couldn't hope to enact all of the reforms I wanted. But I could help create a climate of change and lay the groundwork for future reform.

Fortunately, we are now beginning to see signs that the American people are demanding more consumer information, more truth in advertising from colleges and universities. For a long time American higher education operated in a sort of black box; it was very hard to know what was actually going on inside. We had very little means of assessing what was being achieved. Now universities are being forced to open the black box. They're having to demonstrate their performance, their worth, their influence.

In short, we're witnessing a long overdue change in the public's perception of American higher education. This is the area where I believe the most dramatic change has occurred over the last five to seven years. Once upon a time universities seemed above it all, virtually immune to criticism. But now, for the first time in a very long time, universities and colleges are on the defensive.

In recent years higher education has been rocked by scandals, a Justice Department investigation of price fixing among Ivy League schools, congressional investigations into student loan default rates, and a growing sense among the American people that they are not getting their money's worth.

We've also seen the publication of several widely acclaimed books that are compelling, fierce, and well-documented indictments of higher education. In 1987 Ernest Boyer, one of the nation's leading educators, wrote *College: The Undergraduate Experience in America* (New York: Harper & Row, 1987). According to Boyer, "The undergraduate college, the very heart of higher learning, is a troubled institution." Driven by careerism and overshadowed by graduate and professional education, "many of the nation's colleges are more successful in credentialing than in providing a quality education for their students."

Nineteen eighty-seven also saw the publication of Allan Bloom's extraordinary book *The Closing of the American Mind: How Higher Education Has Failed Democracy and Impoverished the Souls of Today's Students* (Simon & Schuster). Professor Bloom's book was a brilliant, devastating criticism of contemporary higher education. "The university now offers no distinctive visage to the young person," Bloom wrote. "There is no vision, nor is there a set of competing visions, of what an educated human being is." *The Closing of the American Mind* was on *The New York Times* best-seller list for almost a year.

Nineteen ninety-one saw the release of Dinesh D'Souza's *Illiberal Education: The Politics of Race and Sex on Campus* (New York: Free Press), another critically acclaimed best-seller. D'Souza did an in-depth case study of six leading universities—Michigan, Howard, Berkeley, Duke, Stanford, and Harvard. The American academic world, according to D'Souza, "might be the most closed and intolerant sector in American life."

Some academics recognize the threat they now face and have decided to stand up and be counted (most notably the members of the National Association of Scholars). But on some elite campuses today it is still the case that the voices of reason are being shouted down by the mob. If the intellectual trends that we're now seeing among the elite universities continue, the enterprise may well be ruined—not for lack of money, not because of public indifference, not because of a hostile takeover by the state. If the university is ruined, it will be because of degeneration from within.

6

RACE AND THE NEW
POLITICS OF RESENTMENT

I view politics as a contact sport, and I think it should be played with vigor and gusto. But politicians shouldn't make it personal; at the end of the day, you should be able to go out and have an amicable conversation with at least some of your critics and people of different political beliefs. Separate people's character from their political persuasion. But in our day, I think there's probably something wrong if a political figure doesn't offend some people. In a tribute to Franklin Roosevelt, Democrats once hung a banner in Madison Square Garden that said, "We love him for the enemies he's made." There's nothing wrong with offending people if you're offending the right people.

On November 19, 1990, I was the guest at a luncheon hosted by David Broder of *The Washington Post*, and attended by a dozen or so bureau chiefs. When Broder invited me, the subject was to be my tenure as drug czar. But in the interim I had been asked by President Bush to be his candidate for chairman of the Republican National Committee, replacing Lee Atwater, who had been stricken by a severe (and ultimately fatal) illness.

Because I had not yet been officially elected chairman of the RNC, I told Broder that it would be inappropriate for me to discuss the job during the luncheon. And I didn't. But the bureau chiefs, being an enterprising and persistent lot, pressed me for my views on a range of issues. At the end of the luncheon, one reporter asked about my views on racial quotas. It was an issue I had addressed many times before; in fact, I had co-written a book on the subject eleven years earlier. So I wasn't shy about restating my long-held views.

"Giving people . . . a job in the absence of the showing of prior discrimination, simply on the basis of their race or sex, is wrong," I said. "It's a fundamental violation of the way most Americans think and of the most basic value of this democracy."

I was then asked if there would be a big debate about quotas in the 1992 presidential election. "It all depends on how much the Democrats want to do about it," I said. "If the Democrats want to favor by race, whether by quotas or goals disguised as quotas, then there will be a big debate about it."

A debate did ensue, but it didn't wait for 1992. Within twenty-four hours, my comments had touched off a small firestorm of controversy among the media and inside the Beltway. It was becoming "an insider's article of faith," according to Laurence Barrett of *Time* magazine, "that George Bush and his party would create a powerful 1992 campaign issue from the resentment of white voters toward programs that seem to benefit minorities unfairly." And "the main dealer of that racial card was William Bennett." An item in *The Wall Street Journal* said that I seemed "determined to counter Democrats' gains on economic class difference with appeals to racial fears." The *St. Louis Post-Dispatch* accused me in an editorial of being "The New Civil Rights Hatchet Man." And Democratic House Majority Leader Richard A. Gephardt charged in a speech that "the ideologues on the right are following a new trail of racial resentment and recrimination blazed by David Duke, then trod successfully by Jesse Helms, and now given a tarnished patina of intellectual respectability by William Bennett."

Along with abortion, race has become the most divisive issue in contemporary American politics. The great body of the American people believe in *individual* rights, not group rights, not rights conferred by sex, race, or religion. But the liberal elite think otherwise, and have pounded the American people for their beliefs. Racial preferences and quotas should be legitimate issues of debate. But in the current climate, there has been an attempt to muzzle a candid and straightforward debate. The "muzzle" is the growing threat of being accused of (at best) racial "insensitivity" and (at worst) out-and-out racism.

Once upon a time, charges of racism followed sentiments and expressions of actual racism. But not anymore. In some quarters today, it is virtually beyond the pale to discuss legitimate public policy issues about race. This is absurd. It is also, in many instances, a calculated, cynical, and disingenuous ploy. Synthetic moral outrage is the best means the left has to try and preempt a debate about a position they cannot adequately defend.

I could not publicly express my opposition to hiring on the basis of race, without becoming the object of a smear campaign and without some newspaper columnists and politicians getting out a racist branding iron. And as the controversy swirled, and the charges flew, and the rhetoric grew more heated, I thought back to a school visit I had made almost five years earlier.

On January 14, 1986, I ventured to John Hope Elementary School in Atlanta to teach black third-grade children about the meaning of Martin Luther King, Jr.'s life. I had long admired King for his contributions to civil rights and for his grasp of the true meaning of equality in American political thought. The visit to Atlanta—at the invitation of Coretta Scott King, Dr. King's widow (her second or third invitation to me in as many years)—was one of the events I most looked forward to as Education Secretary.

I found out that the well-prepared students at John Hope Elementary were way ahead of me.

"Why are all these cameras here and what makes Dr. King so important?" I asked the children.

"He changed the laws to make things better for black people!" answered an eight-year-old.

"What was Dr. King's dream?" I asked.

"That black people don't get judged by the color of their skin," another child answered.

"How *should* we judge a person? How *should* we decide if we like somebody?" I pressed them.

"By the content of their character," came the answer—a direct quotation from King's "I Have a Dream" speech.

The children of John Hope Elementary School, most of them from low-income families and many from single-parent families, were eager, well prepared, and not in the least intimidated by the reporters, camera crews, and dignitaries at the back of the room—who vastly outnumbered them. They kept stealing my lines, raising their hands, and volunteering answers before I had finished my questions.

I told the class that while segregation hurt black people most, it also made white people "less than they should be." Martin Luther King was working for the moral improvement of whites as well as the equality of blacks.

After nearly an hour of banter and instruction, I gave the class an A plus. They gave me a medallion and a King T-shirt signed by class members. Afterward, eight-year-old Lawrence Carter told reporters, "Mr. Bennett was a good teacher. I learned some things I did not know."

But a thin, serious, bespectacled ten-year-old boy with the makings of a critic, gave me only a grade of B. He explained, "There were some answers he didn't know"—among them, how long it took to arrest James Earl Ray, who was convicted in King's death. (Ray was arrested on June 8, 1968, about two months after the April 4 assassination—a fact I indeed had to look up later.)

At a news conference later, I said I saw no conflict between my embrace of King's teaching and my support for the Reagan administration's efforts to phase out certain forms of affirmative action, efforts which had drawn criticism from some civil rights leaders.

While "people of good will disagree about the means," I said, "I don't think anybody disagrees about the ends. I think the best means to achieve . . . a color-blind society is to proceed as if we are indeed a color-blind society. . . . I think the best way to treat people is as if their race did not make a difference."

In 1968, the year of Martin Luther King's death, I was teaching at the University of Southern Mississippi in Hattiesburg. My views on race were the same then as they are today: America should be a color-blind society in which we do not discriminate, or give preference, based on race. Among whites, at least, this view was clearly a minority opinion, and a very liberal one, in Mississippi in 1968. But I believe it was right then. And it is still right today. To hold to that view in the late 1960s meant you were likely to be criticized by bigots from the South. But to hold to that view today means you are likely to be criticized by race-conscious liberals from the Northeast.

I ended up in Hattiesburg after studying for my doctorate in philosophy at the University of Texas. I had walked into the office of the chairman of the Philosophy Department, John Silber, one of the best teachers I ever had. He had a letter on his desk. "Now here's a job for someone who wants to test his mettle," he said. An administrator at the University of Southern Mississippi had written Silber asking if he knew somebody who might be interested in teaching social and political philosophy in Hattiesburg.

"This would really give somebody a chance to find out if he could really teach," Silber said. "But do you think any of my graduate students want it? Hell, no. They all want to go and teach at Oberlin."

Well, I was actually scheduled to spend the 1967–68 school year in Bonn, Germany, studying German Idealism, Kant and Hegel. But Silber put the bait on the hook and I bit—swallowed whole, in fact. Full of idealism and full of the expectation that I could become a good teacher—and ignited by Silber's challenge—I found myself on a plane for the interview. The chairman of the Religion and Philosophy Department in Hattiesburg offered me the job on the spot. I accepted. So began one of the most interesting years of my life.

While I was in Mississippi, I got into some fairly heated exchanges on the issue of racial equality. One evening, while watching a baseball game on television at a store with a small beer bar in the back, I was challenged on the issue of race by a local guy sitting nearby. "Hey, whadya think of that nigger?" the guy demanded, gesturing toward the screen image of the St. Louis Cardinals' Bob Gibson.

"I think he's a helluva pitcher, probably the best in baseball," I said.

This exchange was followed by a "dialogue" on the equality of the races. I was eventually jumped by my interrogator and a couple of his friends and beaten up.

Several of my University of Southern Mississippi colleagues and I held a teach-in the night after Martin Luther King was killed and we went from there to a memorial service. I was marked by some of the more rabid members of the community as "a Northern liberal," something my long-standing critics may find hard to believe. (They may also find it hard to believe that I was denounced at the 1991 Louisiana State Republican Convention as a "f——ing liberal" by supporters of David Duke.)

But even in southern Mississippi in 1967–68, things were beginning to change. What people had seen on television, combined with their own sense of justice, was beginning to make them much more open to the idea of integration, to equality, and to civil rights. The South was changing. In my view, the South did change more dramatically, more deeply, and more significantly than the North over the next ten years. And today, the South is essentially a transformed society on the issue of race.

But the urban centers of the liberal Northeast have lost ground over recent years. Racial tensions have increased. Dinesh D'Souza, in *Illiberal Education,* points out that "the vast majority of racial incidents have been recorded at northern campuses with a progressive reputation. The South, ancestral home of socially sanctioned bigotry and segregation, seems to have accommodated minority students on its campuses relatively well."

The events in Mississippi were only the first in a series that galvanized my thinking about race in America in the late 1960s. I will never forget entering the Harkness Commons, the Harvard Law School lunchroom, after my first day of class in 1968. In front of me was an array of tables. At most of them sat white students, but at three tables sat black students. No white student was sitting with a black, and no black student was sitting with a white. I remember thinking that this was exactly what I had seen in Mississippi only one year earlier. In Mississippi, it was because of old-time segregation. But at Harvard, it was because of new-time segregation. The next year, in 1969, I became a proctor in the Harvard Yard. I became friends with all my freshmen and spent a lot of time with one black freshman who had entered Harvard from Harlem. He had had the benefit of an excellent high school education, and had entered America's greatest university with advanced placement in math and science. He was planning to major in chemistry as a pre-med student. After six months, however, because of the influence of several other students who were not his intellectual equal, he shifted his major to Social Relations. This was a "politically correct" major, not too demanding, and the minority students could group together in it and be regarded as authorities. Social scientist David Riesman of Harvard has referred to this as "ethnic thumb-sucking."

The student came to me to get my signature on his course card, but I refused to sign it. I told him he could appeal to the dean, but I wasn't going to take part in a decision in which he gave up his life's ambition to be a doctor because of political pressure from other students. We were talking about it when we went together through the cafeteria line in the Harvard Freshman Union. I followed him to his table. When I moved to sit down next to him, he told me I should leave because this was the "brothers' " table; apparently it was understood in the Union that it was for blacks only. I told him I wasn't going to leave. I had been through this before, I told him, when I was a faculty member at the University of Southern Mississippi and I had been urged not to sit with black students or encourage black and white students to sit together (something which I assiduously tried to do during my time in the South). I told him and others at his table that I didn't like separation by race in Mississippi and I didn't like it at Harvard, either. It was wrong at both places. A number of black students at the table went silent and stared at me. I said again, "I'm not leaving." When one or two insisted, I said, "Look, if you want me to go you'll have to carry me out of here. But I'll go limp and I'll sing 'We Shall Overcome' the whole time." They left me alone for the remainder of the meal. Later I got a note from the dean of freshmen, asking me to come to his office. He scolded me for "racial insensitivity," and told me I should never do that kind of thing again. I replied that I would do it again under similar circumstances. But my friend got the dean to sign his card and this particular incident was closed.

The larger issue of race-consciousness gone crazy, however, remains. Forty years ago, in the landmark *Brown v. Board of Education* decision, Chief Justice Warren asked—and answered—the fundamental question: "Does segregation . . . on the basis of race, even though the physical facilities and other tangible factors be equal, deprive the children of the minority group of equal education? We believe that it does." Yet today we're seeing a revival of the concept of "separate but equal." And this movement is being led by the institutions—universities—which are supposed to be among the most thoughtful in American society.

For supposedly noble reasons—including the wish to instill ethnic and racial pride—universities are drawing more and more attention to race. Increasingly we've gone from putting a premium on being color-blind to putting a premium on being *color conscious.* Twenty-five years ago, as a society we sought to stigmatize the whole idea of color consciousness. It was thought correctly to be a character flaw; it meant you were backward, unenlightened, and probably a bigot. Today, among many elites, the situation is exactly reversed: to be color conscious is trendy, a sign of being socially aware, and avant-grade. It is an incredible irony that in the name of a "progressive enlightenment," we are recreating the very institutions, practices, and mind-set we sought to extirpate in the Civil War—"the great moral wrong and injustice" of slavery, in the words of Lincoln—and later, during the civil rights struggle.

Starting with ethnic houses, ethnic studies centers, and black student unions, there has even been a movement to separate seating sections for sports events, as *The New York Times* reported in 1988 in a story on Berkeley, the flagship campus of the University of California:

> Students congregate in racial groups, the blacks in one part of the great flagstone expanse, the whites in another. They say here that if you attend football games, you will find Berkeley blacks and whites rooting for the same team but sitting in different sections. Floors in the undergraduate library are, in practice, segregated by race, and rarely does a single white or two comfortably join a dining room table occupied mostly by blacks.
>
> Students at Berkeley and other universities around the country affirm that they have become accustomed to a kind of voluntary segregation as a normal, or at least inevitable, part of the way of life. . . . The unforced inclination toward separateness . . . indicates that the goal of an easy commingling of races has generally eluded university administrators.
>
> "On the whole, blacks and whites don't have relations with each other on this campus," said Carline Davis, a Berkeley senior.

What follows from here? Separate dormitories? Will we soon see separate washrooms for blacks and whites? In some places, primarily in the North, we are seeing the reinstatement of practices of the Jim Crow South. Is this what we fought the civil rights struggle for? Is this what Dr. King marched to Birmingham to achieve? Is this the reason President Lincoln signed the Emancipation Proclamation?

This need not be the case. There is one institution in particular, the military, from which the modern university might learn. Ironically, the institution trained for war can teach a lesson about race relations to the institution dedicated to thought and reason. While racial tensions have increased in society in general, things have gotten much better within the military. According to Charles Moskos, a professor of sociology at Northwestern University and author of *A Call to Civic Service,* the reason for the military's success includes "a radical meritocracy" (in the words of sociologist Marion J. Levy, Jr.); a stated goal of nondiscrimination and absolute commitment to equal opportunity; an absence of quotas; solid race-relations programs; and highlighting blacks in leadership roles.

In 1991, of the seven thousand blacks who served in the Army officer corps, twenty-six held flag rank (6 percent of all Army generals), and Colin Powell, chairman of the Joint Chiefs of Staff, was the first black to head the American military. According to Moskos, "The point that distinguishes [black military role models] from black role models in civilian life is that senior Army blacks tend to eschew any social agenda that promises black advancement on racial politics and supplication to benevolent whites. In their bootstrap conservatism and rejection of the ideology of victimhood, senior black sergeants and officers differ from an important segment of the black civilian leadership." The broad lesson from the military, Moskos says, is "race relations can best be transformed by an unambiguous commitment to nondiscrimination coupled with uncompromising standards of performance."

At my confirmation hearings in 1985 Senator Paul Simon (D-Illinois) accused me of being "not so strong in the area of civil rights" because as chairman of NEH I had refused to provide the Equal Employment Opportunity Commission and its chairman, Clarence Thomas, with goals for the hiring of women and minorities. I responded that I had always opposed goals and quotas but also pointed out that one-quarter of the top wage earners at NEH were black, three times higher than the government average.

My position was clear, and since then I have restated it time and time again: "We will neither favor nor slight anyone because of race, color, national origin, religion or gender," I told Senator

Simon. "To believe in human equality and equal liberty can mean nothing less than to treat white and black, male and female, Jew and Gentile as morally equal."

I am a strong supporter of affirmative action in its *original* intent: to cast a wide net, to reach out and to recruit aggressively, to be sure that women, minorities, and the handicapped are made aware of jobs and encouraged to apply for them. This we did, and did aggressively in the government agencies I ran. But to discriminate by either giving or taking points from someone because of race or sex is inherently inequitable and wrong. I believe counting by race is a clear violation of the Fourteenth Amendment ("No State shall make or enforce any law which shall abridge the privileges of immunities of citizens of the United States; nor shall any State deprive any person of life, liberty, or property, without due process of law; nor deny to any person within its jurisdiction the equal protection of the laws") and of Title VI of the Civil Rights Act of 1964 ("no person . . . shall, on the ground of race, color, or national origin, be excluded from participation, or be denied the benefits of, or be subject to discrimination under any program or activity receiving federal financial assistance.)" It was the liberal Democrat Hubert Humphrey, one of the congressional authors of the Civil Rights Act of 1964, who said that the law guaranteed equal opportunity, and that no court could "require hiring, firing or promotion of employees to meet a racial 'quota.' " Senator Humphrey's reasoning was sound in 1964, and it is sound in 1992. Martin Luther King put it well in his 1961 commencement address at Lincoln University:

One of the first things we notice in this [American] dream is an amazing universalism. It does not say some men [are created equal], but it says all men. It does not say all white men, but it says all men, which includes black men. It does not say all Gentiles, but it says all men, which includes Jews. It does not say all Protestants, but it says all men, which includes Catholics. . . . It says that each individual has certain basic rights that are neither conferred by nor derived from the state. To discover where they come from, it is necessary to move back behind the dim mist of eternity, for they are God-given. Very seldom, if ever, in the history of the world has a socio-political document expressed in such profoundly eloquent and unequivocal language the dignity and the worth of the human personality. The American dream reminds us that every man is heir to the legacy of worthiness.

A color-blind society is the hope of most of the American people and of the black students of John Hope Elementary School. It was Dr. King's dream. And the way to achieve a color-blind society is to actually *be* a color-blind society, in law and in spirit. The way to get beyond treating people as if race makes a difference is actually to treat them as if race does not make a difference.

But why do some of the elite think otherwise? In part, because they believe that since America was once a racist society, race preference and quotas are a necessary corrective.

Slavery is indeed an ugly stain on American history. But you do not undo one wrong by committing another, particularly when the same principle is violated in both instances. Equality is one of the founding principles of our Republic, the issue on which Lincoln and Douglas debated. And we succeeded in abolishing slavery precisely because we upheld the principle—the "self-evident" truth, in the words of Jefferson—of equality.

If the argument is that if there ever was discrimination then there is always reason for race preference, now or in the future, then we will never act as if we really mean the Fourteenth Amendment. We need to say that no person will be discriminated against on the basis of race, sex, ethnicity, religion, or background. We should say it now. And we should mean it.

It is also worth keeping in mind some of the unintended side effects of preference by race. "Much of the 'subtle' discrimination the blacks talk about is often (not always) discrimination against the stigma of questionable competence that affirmative action marks blacks with," according to Shelby Steele, author of *The Content of Our Character*. "The effect of preferential treatment—the lowering of normal standards to increase black representation—puts blacks at war with an expanding realm of debilitating [self-] doubt."

Charles Krauthammer, a syndicated columnist and an original supporter of affirmative action, has written, "Affirmative action has turned out to be far more costly than had previously been thought. It dispenses unequal justice. It Balkanizes communities. It distorts the merit system. It pits group against group. And now, it attaches a question mark to every real black achievement."

But many elites believe that America is still a deeply racist society in which blacks cannot advance without the help of race preference. On this score they are wrong. Of course bigotry and racism still exist among Americans of all color. And there are shameful incidents of racism that we need to denounce. But overall, America has come an enormous distance in law, attitude, individual actions, and economic opportunities. We have basically overcome the legacy of slavery. In fact, we are bending over backward to make amends.

The 1980s, for example, witnessed some extraordinary economic gains for many blacks. In a survey published by the Joint Center for Political Studies (a Washington-based black political think tank), two-thirds of blacks said they had kept pace economically or moved ahead during the 1980s. Joseph Perkins, then a *Wall Street Journal* editorial writer, reported in 1988:

> More blacks are working today at higher wages than ever before. The black middle class has grown by nearly a third since 1980, and is now, for the first time ever, the dominant income group in black America. Black family incomes are at an all-time high, having increased by roughly 6% in real terms. . . . The number of black professionals has increased an amazing 63% since 1980. Black managers and officers in corporate America increased in number by 30% over the same span.

In 1991 the Population Reference Bureau released a report, "African-Americans in the 1990s," which showed that after adjusting for inflation, the number of affluent black families doubled during the 1980s and has quadrupled since the late 1960s (although the poverty rate among blacks has remained relatively constant during the past two decades).

But these economic gains don't stop a very active and voluble civil rights lobby from continuing to live in the past, as if we were still in the era of Jim Crow. Too often the so-called civil rights leadership is causing unnecessary divisions among the races. And this, fundamentally, is a failure of leadership.

Take as an example some of the civil rights legislation of the last couple of years. The bills put forward by the civil rights leadership became one of the most hotly disputed pieces of legislation in recent times. The effect of their "civil rights" bill would, for all intent and purposes, lead to racial quotas. Given the burden of proof on employers in this legislation, employers will adopt de facto quotas to avoid lawsuits. It would lead to a bonanza for lawyers. A few middle- and upper-middle-class blacks might benefit. But for the poor black, Hispanic, or other poor minorities, very little would be won, since it neglects the most serious problems facing black America (dissolution of the family, births to unwed mothers, black-on-black violence, low academic achievement, the number of young black men dropping out of the economy). The Civil Rights Act of '91 "won't do a blessed thing" for the most serious problems affecting black Americans wrote *Washington Post* columnist William Raspberry. "Worse, it threatens to divide America along racial lines."

The self-appointed civil rights leadership isn't facing up to the real issues. Arch Puddington, a former aide to Bayard Rustin and author of *Failed Utopias,* describes the effects of their leadership (*Commentary,* January 1991):

Today's race leadership has largely abandoned the role of moral arbiter for a single-minded focus on the politics of racial resentment. This is nothing less than a tragedy. For black neighborhoods will not be revived by attacking white society or through affirmative action or ten-point political programs, of either the liberal or conservative variety. The beginning of a solution will come about only when black leaders insist that the lying be stopped: about American society; about whites; about crime, work, family responsibility, and the treatment of women.

Or as Walter Williams, a professor of economics at George Mason University, has pungently put it:

The fact that Washington and Harlem have 80 percent illegitimacy has nothing to do with racism in America. It has to do with 13-, 14- and 15-year-old girls having sexual intercourse without benefit of marriage. In 1925, 85 percent of black kids lived in two-parent families. Surely in Harlem in 1925, blacks were far poorer and there was more discrimination.

The civil rights leadership is ignoring the most important realities of the underclass. It is promoting a narrow, divisive agenda.

And their agenda needs to be rejected. If it is not, race relations will get worse, not better; and while the status of the civil rights establishment may improve, the status of those for whom they profess to speak will continue to deteriorate.

The so-called civil rights movement is becoming increasingly marginalized and is now breaking apart. Twenty-five years ago, when Martin Luther King, Jr., symbolized the movement, there was a dignity to it, an appeal to equality and conscience. What many Americans see in the modern-day civil rights movement (perhaps best symbolized by Jesse Jackson) is an appeal to special rights instead of equal rights, an appeal to advantage instead of principle. At its worst, it is a power grab, a scam.

A 1991 public opinion study commissioned by the Leadership Conference on Civil Rights, a coalition of liberal groups, found strong support for the principles of equal opportunity, efforts to expand opportunity for the disadvantaged, reward for merit and hard work, and fairness in the workplace. It also found (to the dismay of the groups commissioning the study) a widespread view that civil rights organizations are *not* committed to those same principles. According to Celinda Lake, one of the authors of the study, "the civil rights organizations and proponents of civil rights were no longer seen as . . . addressing generalized discrimination, valuing work and being for opportunity."

When we listen to many of the new civil rights leaders, it is clear they have lost their moral base. Dr. King's principle of color-blindness is now an embarrassment to the civil rights leadership. And so these leaders are about done; their day is over.

During a television discussion with Eleanor Holmes Norton, delegate to the House of Representatives from the District of Columbia and a major figure in the civil rights establishment, I quoted Dr. King, who in 1963 said that persons should be judged by the "content of their character" and not by the "color of their skin." Mrs. Norton, angry, rebutted me by telling me to "stop quoting dead saints." When I used Dr. King's quote during a debate with Jesse Jackson, he accused me of "intellectual terrorism" for taking the comment "out of context"; Dr. King, Jackson explained, was a "context theologian." When this phrase of King causes cognitive dissonance to the "civil rights leadership," they are out of steam, moral steam. There is some ground which, when you remove it from beneath your feet, leaves you not on other ground, but in thin air.

Sound civil rights policies must be based on the facts. Glenn C. Loury, a professor at the John F. Kennedy School of Government at Harvard University, gives us a graphic summary of the circumstances of poor black Americans (*First Things*, June/July 1990):

- In big-city ghettos, the black youth unemployment rate often exceeds 40 percent.
- Over one-quarter of young black men in the critical age group 20 to 24 have dropped out of the economy, in the sense that they are not in school, not working, and not actively seeking work.
- In the inner city far more than half of all black babies are born out of wedlock.
- The level of dependency on public assistance for basic economic survival has essentially doubled since 1964; almost one-half of all black children are supported in part by transfers from the state and federal governments.
- Over half of black children in public primary and secondary schools are concentrated in the nation's twelve largest central city school districts, where the quality of education is poor, and where whites constitute only about a quarter of total enrollment.
- Only about one black student in seven scores above the 50th percentile on standardized college admissions tests.
- Blacks, though little more than a tenth of the population, constitute approximately half of the imprisoned felons in the nation. Roughly 40 percent of those murdered in the United States are black men killed by other black men. In some big cities black women face a risk of rape that is five times as great as that faced by whites.

In addition, from 1970 to 1990, the proportion of two-parent black families with children under eighteen fell from 64 percent to 39 percent. Most black families today are headed by women.

In my tours as drug czar, I visited many public housing projects and saw many of those women and their children. The civil rights elites' thinking and solutions are far removed from the realities of these stricken people. But is there an alternative? Absolutely.

We can replace the negative agenda of race stigmatization and counting by race with a positive agenda for the poor and disadvantaged—many, although by no means all, of whom are minorities—who are willing to take advantage of opportunities.

First, we should ensure equal protection of the laws. We must make minority neighborhoods safer than many of them, especially in the inner city, are now. The main environmental difference between the nonpathological poor and America's middle class is the presence of crime. When some people ask, "What's wrong with these people?" the answer should be, "Many of them are scared to death; they live in fear for self and child."

John DiIulio, Jr., of Princeton argues that the underclass problem is mainly a crime problem. "Those closest to the problem," DiIulio has written, "understand that improving the response of criminal-justice agencies is the *sine qua non* of progress on other fronts," such as schools, jobs, and delivery of social services. The vast majority of inner-city residents are decent, law-abiding individuals. They suffer disproportionately from predatory criminals. A civilized, humane civil rights agenda must include a more effective criminal justice system. That means, among other things, tougher laws, more cops, more courts, more prosecutors, and more jails and prisons.

As *The Federalist Papers* explain, government's clear, first, and distinct responsibility is to provide for the security of its citizens. With crime rampant, many of the poor will not or cannot take the steps necessary to improve their condition. With crime under control, people are more likely to feel safe, stay later at work, take school courses at night, and gain self-confidence as citizens who do not have to cower in their homes or apartments.

Second, we need better schools. One of the strongest cases for overhauling the current system is the lousy education the poorest among us are receiving. The underclass are least able to afford a bad education, since "the safest and surest route to permanent black economic mobility lies in additional education in a good school," according to a Rand Corporation study of the economic progress of blacks since 1940. And the best way to improve American education is to support a reform agenda based on parental choice, accountability, merit pay, alternative certification and a solid core curriculum.

Far too many disadvantaged minority students are not being provided a challenging curriculum. They are victims of unwarranted pessimism, low aspirations, and a subtle form of discrimination. Poor minority students deserve the same kind of education that upper-class white kids get.

What disadvantaged black children definitely do *not* need is to be subjected to the most pernicious version of the newest trend in American education: the "multicultural" curriculum. Not all efforts at introducing a multicultural curriculum in our schools are bad. Indeed, some can be good. To develop a curriculum that better reflects the contributions of individuals of different races and backgrounds to the richness of America is a worthy goal. The history of slavery and the achievements out of suffering of many black Americans must be part of the history we teach. The names of Benjamin Banneker, Frederick Douglass, Harriet Tubman, W.E.B. DuBois, and Martin Luther King, Jr., must be familiar to all students. We should insist on honesty in telling about this country and its history, its long record of glories and failures, aspirations and sins, achievements and victory; America in the totality of its acts.

But for many other advocates of a multicultural—or more precisely, "Afrocentric"—curriculum, the purpose is the politicization of the curriculum, the promulgation of cultural myths, the distortion of American history, and the primacy of ethnic and racial thinking (the "new tribalism" as it's been called). In this version, identity is reduced to ethnicity; identity is determined by race.

As Secretary of Education the thing that I most objected to in the education of poor Americans, particularly poor blacks, was that they were given "back-of-the-bus" math and "Jim Crow" science because of the assumption by some people in the school that these kids couldn't handle a challenging curriculum. But now some would have them thrown off the bus completely. The new, divisive, ethnicity-is-identity multicultural curriculum is poison for these children. Its effects will be to divorce blacks completely from the mainstream of American life and increase the alienation that many blacks feel toward the rest of our society and our central civic institutions.

In 1991 historian Arthur Schlesinger, Jr., wrote *The Disuniting of America*. According to Schlesinger:

It is hard to imagine any form of education more likely than Afrocentrism to have a "terribly damaging effect on the psyche." The best way to keep a people down is to deny them the means of improvement and achievement and cut them off from the opportunities of the national life. If some Kleagle of the Ku Klux Klan wanted to devise an educational curriculum for the specific purpose of handicapping and disabling black Americans, he would not be likely to come up with anything more diabolically effective than Afrocentrism.

Our origins are diverse, yet we live together as fellow citizens. In America, we can say proudly "E Pluribus Unum"; out of many, we have become one. This has been the great unifying sentiment of the American experiment. Unfortunately, during the last two decades we have celebrated what divides us to the neglect of what unites us. As Professor Schlesinger has written:

> Should public education move in this direction [a primary concentration on race], it will only increase the fragmentation, resegregation, and self-ghettoization of American life. The bonds of national cohesion in the republic are sufficiently fragile already. Public education should aim to strengthen those bonds, not to weaken them. Of course Americans should be free (as they always have been, and have often done) to cultivate ancestral customs and traditions. But the function of the schools is surely to teach what holds Americans together as well as to teach what sets them apart. The alternative to integration is disintegration.

One of the things that has kept America from fragmentation (as is happening in Canada), dissolution (as is happening in the Soviet Union), and even breaking up into warring nationalities (as has happened in Lebanon and Yugoslavia) is that we share a common culture. It is our civic glue. Our common culture serves as a kind of immunological system, destroying the values and attitudes promulgated by an adversary culture that can infect our body politic. Should our common culture begin to break down, should its fundamental premises fail to be transmitted to succeeding generations, then we will have reason to worry. One vital instrument for the transmission of the common culture is our educational system, and we need to ensure that our schools meet that responsibility.

All Americans can learn from the successes of the Asian-American community. There is ample evidence of the success of Asian-American children, many of whom are children of immigrants, in American schools. Studies show that they outperform all other major population groups in education attainment. The "secret" of their success is the high value Asian parents put on educational achievement, homework, an ethic of hard work, and strong family ties. Asian-American children are taught that schools are not repressive institutions, but places to learn; America is not a racist society, but the land of golden opportunity. The attitude of many Asian Americans was captured by Nancy Kwan, perhaps the best-known Asian-American actress, who told the Asian-American Voters Coalition in 1990, "We will honor your government and your history and your ways. We will be part of your schools and your universities and your workplaces. We treasure what you are, for we know—perhaps even more than you do sometimes—what the word freedom really means. We know what it is not to be free."

The so-called civil rights leadership could serve its children very well by stressing the same values. What children are taught they will come to believe, and they should be taught to believe that this country and its institutions are for them, not against them.

A 1991 Gallup Organization public opinion poll asked of both whites and blacks, "In which one of the following areas do you think blacks should focus most of their efforts for improvement?" The areas most often cited was *education,* with a positive answer from 71 percent of whites and 68 percent of blacks. Next came antidrug efforts: whites, 10 percent; blacks, 15 percent. Then came anticrime efforts: whites, 9 percent; blacks 6 percent. *Affirmative action received a positive response from only 2 percent of whites and 4 percent of blacks.*

One of the most compelling discoveries we made at the Department of Education was that a black high school graduate with a B average is more likely to go to college than a white high school graduate with a B average. But there are many fewer black students with B averages than white students, and there are fewer yet as a percentage of the population because proportionally more black students drop out of school, especially black males. Those who do finish and complete school in good standing are *more* likely to go to college than their white counterparts. These students do not need affirmative action, most do not need special programs, they do not need a handout. What they need is to be given a fair chance for a good education, and then they will make it on their own. Even if they don't go to college, if they only complete high school, their odds of doing well in this society are substantial.

In 1986 the distinguished social analyst Charles Murray issued a report on the Family and American Welfare Policy. Murray's findings show the powerful positive effect of merely attaining a high school diploma. Only 4.7 percent of black male heads of households with no more than a high school education were in near-poverty by 1980. Among adult black males, 86 percent had family incomes greater than twice the poverty level. American society has such a capacity for social buoyancy that even at current low standards of achievement—a high school diploma in many cases certifies not knowledge and grasp but merely attendance—the diploma alone enables significant social mobility. Merely ensuring that the diploma truly signifies achievement, curricular coherence and thereby grasp of the disciplines of math, English, history and science, would be a powerful policy.

For black women with a high school education, 91.5 percent live above the poverty line. But for a black woman to attain this, she has to avoid becoming pregnant before marriage. "A poor woman who wishes to get out of poverty ought not have a baby out of wedlock" reads the Murray report. "This is not a moral statement but an empirical one."

But of course it is a moral one as well. This is just one obvious example of the intimate link between educational attainment and success on the one hand, and values on the other. Behavior affects attainment, and nothing—race, class, or family background—more powerfully affects behavior than one's beliefs and convictions.

It is precisely on this kind of point that we can expect to hear the complaint from some quarters that this is typical conservative cant, seeking to impose its ideas of morality on others. But the issue is not what to impose; the issue is what to do. The argument for delaying pregnancy until after marriage is not the arbitrary impositon of a moral principle; it is a statement of common sense and social sense. Like the coach who wisely insists his athletes not smoke or drink because of the risk to their performance, adults and community leaders should strongly advise young women to avoid the easy course of premarital pregnancy—again, for their own sake. It's a statement about survival and progress and the possibilities of a good life, not a self-serving arbitrary moralism.

A third cornerstone of a new civil rights agenda is greater economic opportunity for the underclass. That means vigorously promoting an "empowerment" agenda that stresses market-oriented solutions, choice, decentralization, and accountability—for example, the agenda of Secretary of Housing and Urban Development Jack Kemp to achieve tenant ownership of public housing, investment in low-income housing, tax incentives to businesses located in "urban enterprise zones," community reinvestment, and the like. We need to tear down the economic barriers that keep the underclass in poverty.

A fourth cornerstone is affirming individual responsibility. The most serious problems plaguing the black underclass have to do with a breakdown of the family. Too many young black children are being raised without the presence of good men in their lives. How do we begin to reverse this fact? By crafting economic and social policies that support the two-parent family; fashioning public policies that reward right behavior and penalize wrong behavior; using all the means at our disposal—in our public, private, and social spheres, through law and moral suasion—to condemn irresponsible acts (for example, fathering children and not supporting them); putting young men in the presence of positive male role models; and insisting that people in responsible positions affirm the right things (honoring commitments, individual responsibility, hard work, community norms, and virtue, to name a few). Some of the solutions involve government action. Many do not. And while none of these things alone is sufficient to the task, each is necessary.

In Atlanta, I had a memorable experience at another high school named for another distinguished black leader, Benjamin Mays, a mentor of Dr. Martin Luther King, Jr. Mays used to say when he presided at Morehouse College that he was not turning out doctors or lawyers or preachers; his aim was to "turn out men."

At Mays High School, an all-black school, I was greeted by a squadron of ROTC student cadets. I then met with the principal, an extraordinary woman named Rubye McClendon, and some of her staff. She stressed that she agreed with me on the importance of what I described as the three C's of American education: content, character, and choice. But she then scolded me and said, "But you forgot the big D that is so important to us here at Mays."

"What's that?" I asked.

"*Discipline*," McClendon said. "Discipline is at the heart of it;

these children need it more than anything else. When they get it they can make it on their own."

It's hard to estimate what self-discipline and the ability to commit to a task could bring about if every child in America had them. At least they would eliminate much remedial education, much of our dropout problem and much social pathology among the poor. But one cannot simply wave a wand and create virtue and sound character in people. It takes real effort over time, effort of the sort Rubye McClendon and her staff make daily. And it makes a difference.

Soon after I left my position as Secretary of Education, I received a call from a young woman who said she was representing the Harvard Law School fund. It was a dunning call, intended to get me to cough up some money for my alma mater. I resisted the request, explaining that I gave money to my high school and to my church, both of which needed it more than Harvard and which I thought had better moral standards. But she was persistent.

When I finally surrendered to her entreaties and said, "All right, send me the form and I promise I'll think about it," the young woman thanked me very pleasantly and then promptly changed the subject.

She said that she wanted to tell me how much she enjoyed my visit to her high school the year before. She was a graduate of Mays High School and was now a freshman at Harvard, working the phones for the law school to make some extra money. I asked her what she was studying. "I want to go into biomedical research," she said, "so I'm taking a lot of biology and chemistry."

"Is it tough?" I asked her. "Any problems?"

"No," she said, "it's not too bad. Mays prepared me very well. Some of my classmates are having some problems, but so far it's not too hard. I'm helping some of them."

Here was this young woman helping some of her Harvard classmates in biology and chemistry because of the education given her at Mays High School. This is how it works, when it works.

Another success story is A. Philip Randolph High School in New York City. One thousand five hundred blacks and Hispanics, half of whom are disadvantaged, comprise the student body. But students follow an extremely rigorous college preparatory program— eight academic classes a day, five days a week. To graduate they must complete four years of English; three and one-half years of history; three years each of math, science, and foreign language; one year of computer science; a quarter year of community service; and three additional college-level credits. Course material is intensive, challenging, and complete.

"Our students are familiar with the classics—they are able to use the image of the shadows in Plato's cave to relate to their everyday experience," Lottie L. Taylor, the principal, told me. "What is truth, perfection, and beauty? These are familiar questions to them."

Daily attendance and graduation rates are well over 90 percent. "My students are so eager to learn," says Taylor, "that I think I'm the only principal in the city who at night must ask students to please go home." Ninety-three percent of Randolph's students voluntarily attend summer school. There are no dropouts, and test scores are extraordinarily high. Almost nine out of ten students are accepted by four-year competitive colleges and universities. Most of the rest attend two-year institutions for specialized training in nursing or other professions. Mrs. Taylor has little patience with doubters and nay-sayers. "Don't say it can't be done," she insists. "We have done it and will continue to do it."

And yet this agenda is not the conventional wisdom about how disadvantaged black people can achieve full equality. Many people have not seen or heard of such places, and so they persist in believing that poor black children are not capable of learning and therefore must be given a special crutch of racial preference. This stems not from bad will but from ignorance of what actually works for whites, for blacks, for everyone. But while well-intentioned, this negative agenda contributes to the stereotyping of the poor and blacks in a way that undermines both their interests and the wider interests of our society. Poor black children don't need many of today's so-called civil rights leaders to help them. Neither do they need any new theory of education in order to perform and get ready for college. What they need are Jaime Escalante, Lottie Taylor, Rubye McClendon. They need the same kind of attention, concern, standards, and high expectations that other kids get.

In January 1988 at a meeting of the American Council on Education (ACE)—the lobbying voice of higher education in

Washington—minority recruitment in higher education was the topic. This was to be a priority for the hundreds of colleges that form the membership of the ACE.

I was asked to address the meeting, and I stressed what I had learned: "Most higher-education institutions have been diligent about recruiting black students," I said. "The problem is enlarging the pool. Where schools do a good job by those students, they go to college.

"The main problem of access is the kid who doesn't have the stuff to go. I don't mean Pell Grants and loans. I mean the academic background." Some schools send a message to kids that they can learn, but other places send the message that you're poor, you're black, you're not going to make it. So they put the kids into dummy math and dummy English, and do not push them too hard.

"Take a look at what minorities are studying," I told members of the ACE, "and that will.be a pretty good predictor. Only 25 percent of our high school graduates have taken a course in physics or chemistry. Now we talk about access to a college program in science and engineering. The kid's going to go nowhere near it. He's scared to death of it."

Percy A. Pierre, president of Prairie View A&M University in Texas, said he was "appalled" that I would say there is "no problem of access for minorities." Reginald Wilson, director of ACT's Office of Minority Concerns, characterized my remarks as "cavalier." Yet only one year later, Wilson wrote a report citing a number of factors that put black males at a particular disadvantage. "Poor elementary and secondary school preparation makes success in higher education difficult even for highly motivated students," the report said.

Deborah J. Carter, who co-authored the ACE study with Wilson, said, "What we find is that early on, students make their choices as to whether they think they're capable. . . . We need to reach into our junior high schools and high schools to give students some incentive to hang in there and to make sure they take the kinds of courses they need."

It is time we concentrate our efforts in that direction. Institutions competing harder for a small number of well-prepared black students will not produce any more qualified students. What higher education should do first is to join with other institutions in creating greater accountability in all schools; better and more rigorous content; and more choice for parents to select for their children, particularly more choice for the poor. Rather than pursuing a negative agenda of color consciousness, universities should join the rest of us in a new, positive, soundly based civil rights movement. One of the most important battlegrounds for civil rights is in America's classrooms, and one of the great civil rights issues for the 1990s is equal intellectual opportunity for all students.

It is time we give all our students the best we have to offer. It is time we put an end to "separate but equal" class curriculums—a middle-class white curriculum on the one hand, and a lower-class black curriculum on the other. If we believe in equal opportunity, then all our children deserve the best we have to offer—from literature to calculus to science to history. Patronizing attitudes only maintain the barriers and limits to escape from the ghetto.

The condescending attitude of the elites toward minorities, and toward blacks in particular, is a prescription for disaster. The only way to get beyond race is to get beyond race. The way to get beyond race in the future is to get beyond race now. It is time for us to tell the truth and to get on with our common business.

7

THE GREAT CULTURAL
DIVIDE:
RELIGION IN AMERICAN
POLITICAL LIFE

*I've been called "combative." I don't mind; I've always tried to be
very direct and candid. Americans like straight talk. They're smart,
sovereign citizens. And public officials shouldn't talk down to them.
I was trained under the Socratic dictum that three things are
necessary for good conversation: intelligence, candor, and good
will. I always speak with good will—that is, with the hope of
arriving at a conclusion that we can all share. I think I speak with
intelligence most days that I'm alert—at least I aspire to. And I've
always been straightforward. If the choice is between gobbledygook
and being "combative," I'll take combative.*

In 1985, shortly after I became Secretary of Education, I had a
long interview with Mike Wallace of "60 Minutes." For more than
three weeks a "60 Minutes" camera crew tracked me on virtually
every trip I took. I was told they were preparing a "profile" on me.
But what they hoped for was more on the order of a public suicide, offering me the rope with which to hang myself. The rope
came in the form of a question on religion.

For ninety minutes, Wallace peppered me with a lot of questions on a lot of different subjects. But at the end of the interview,
he dangled the noose. Leaning in, moving his face close to mine,
Wallace asked me if I believed an American child should be able

to leave an American public school without the belief that Jesus Christ "was his personal Lord and Savior."

I answered, "Absolutely. That's not the purpose of a public school. Unfortunately, he can leave many of our public schools and not know lots of things that school *is* supposed to teach him."

Wallace was clearly upset. He picked up his stack of papers, tossed them in the direction of his producer, and said, "We don't have anything." By the way, "60 Minutes" never ran the "profile."

This interview, like much of the criticism I received, was based on the simple fact, unforgivable to some of my critics, that as Secretary of Education I had some good words to say for religion. Even people who were generally supportive of much of what I had to say on other issues became extremely uncomfortable with my sympathetic views on religion. Former colleagues and generally tough-minded academics, ready to battle alongside me over the core curriculum, higher standards, and the debasement of our schools and colleges, drew back from me with a shudder or in silence on the issue of religion.

An old friend and classmate, for example, called to tell me how he agreed with much of what I was saying and doing as Secretary of Education. We had a pleasant talk, and then he added, "The only thing you've done that I really disagree with is that you've allied yourself with the religious right."

"What specific position troubles you so much?" I asked.

"I don't remember. But that's not the point," was the response. "If you're with those people on anything, I can't agree with you; you're an educated man, you have a Ph.D. in philosophy, for God's sake. You should *never* be an ally of those people."

Yet however nervous some may be about religion, they must acknowledge certain facts about religion in American history and its role in our society.

The problem isn't that public schools don't teach that Jesus Christ is the Lord; they shouldn't do that, and they are constitutionally prohibited from doing that. "What the American people don't understand," I said in a speech a year after the Wallace interview, "and I think they are right not to understand it, is that a group of students can, [by] law, get together and say, 'We must all advance the Marxist revolution.' A group of students can get together and say, 'I don't like reds, I like green drugs. What kind of drug do you like?' A group of students can get together and talk about various methods of birth control. But they can't get together and say, 'Our Father, who art in heaven, hallowed be Thy name.' "

In too many places in American public education, religion has been ignored, banned, or shunned in ways that serve neither knowledge, nor the Constitution, nor sound public policy. There is no good curricular or constitutional reason for textbooks to ignore, as many do, the role of religion in the founding of this country or its prominent place in the lives of many of its citizens. We should acknowledge that religion—from the Pilgrims to the civil rights struggle—is an important part of our history, civics, literature, art, music, poetry, and politics, and we should insist that our schools tell the truth about it. As I told the American Jewish Committee, "there is a confusion among some teachers and some principals that, because the schools should not be used to encourage people to be members of one religious faith or another, . . . the whole question of religion in our society is out of bounds." That, I said, "is wrong-headed and silly."

If students are learning about Western art, how are they to understand the paintings of Michelangelo, Raphael, or Fra Angelico, which depict religious figures and events?

The extreme to which some will go to deny the place of religion in American life is mind-boggling. A 1986 study of New York University professor Paul Vitz, for instance, found that the overwhelming majority of elementary and high school textbooks go to extraordinary lengths to avoid *any* references to religion. One sixth-grade reader, for example, includes a story called "Zlateh the Goat," by the late Nobel Laureate Isaac Bashevis Singer. In Singer's story, a boy named Aaron is told to take Zlateh, the family goat, to a butcher in the next village to be sold. On the way, Aaron and Zlateh get caught in a three-day blizzard and are lost in the snow. At this point, Singer writes, "Aaron began to pray to God for himself and for the innocent animal." But in the school reader this has been changed to: "Aaron began to pray for himself and for the innocent animal." Later, after Aaron and Zlateh have found shelter in a haystack, Singer writes, "Thank God that in the hay it was not cold." But in the reader this had been changed to: "Thank goodness that in the hay it was not cold."

"This would be funny if it were not so serious," I said in a 1986 speech. "Has the very mention of God's name in public become an offense?" Among Orthodox Jews, it has always been considered blasphemous to write the name of God in full. Well, I asked, "Have we come to the point where, in school textbooks, it is now considered a secular blasphemy to write the name of God, even if omitting His name does violence to the original text? Have we come to the point where it is now considered a secular blasphemy to acknowledge the name of God at all? Have we come, in some bizarre way, full circle, from scrupulous piety to fastidious disdain?"

Professor Vitz's study documents case after case of exclusions, misrepresentations, and distortions. One world history book completely ignores the Reformation. An American history textbook defines pilgrims as "people who take long trips." Another defines fundamentalists as rural people who "follow the values and traditions of an earlier period." Even a study by Norman Lear's liberal People for the American Way found that "with only rare exceptions," American history textbooks for junior high school students "treat religion by exclusion or by brief and simplistic reference."

I was asked in an interview why this happens.

"Fear. Worry. Overinterpretation, misinterpretation of the First Amendment," I said. "Some people got so scared about the whole idea of church and state, and values, and whose values, that they backed off completely, which has led to an attempt to sanitize. But it ended up distorting."

Everyone, including "First Amendment" liberals, agnostics, and atheists, must concede that the Judeo-Christian tradition is a major formative influence on American life, on our law, ideals and principles as a free people. Even a rudimentary knowledge of American history makes that clear.

George Washington warned in his Farewell Address, "Of all the dispositions and habits which lead to political prosperity, religion and morality are indispensable supports. . . . And let us with caution indulge the supposition that morality can be maintained without religion." Our other Founders agreed. John Adams, a Massachusetts Unitarian, agreed in no uncertain terms: "Our Constitution was made only for a moral and religious people. It is wholly inadequate to the government of any other." James Madison, an Episcopalian, insisted that "before any man can be considered as a member of Civil Society, he must be considered as a subject of the Governor of the Universe." And even Thomas Jefferson, the great deist who was deeply skeptical of sectarianism in any form, agreed. He asked, "Can the liberties of a nation be thought secure when we have removed their only firm basis, a conviction in the minds of the people that these liberties are the gift of God?" Religion, he concluded, should be regarded as "a supplement to law in the government of men," and as "the alpha and omega of the moral law."

From Sam Adams to Patrick Henry to Benjamin Franklin to Alexander Hamilton, all of the Founders intended religion to provide a moral anchor for our liberty in democracy. And all would be puzzled were they to return to modern-day America. For they would find, among certain elite circles in the academy and in the media a scorn for the public expression of religious values that clashes directly with the Founders' vision of religion as a friend of civic life. But it is not enough merely to identify the intent of the Founders. It is also necessary to defend it.

The first question we should ask ourselves is: Why did the Founders see a connection between religious values and political liberty? Alexis de Tocqueville, the French statesman, historian, and author of the classic *Democracy in America,* points to an answer. "Liberty regards religion . . . as the safeguard of morality, and morality as the best security of law and the surest pledge of the duration of freedom." In short, Tocqueville concluded, religion "is more needed in democratic republics than in any others." Americans today agree with Tocqueville. We are among the most religious people in the world (a City University of New York study done in 1991 revealed that nearly 90 percent of the American people identify themselves religiously as Christians or Jews, while only 7.5 percent claim no religion.)

Our very commitment to liberty of conscience—including the freedom to believe or not to believe and many other liberties—follows, in good part, from the respect for religion still felt by the majority of Americans. It is ironic that anyone who appeals to religious values today runs the risk of being called "divisive" or attacked as an enemy of pluralism. For the readiness of most Americans to defend tolerance and equality does not derive only from an abstract allegiance to Enlightenment ideals. It also comes from a concrete allegiance to the Judeo-Christian ethic. That faith is deep, alive and important in and to America.

Moreover, at its best, religion deepens politics. It is a wellspring of the civic virtues that democracy requires in order to flourish. At its best, it promotes hard work and individual responsibility. It lifts each citizen outside himself and inspires concern for community and country. It is a call to kindness, decency, and forgiveness in our homes, our schools, and our communities. At the same time, it offers a sense of purpose and a frame of reference for claims that transcend everyday politics, such as our collective responsibility to foster liberty around the globe. As Pope John Paul II's extraordinary encyclical, *Centesimus Annus* ("The Hundredth Year"), states:

> The theological dimension is needed both for interpreting and solving present-day problems in human society. It is worth noting that this is true in contrast both to the "atheistic" solution which deprives man of one of his basic dimensions, namely the spiritual one, and to permissive and consumerist solutions, which under various pretexts seek to convince man that he is free from every law and from God himself, thus imprisoning him within a selfishness which ultimately harms both him and others. . . . If there is no ultimate truth to guide and direct political activity, then ideas and convictions can easily be manipulated for reasons of power. As history demonstrates, a democracy without values turns into open or thinly disguised totalitarianism.

American culture and American greatness—perhaps more accurately American *goodness*—draw strength and direction from the Judeo-Christian tradition. There have been times in American history where the face of religion was ugly. And there are even some ugly sides to the way religion is practiced today. But if we add it all up, if we consider everything religion has given us—the good and the bad—America owes much to the faiths of its Founders, and the faiths of the millions on whom the Founders built our republic.

America is not a theocracy, nor does this country seek as some others have done to extinguish the faith of its people. Religion is not at risk *in* America, and the religion of our people is not a risk *to* America. Yet in recent times many individuals and even some key institutions took a distorted view of religion in America. At the heart of the distortion was the refusal to recognize, in the words of the distinguished constitutional historian Edward S. Corwin, that "the historical record shows beyond peradventure that the core of 'an establishment of religion' comprises the idea of preference; and that any act of public authority favorable to religion in general cannot, without manifest falsification of history, be brought under the ban of that phrase." In other words, our political order has never been simply neutral toward, or separate from, religion.

One case in particular thrust me in the center of the church-state debate. In *Aguilar v. Felton* (1985), the Supreme Court forbade public school teachers from teaching poor children in remedial classes in parochial schools. This decision greatly impeded efforts to fulfill the congressional mandate, dating back to 1965, to provide compensatory services to all needy students, whatever school they attend.

The Court was not bothered by the fact that not one complaint of improper indoctrination had been filed; that this program had, in the words of the court of appeals, "done so much good and little, if any, detectable harm"; or that it had ignited no divisive controversy beyond the lawsuit itself. Nonetheless, the program was ruled unconstitutional. According to the majority opinion, "Administrative personnel of the public and parochial school systems must work together in resolving matters related to schedules, classroom assignments, problems that arise in the implementation of the program, requests for additional services, and the dissemination of information regarding the program. Furthermore, the program necessitates frequent contacts between the regular and the remedial teachers (or other professionals), in which each side reports on individual student needs, problems encountered; and results achieved." In other words, the offense was that public and parochial school teachers were "working together" in educating poor children.

The day after the Supreme Court decision I termed it a "ridiculous" expression of the Court's "fastidious disdain for religion that is hard to fathom" and described as "utter chaos" the general line of Supreme Court decisions in this area. "Aid for parochial-school textbooks is fine; aid for school supplies such as maps is not," I said. "Bus transportation to and from school can be provided for parochial-school students, but bus transportation to and from field trips cannot be provided. State money can pay for standardized tests in parochial schools, but not for teacher-made tests." I concluded by quoting Senator Daniel Patrick Moynihan (D-New York): "What do you do with a map that's in a textbook?"

In August 1985 I spoke before the Knights of Columbus on the relationship of our political and social order to religious belief. I stated that the history of our nation is intertwined with a certain religious tradition, and that the First Amendment was not intended to result in the complete exclusion of religious beliefs from our public classrooms. I then addressed the broader implications of the *Felton* decision:

> The fate of our democracy is intimately intertwined— "entangled," if you will—with the vitality of the Judeo-Christian tradition. . . . The attitude that regards "entanglement" with religion as something akin to entanglement with an infectious disease must be confronted broadly and directly. . . . It would be—it is—tragic indeed to find that the passing of old-fashioned suspicion of particular religions has been followed, with barely an interruption, by a new suspicion of our broad religious tradition on the part of secularized elites, far more sophisticated, a bit better disguised, but no less divisive, no less reprehensible, no less damaging [than the old divisions between Protestant and Catholic, Gentile and Jew]. . . . The Judeo-Christian tradition is not a source of fear in the world; it is a ground of hope. . . . No one demands doctrinal adherence to any religious beliefs as a condition of citizenship, or as proof of good citizenship, here. But at the same time we should not deny what is true: that from the Judeo-Christian tradition come our values, our principles, the animating spirit of our institutions. That tradition and our tradition are entangled. They are wed together. When we have disdain for our religious tradition, we have disdain for ourselves.

The national debate the speech triggered was a good thing. I was glad to see discussion of our tradition in the daily newspapers, and to read serious accounts of the deliberations of the First Congress and of the role of religion in our national history. Taking these questions seriously is a sign of political health and intellectual vigor.

Yet some of the reactions to my remarks were less encouraging. Some critics spoke as if those of us who call attention to the claims of religion and the Judeo-Christian tradition were partisans of intolerance and bigotry.

So my criticism of the Court's decision impeding aid to needy students in parochial schools led some people to say that I was illegitimately trying to promote my "brand of Christianity," and that I thought of myself as a messenger "heaven-sent to silence the heathen." A *Baltimore Sun* cartoon had me walking away from the Supreme Court saying, "If we could close it down it would make a great cathedral." And for my support of voluntary school prayer in our public schools—or of allowing the posting of the Ten Commandments in a classroom—made me an "ayatollah." In sum, my position was characterized as an invitation to "Khomeinism and Kahaneism."

I referred to this whole line of argument—if one can call it that—as *reductio ad Khomeini*. It assumed that my statement of this nation's commitment to the principles of tolerance and equal rights for all—for the believer and no less for the nonbeliever—was mere window dressing. It ignored my statement that "no one demands doctrinal adherence to any religious beliefs as a condition of citizenship, or as proof of good citizenship, here." Some of my critics seemed to believe that Americans are a people primed for a campaign of intolerant oppression, led by "the sectarian elites of religious fundamentalism." And they assumed that describing the intimate relationship between the Judeo-Christian tradition and our public life is a step down the path toward Lebanon or Iran.

This vision said more about its beholders than about this nation. America is both religious and tolerant; what the American experience shows is that one of these qualities need not flourish at the expense of the other.

The real danger, then and now, is an impoverishment of our public life by a disdain for religion. "The trouble when people stop believing in God is not that they thereafter believe in nothing," G.K. Chesterton said, "it is that they thereafter believe in anything." Neutrality to religion turns out to bring with it neutrality to those values that issue from religion. The new source of divisiveness is the assault of secularism on religion. We need not distance ourselves from some of our best beliefs and traditions in order to protect the First Amendment. Justice William O. Douglas put it well over thirty years ago. If the First Amendment is interpreted to mean that "in every and all respects there shall be a separation of church and state," then "the state and religion would be aliens to each other—hostile, suspicious, and even unfriendly."

On "Meet the Press" the Sunday following my Knights of Columbus speech, Ken Bode's lead-in described me as a "lightning rod for controversy." Garrick Utley of NBC led off the questioning by asking whether I was "confusing . . . religious practice and religious belief." I responded, "Before I came to this job, I was a scholar, a university professor. I've studied these things for some time, and I think I know something about American history, and I have put forward my position, and now I would welcome further conversation about it. If I am mistaken, I would like to be corrected."

When pressed about criticizing a Supreme Court decision, I said, "It is my responsibility, it is every citizen's responsibility, when the Supreme Court has spoken, to adhere to its ruling, to obey it, and for us, the Department, to enforce its decision. But we're not obligated to agree with the decision. . . . These [issues], in a democracy, are continuing matters of concern and we cannot say, as Abraham Lincoln taught us [in the wake of the Dred Scott decision] . . . that because the Supreme Court has spoken, the issue is no longer one that we can discuss."

I made the point during the interview that "it's easy to throw around the phrase 'the separation of church and state,' but does the Court really . . . have a consistent view? In the area of higher education we give out several hundred million dollars, billions . . . to students so that they can enroll at Georgetown University [Catholic] or Yeshiva [Jewish], or Southern Methodist University, and there's no problem." But in *Aguilar v. Felton*, "the Court says 'No, you can't do that.' The money isn't even going to the students, the money is going to public school teachers. There's not a consistent pattern upon which we or our school systems can rely. . . . I think this is a mistake and a tragedy."

One of the more revealing aspects of the whole controversy was the reaction to a sentence from my Knights of Columbus speech that read, "Our values as a free people and the central values of the Judeo-Christian tradition are 'flesh of the flesh, blood of the blood' with our tradition." *The Washington Post* incorrectly described this as "borrowing words used during the consecration at a Roman Catholic mass."

During the Consecration in the Catholic mass the priest, quoting Christ, says, "This is my Body; this is my Blood." But I had not quoted from the Mass; I had quoted from an 1858 speech by Abraham Lincoln. Lincoln talked about the men and women who had come to America in recent years seeking freedom and liberty.

And he said that though their ancestors might not have signed the Declaration, they were nonetheless "flesh of the flesh, blood of the blood" of those who signed that document.

Lincoln had embellished a phrase from the Book of Genesis. The fact that so many journalists missed that reference proved my point. What Lincoln said cannot be understood without reference to the Judeo-Christian tradition. And what was true of Lincoln's statement was true of much of American history. Why, then, is there so much animosity toward religion? Why such willful misunderstanding of what I was saying?

Religion seemed to be the cultural dividing line of the past decade. Much of the left-liberal elite despise traditional religious beliefs (although they can be very sympathetic to religion when left-wing groups, such as the National Council of Churches, speak for it). The elite generally take a religious position seriously only when it accords with their ideology—for example, promoting "liberation theology." But in general they are profoundly uncomfortable with religious institutions and the traditional values they embody.

Sociologists tell us that when groups of like-minded people gather, they do so with tacit understandings. There are certain things that don't have to be discussed if they are already settled in advance. There are certain words or phrases that are accepted without examination; these are considered "argument closers." Among many academics, liberal segments of the media, and intellectuals, these words are "fundamentalist," "born again," and "the religious right." In their minds, these words put an end to the argument. Any serious nod in the direction of spokesmen for "the religious right" is guaranteed to call forth not simply criticism but also ridicule, and an attitude of intellectual superiority. Anyone who actually takes "the religious right" seriously on anything automatically forfeits his intellectual respectability. But while in office I took seriously the concerns of people such as Paul Weyrich, Phyllis Schlafly, James Dobson, and my colleague Gary Bauer, and I'm glad that I did.

I crossed the line again, at least in the eyes of some, when I agreed to give the commencement address at Liberty University on April 23, 1986, at the invitation of its president, Jerry Falwell. As we sat on the podium with the audience gathering, Falwell leaned over to me and with a smile said, "I understand a reporter from *The Washington Post* is in the audience. Maybe I should put my arm around you and embrace you—and destroy your career forever."

I began my remarks at Liberty with a rhetorical question: "What's a nice Catholic boy from New York doing at a fundamentalist university in Virginia?" (A Liberty student later told reporters, "I was shocked that he said he was Catholic—that he just came out and said it. Yet I was really impressed with his moral views. I was impressed that he seemed so family-oriented.") I spoke on the family as the first teacher, the most important educational institution, the place where children first learn.

My support of voluntary school prayer also made me a bogeyman in certain circles. Fred Hechinger of *The New York Times,* for example, wrote that "President Reagan and William J. Bennett, his Secretary of Education, have recently accused the schools of being 'value neutral,' but their plea for teaching of moral values has aroused controversy because it was linked to their quest for prayers in schools. This makes many parents and others nervous because they believe in the wall that separates church and state"— implying, of course, that by virtue of our support of school prayer neither the President nor I believed in the separation of church and state. Of course we believe in church–state separation. As Irving Kristol has pointed out, the problem is "efforts by liberals . . . to establish a wall between religion and society, in the guise of maintaining the wall between church and state."

My view on voluntary school prayer is that it is important to reestablish what was believed by almost everybody for a very long time, that people do not give up their First Amendment rights when they enter a classroom. The spirit of our proposed constitutional amendment, that students will be neither required nor prohibited from praying in school, was consistent with that.

Many "sophisticated" political and social commentators complain that issues like school prayer and whether or not students should be allowed to recite the Pledge of Allegiance are not serious and are unworthy of serious attention: they are viewed as "distractions" that have nothing to do with the most pressing issues of the day. What they fail to recognize is that these kinds of issues have resonance because they touch on deeper, more fundamental issues. In this case, the large issues involved in these debates have to do with the interest the American people have in

restoring a sense of moral seriousness to the school. A large part
of the American people think that this can be aided by allowing
students to begin the day with prayer. And I think they're right.

All religious faiths are concerned with the moral and religious
training of the children of their faith—that is, with education.
And at the Department of Education, we had some profitable
meetings on education and later on drugs with representatives of
religious groups. We enjoyed close cooperation with, and received
welcome support from, evangelical Protestants and conservative
Jews on both issues. We emphatically agreed with those who came
to see us that contemporary American education needed, and yet
had drifted away from, a firm belief in traditional moral values:
right and wrong, the importance of character, a concern for the
hearts of children as well as their minds. I think the record will
show that religious conservatives saw us as a Cabinet department
not only unafraid to talk about these matters, but eager to do so.
Where many evangelical Christians and conservative Jews had felt
much aggrieved by the aggressive and intolerant secularism of
many governmental and political players and agencies, they felt
comfortable with our respect for, and insistence on, the importance of teaching "the Judeo-Christian tradition."

Another area of controversy has been public support of parochial schools. Congressional interest and intent to aid children in
all schools has been part of federal legislation since the mid-1960s,
when efforts were made to aid poor children, whether attending
public, private, or parochial schools. I often used Catholic schools
as an example of the educational good works private schools can
accomplish.

Speaking before the National Catholic Education Association, I
made the case that religion is "fundamental" to a vital society.
Catholic schools "are a living reminder of the moral and intellectual vision behind our public system itself." I particularly praised
the Catholic church's commitment to educating the disadvantaged, the urban poor and non-Catholics, especially non-Catholic
black and Hispanic students.

In New York City, according to *Time* magazine, Catholic
schools graduate 99 percent of their students on time, while
public schools graduate 38 percent of their students on time.
Catholic schools educate at a cost of $1,735 per student, while
public schools spend over $7,000 per student. The average pub-
lic school teacher in New York City makes just under $40,000

per year, while the average Catholic school teacher makes $22,500 per year. And the New York City public schools employ 4,000 administrators at headquarters, while Catholic schools (which teach about a quarter as many students) employ 33.

How do Catholic schools do it? According to *Time* (not exactly a Catholic mouthpiece), "Mostly by practicing and preaching old-fashioned stuff: values, discipline, educational rigor and parental accountability, coupled with minimal bureaucracy." In other words, the advantage of Catholic schools is they are based on a core set of solid values. "For schools operated by a religious community," University of Chicago Professor James Coleman wrote, "school is not regarded as an agent of the larger society or of the state, to free the child from the family. Rather, it is an agent of the religious community of which the family is an intrinsic part. The religiously based school is thus in a better position than is the public school to support and sustain the family in its task of raising children."

Whatever one's theological position is on Catholicism, the Catholic Church holds strong views on morality, self-discipline, self-control, and high aspiration—all of which are valuable for young students. Catholic schools do not take on a self-defeating posture of "value neutrality"; no moral vacuum surrounds the students. That is why so many people, Catholic and non-Catholic, accurately understand Catholic schools to "mean business." What is particularly striking and important, but often overlooked, is the number of poor and disadvantaged children—Catholic and non-Catholic—who are well educated in Catholic schools. For children for whom education matters the most, and who it is said are the hardest to educate, Catholic schools do very well indeed.

The National Catholic Education Association's report, "Catholic High Schools: Their Impact on Low-Income Students," testifies to the remarkable commitment and effectiveness of these schools. It shows the great number of children from poor families, from broken families, and from families that speak no English who have turned to the Catholic schools for their education. It is a resounding rebuke to the notion, still dear to some, that Catholic schools are bastions of privilege and elitism.

In 1990 the City University of New York conducted a national survey that "demonstrates the remarkable educational achievements of the 2.4 million black Roman Catholics," according to Seymour P. Lachman, dean of the City University of New York, and Barry A. Kosmin, who directs the City University Graduate

School's national survey of religious identification. The survey found that the graduation rate of black Roman Catholics from high school and college is greater than that of other blacks, equal to that of other Catholics, and higher than the overall American average regardless of race. Black Catholics are 40 percent more likely to graduate from college than other black Americans, are more likely to be employed full time than blacks as a whole (66 percent to 55 percent), and have 50 percent more households earning more than $50,000 a year than the rest of the black population.

Nevertheless, despite this record, Catholic education is in decline; indeed, many Catholic schools are closing. Although Catholic schools are still the single largest provider of private education, they have lost half their students and 2,500 of their schools during the past twenty-five years. This is not a sensible way to run an education system.

The point is this: if society recognizes the education of the poor and disadvantaged as one of its most pressing problems and Catholic schools do it well, shouldn't we rally to their support and do what we can, constitutionally, to support them? After all, we support religious institutions in other areas. There is little resistance to support of medical efforts at religious hospitals that treat sick babies, care for AIDS patients, or take care of the elderly. All of these patients are part of the public, too. Large and generous federal financial aid in grants and loans supports students at Catholic and Jewish colleges and at Protestant seminaries. For reasons of consistency as well as compassion, public support for schools that teach children who are intellectually at risk shouldn't be beyond the pale, either.

But during many congressional committee and subcommittee hearings on this and related issues, liberal Democrats—be they Senate or House members—usually behaved as one, shaking their heads back and forth solemnly, accusing us of being enemies of public education and despoilers of the Constitution. One exception was Senator Barbara Mikulski of Maryland, a very liberal Democrat.

Senator Mikulski listened attentively to our arguments and talked with us about trying to find ways to help keep the good but poor religious schools alive. Mikulski, herself a Catholic raised in the working class section of Baltimore, knew what was involved and what was at stake.

Shortly before I left my job as Education Secretary, I visited

Capitol Hill and made a special point of seeing her and telling her that despite our enormous differences on so many other things, I appreciated her genuine concern on this issue. I "bequeathed" to her (unofficially of course), as one of my last acts in office, the care and guardianship of these poor but effective schools. Not much has come of it. She may be sympathetic to the idea of supporting these schools but perhaps the pressure from her colleagues on the left has kept her in place.

There is much validity to the concerns of many on the "religious right," such as the drift and decline in the teaching of traditional values, and the erosion of the family, and in calling for the spiritual and moral instruction of children. Sadly, on some occasions, some of their spokesmen present their views in ways that are unnecessarily narrow and seemingly hostile to those outside the group. I emphasize the word "unnecessarily." Just as we speak differently to our families and to the public, conservative Christians need to appeal to the *general* moral conscience of most Americans. This does not mean compromising their principles, which the majority of Americans doubtless share. It means only to recognize that in public discourse one of the priorities is to persuade those who don't share your views, and not simply to speak to those with whom you have an affinity.

At the Department of Education we offered a sympathetic ear to their concerns, but took our own way of speaking of their concerns, consistent with our obligation to serve all the people whatever their religious beliefs, and to honor the spirit, as well as the letter, of the Constitution and the First Amendment.

Public schools should not indoctrinate anyone in any particular set of sectarian beliefs. One must always recognize that in a public setting, there are people of different beliefs. But this does not mean we have to stop teaching history, stop teaching what we know to be true, stop teaching the difference between right and wrong, or disparage the efforts of deeply committed religious people to have their ideas respected. I have no doubt that the real irritation of those on the religious right is not that their particular creed is not embraced by the schools, but that often their creed is the only one singled out for contempt.

A convulsive shock went through the evangelical community after the revelations about the well-known television evangelists

Jim Bakker and Jimmy Swaggart. I had never had any doctrinal, personal, or philosophical affinity with either Bakker or Swaggart. And as Secretary of Education I found what they had done to be very damaging. It was not just their obvious hypocrisy, duplicity, and the violation of the trust and confidence placed in them by their followers. Bakker and Swaggart also gave the moral cynics a golden opportunity to caricature people who have a deep religious faith and stand up for decency. They undercut the entire effort. I told the annual meeting of the National Association of Evangelicals that the national conversation on values, public morality, and the proper role of religion in public life was hurt "when those who protest the loudest fail to live up to morality in their own lives." My remarks were well received. The members of that audience had every reason to be angry; strong, decent, responsible religious leaders of all faiths suffered because of those breaches of trust.

Fortunately the public conversation about religion has improved markedly over the last five to seven years. Responsible conversation about the need for moral education in the schools and the critical role religion plays in our society has entered the mainstream; some common ground has been achieved.

The Washington Post described a 1987 conference held in Washington this way: "The need to teach values in public schools, a theme pushed by conservatives for the past several years, is being promoted by liberals and leading educators as well, creating an unusual consensus that the nation's schools should abandon the 'values-neutral' teaching approach widely used for two decades."

"The consensus," according to the article, "is that schools should impart civic virtue and take clear positions on right and wrong behavior and personal morality—teaching, for example, that students should not engage in sex. . . . The reconciliation of normally opposing camps was evident."

According to the *Post,* "The new attention among liberals and educators to values has been prompted by the same social trends that have motivated conservatives such as Education Secretary William J. Bennett: the prevalence of teen-age pregnancy, drug problems, high-school dropouts and single-parent families."

Even Norman Lear conceded that "For all our alarm, it is clear that the religious right is responding to a real hunger in our society . . . a deep-seated yearning for stable values." When conservative Christian groups "talk of failures in our educational system, the erosion of our moral standards, and the waste of young lives," Lear said, "they are addressing real and legitimate concerns." A few years later Lear went even further in his criticism of some on the left. "Among secularists," he said in a speech to religion scholars, "the aversion toward discussion of moral values, let alone religion, can reach absurd extremes."

That it surely can. Consider the reaction to a speech I gave as drug czar to the Baptist Convention in New Orleans. During the speech I encouraged churches to get involved in fighting the war on drugs because, I said, "The drug problem is fundamentally a moral problem—in the end, a spiritual problem. It is seeking meaning in a place where no meaning can come." I then said:

> I continue to be amazed how often people I talked to in treatment centers talk about drugs as the great lie, the great deception—indeed a product, one could argue, of the great deceiver, the great deceiver everyone knows. "A lie" is what people call drugs and many, many people in treatment have described to me their version of crack, simply calling it "the devil." This has come up too often, it has occurred too much, too spontaneously, too often in conversation, to be ignored. So I applaud your effort to bring those in need to the God who heals.

The next day a *San Francisco Chronicle* headline read, "Bennett Blames Satan for Drug Abuse." The *Sacramento Bee* wrote, "Illegal drugs are indeed the devil's handiwork, federal drug czar William Bennett said."

This reaction was absurd, but illustrative. I was reporting what I had heard from people in drug treatment and speaking of drugs in a moral context. But some members of the media couldn't resist trying to ridicule my view—as well as the beliefs of drug addicts who were trying to recover. "What you've got here," I said in response, "is really a case of journalists making fun of people who believe in God and the devil." D. Patrick Miller, writing in the *Columbia Journalism Review,* argues that religion has become "the blind spot of American journalism." And Fred Barnes of *The New Republic* notes:

> Religion's crucial role in the lives of many people . . . is rejected out of hand by the political community, especially the press. This is crazy, all the more so because polls show how

religious most Americans are. Nine out of ten in a new Gallup
Poll say they've never doubted the existence of God. Nonetheless, reporters are indifferent to spirituality and its impact
on folks whose every political twist they cover.

The reaction to my comments was all too typical. Apparently
it is beyond the capability of some cynics to sympathize or understand the simple faith of many, and to appreciate that a deep
religious faith might actually help them to improve their lives.
Not surprisingly, studies show that religious training and a deep
religious commitment are strong safeguards against all sorts of
harmful behavior, including drug use. We should not refuse this
ally; the Founding Fathers were right, the modern-day critics
wrong.

If we have come some distance in recognizing the need for moral
education in the schools, it is still true that there is fear and loath-
ing among a lot of people for the *source* of most people's values—
religion and its institutions.

But organized religion has brought many of its problems on
itself. The leadership of many of the mainline Protestant churches
in America are way out of step with their membership. While
most members of the Protestant denominations remain fairly conservative on social and economic issues, polls done by the Center
for the Study of Social and Political Change show that 80 percent
of mainline Protestant leaders consider themselves liberals. (In a
1988 CBS/*New York Times* poll, 21 percent of Americans called
themselves liberal, and 33 percent considered themselves conservative.) When asked in 1989 to rank twelve public figures, mainline
Protestant leaders answered (in order of best to worst): Andrew
Young; Ralph Nader; John K. Galbraith; Ted Kennedy; Gloria
Steinem; Milton Friedman; Margaret Thatcher; the Nicaraguan
Sandinistas; Jeane Kirkpatrick; Ronald Reagan; Fidel Castro; and
the Moral Majority.

The most avid supporters of Daniel Ortega and the Sandinistas
came from American churchmen. According to Paul Hollander,
professor of sociology at the University of Massachusetts, Am-
herst, and author of *Political Pilgrims,* "Of all the pilgrims to the
Marxist-Leninist regime in Nicaragua, it is church groups who
have become its most active and dedicated supporters."

This predictable political agenda—one wag has said that "the

religious left is the only left, left"—has alienated the church leadership from much of its membership and from most Americans.
The mainline Protestant leadership is out of the mainstream and
is losing church members in droves (today there are one million
fewer Presbyterians and three quarters of a million fewer Episco-
palians than twenty years ago, for example).

Much of the leadership of the Catholic church is no better. Despite our praise for many religious schools, especially inner-city
Catholic schools, we did not get much cooperation and enthusiasm
from the Catholic education leadership. In particular, the National
Catholic Education Association did not seem inclined to tangle with
the education establishment. After several meetings I concluded,
ironically, that the national Baptist leadership was a stronger and
more convincing voice for Catholic education interests than was
the Catholic leadership. The Catholic leadership was not at the
forefront of antidrug efforts, either. For reasons inexplicable to
me, they didn't want to address this as a priority matter.

How far have things fallen? In a well-publicized incident recently, a national committee of Presbyterians, in a majority report
on human sexuality, questioned the importance Americans place
on marriage, approved of masturbation and petting among teen-
agers, and says that "maturity," not marriage, should determine
when teens engage in intercourse. It argued that the church
should endorse "new" family structure (including same-sex
couples with adopted children), and homosexuals should be or-
dained into the ministry. The majority report attacks the sexual
attitudes of the church and this country as "patriarchal, homopho-
bic and biased toward heterosexuality," according to *The Washington Post*. ("Middle-class America had a heart attack," said
committee chairman John J. Carey, a professor of Bible and Religion at Agnes Scott College. "At least we've gotten their attention.") Fortunately, the report was voted down during the General
Assembly of the Presbyterian Church (U.S.A.). But the fact that
this kind of report could get a serious hearing is an indication of
how morally and doctrinally confused some segments of the
churches have become.

In a remarkable bow to "politically correct" thinking, the National Council of Churches has recommended that the 500th anniversary of Columbus's discovery of America be a time of
"repentance" for starting "centuries of genocide."

But if a single recent event most vividly demonstrated the chasm that now separates the values of many church leaders from those of the American people, it may have been the Persian Gulf war. A poll conducted immediately following the January 16 bombing of Iraq found 78 percent of the American people believed the United States did the "right thing." Yet according to nationally syndicated columnist Georgie Anne Geyer, "every major Christian religious denomination was condemning a Gulf war as 'morally unjusti-fied.' " Prior to the beginning of America's involvement in the war, the National Council of Churches charged the U.S. with "weak res-ignation to the illogical pursuit of militarism and war."

What troubled many people was not opposition to the Persian Gulf war per se. The troubling part was that many religious lead-ers seemed singularly unable to make a *principled* case, a morally compelling case, against the war. Instead, much of the opposition can be traced to an almost reflexive anti-Americanism. Many of the Protestant and Catholic statements opposing the war were, according to George Weigel, president of the Ethics and Public Policy Center, "pacifism rooted . . . in a profound alienation from the American experiment and in a deep conviction that American power cannot serve good ends in the world."

During the Persian Gulf war many church leaders demon-strated, once again, that on matters of profound moral impor-tance, they have virtually nothing useful, significant, or specifically religious to say. Their marked inability to make the classic distinc-tions between the use of force in a just manner for right purposes and the use of violence to advance evil is a sign of sheer moral exhaustion. President Bush was widely ridiculed for consulting the Reverend Billy Graham before the Gulf war. But at a time when men of good will, President Bush included, were looking for guidance, the church establishment took a hike.

Faced with declining membership and their increasing irrele-vance to important social and foreign policy issues, many church leaders comfort themselves by telling themselves that they are suffering the fate of the prophet, of those who speak uncom-fortable truths, men without honor in their own land. But the American people know what they know: many church leaders are intellectually and morally depleted. Ironically, at the very moment when people are looking for moral guidance and moral certainty in their lives, many of the churches are looking the other way.

Throughout both jobs, as Secretary of Education and as drug

czar, I was often credited with effective use of the bully pulpit. It was ironic that with only a few exceptions, the people to whom the pulpit was originally given were not committed to its use and to responsibly addressing our most pressing concerns. They didn't seem to view the education and drug problems to be high priorities, worth discussing with the authoritative voice vested in them by their flock.

The politicization of the leadership of mainline religious institutions makes their help on truly pressing social and domestic issues unlikely and unreliable in the future. What would assistance look like? Where might it come from? I believe a great lifeline which could be resuscitated in the future might come from black churches. In Washington, D.C., Bishop Felton May has organized his Methodist church to make a commitment to help poor inner-city communities afflicted by drugs. When the membership of the black churches march in the streets against drugs, or for full educational choice, or for better police protection—all things many inner-city citizens have told me they want—then positive things will begin to happen for the children in those communities. And the churches will be a primary, positive cause of such improvement.

The effective influence of the mainline churches will depend on church members breaking free of the increasingly radicalized political faith of their leadership. In the battle for preserving sound social and moral norms, many religious institutions can no longer be counted as allies. In some instances, they have even hurt these efforts. It is time they return to first principles and use the bully pulpit truly to advance the nation's moral and spiritual life. Otherwise, they will find themselves relegated to the sidelines, an odd institutional relic of the late sixties and early seventies, irrelevant to the resolution of our most pressing contemporary moral issues, suffering the fate not of the prophet who speaks for the ages but of the transient political pastor who parrots only the thin, unexamined sentiments of his time.

Conclusion

REFLECTIONS ON BEING IN THE FIGHT

Who am I? If you believe what I've been called in print, I am: a medieval knight jousting against an immoral world; Knight of the Right; the Reagan administration's principal breaker of crockery; a bull in a china shop; a black sheep; the Lone Ranger; a loose cannon; a Neanderthal; a bully with a pulpit instead of a leader in a bully pulpit; the man who put the bully back into the pulpit; the cowboy in the capital; a noisy ideologue; a motor-mouth; a pain in the neck; sexist; imperialist; bourgeois; ethnocentric; selfish; solipsistic; secretary of ignorance; secretary of private education; secretary smarty-pants; secretary of religion; heaven-sent to silence the heathen; an ayatollah; Bennett the Hun; propagandist and ideological gangster; an ideological samurai; a divisive fearmonger; elitist; populist; someone who rushes in where politicians fear to tread; a political pimp; a husky brawler; a walking rock and roll encyclopedia; philosopher and tough Irish cop; a pit bull with a brain; a tornado in a wheat field; someone who combined the ideals of Erasmus with the tactics of an alley fighter; the Cabinet's resident Dennis the Menace.

During ten years in politics, I have been called a lot of things and I've been at the center of some political storms. But I have had a great time, and I have no large regrets. I believe, as John Buchan, an early-twentieth-century British Member of Parliament, wrote in *Pilgrim's Way*, "Politics is still the greatest and most honorable adventure." Traveling across this country, talking to the American people about things that matter has been a privilege. I loved it, was energized by it, and engaged in it full tilt. Arguing about

225

the ideas that rest behind some of the passions of our time is deeply rewarding and enriching work. Politics is an adventure. Aristotle taught that "man is by nature an animal intended to live in a *polis* [city-state]." Political debates about the way in which we order our social life together are among the most consequential of human activities. But severed from principles, from debates that matter, politics becomes trivial. The problem is not (as many political commentators assert) that modern-day politics has become particularly uncivil and nasty. After all, there has always been a lot of incivility in American politics. In 1800, for example, a Federalist pamphlet said that if Jefferson and his "Jacobins" were elected they would "trample upon and explode" the "morals which guard the chastities of our wives and daughters from seduction and violence, defend our property from plunder and devastation, and shield our religion from contempt and profanation." Lincoln was referred to as a "baboon." And many other presidents and public officials have been called things equally bad and worse.

The problem today is that politics has become boring, predictable, and unengaging. Too much political discourse is lame, mushy, and vapid. The explanation for this has to do with the fact that many of our contemporary political debates, over the still great issues facing our nation, lack any philosophical underpinnings—a "sheet anchor" (in a phrase used by Lincoln), a commitment to principles that inform the particulars of policy.

I think the Founding Fathers would think that today's political soup is too thin, and they would see the need for a more vigorous and thoughtful political discussion. "In a nation of philosophers," Madison wrote in *Federalist* No. 49, "a reverence for the laws would be sufficiently inculcated by the voice of an enlightened reason." In the United States, he believed, reverence would have to be inculcated primarily by study and by debate. Hamilton writes in *Federalist* No. 22, "The fabric of American empire ought to rest on the solid base of THE CONSENT OF THE PEOPLE." But only informed consent and studied reflection can buttress the "pure, original foundation of all legitimate authority." Jefferson closed one of his letters to Madison on the Constitution with the hope that "the education of the common people will be attended to; convinced that on their good sense we may rely with the most security for the preservation of a due degree of liberty." And Madison, looking back on his achievement twenty-eight years later, echoed the sentiment: "The diffusion of knowledge is the only guardian of true liberty."

The popular debates of the early republic had done much to justify the Founders' faith. The adoption of the federal Constitution, the state constitutions, and the Declaration of Independence were accompanied by an outpouring of political literature unmatched in sophistication, variety, and quantity. In newspapers, pamphlets and almanacs, the framers took their case to the people and the people responded—in referenda, in town meetings, and in heated debates among themselves. The citizens shared with their leaders a common determination to ask hard questions, to confront and to resolve the moral tensions at the base of the new republic—the tensions between liberty and equality, between individualism and community, between executive and legislative, and between the states and the nation.

In recent years many of us, politicians and citizens, have shown less of an inclination to think seriously about important political principles. Because politicians have avoided serious debate, many of the people have disengaged. But this does not have to be. The greatest debates in American history—between the Federalists and the anti-Federalists, Madison and Jefferson, Jefferson and Hamilton, Lincoln and Douglas—have involved sharp, vigorous, spirited, sometimes "uncivil" clashes. That's fine; politics was never intended to be confused with a garden party. The important thing is that they were battles over large ideas, and they went a long way toward helping us define what kind of people we want to be. And the people were interested in the conversation. Some of the large questions have been settled, but as I hope this book has made plain many others—some direct descendants of the original debates on equality, civic virtue, education, religion, and the line separating liberty and license—remain to be settled by candid political debates. Invited to a serious discussion of serious matters, the people will accept.

As a former professor of political philosophy, I was taught the importance of ideas to the life of a nation, to see the issues of the day in light of enduring principles. Politics properly understood involves the clear expression of deep convictions, and the proper, time-honored task of politicians is to "reinaugurate the good old central ideas of the Republic," as Lincoln said.

*   *   *

I have been accused of liking a political fight. That's true, up to a point. I like a fight if it's worth being in. My jobs have touched on issues that cut deeply, that evoke strong feelings and passions. Fundamental principles are at the heart of almost every one of the jobs I held, and many of the controversies of which I was a part. I took to politics Flannery O'Connor's advice, "You have to push as hard as the age that pushes against you." The modern age and the bearers of some of the modern age's sentiments pushed hard against me. I pushed back.

Politics, then, is a struggle of fighting faiths. Today, as before, many faiths compete for the allegiance of the American people. People disagree, and sometimes they disagree strongly, about first principles. And those disagreements matter.

It is precisely because of my views that I have welcomed a fight over first principles. I wanted to place issues of culture and values at the top of our national political agenda and at the center of our public discourse. In some cases, this meant trying to retake enemy-occupied territory. That was bound to set off alarm bells among some of the liberal establishment. But this cultural war is not an undertaking for people with delicate sensibilities.

Politicians often try to protect their views and themselves by suggesting that sincerity can substitute for sound reasoning. In 1990 I traveled to Denver to campaign on behalf of Hank Brown for the U.S. Senate. During the trip I criticized his Democratic opponent, Josie Heath. As Boulder County commissioner, Heath endorsed a plan to distribute free syringes to 200 intravenous drug users and even offered $5 to junkies willing to swap their used needles for sterile needles. "Her position on free needles is bizarre and grotesque. It's a surrender in the war on drugs," I said. "We need to make needles and drugs more scarce, not more plentiful."

Following my comments, I was asked by a reporter if I doubted her "sincerity." Sincerity has nothing to do with whether she is right or wrong on the issue, I answered. Sincerity is not the test of truth. If something is dubious, believing it "harder" doesn't make it any truer. Sincerity, like conscience, is a reliable guide to action or belief only when it is joined with intelligence. No fact was ever altered by believing it wasn't one, no matter how sincerely.

*   *   *

In Washington, too many people accede to the politics of bribery. They believe that they have to cave in to interest groups on just about every issue, or they will not be elected. They shouldn't do that in any event, even if there is a political cost. In our system, of course, compromise attends politics. That's a good thing, provided one makes the important distinction—best made by Duff Cooper in his biography of Talleyrand—between the willingness in principle to compromise (which is fine), and the willingness to compromise on principle (which is not).

If public officials were more principled, I suspect that they would find they would be elected with pretty much the same regularity. You do not gain people's affection, and you certainly don't gain their respect, by caving in.

Madison said that if every Athenian citizen had been a Socrates, every Athenian assembly would still have been a mob. Needless to say, we do not have an abundance of Socrateses on Capitol Hill. Some good men and women, yes. But as a group, when they act as a group, they do not make the grade.

Congress was the institution in which I was most disappointed. As one writer described it, Congress acts like an overzealous high school student council with unlimited resources. Often it seems that any idea that fits the *zeitgeist*, that can be linked to a "need," anyone's need, anywhere, anytime, is funded. Frequently it is funded at the cost of hundreds of millions, or even billions, of dollars, without the slightest regard to whether the program will work, whether it will be held accountable, whether it is appropriate for the federal government to fund it, or whether it is something people can or ought to do for themselves. For Congress the operative word is input, not output.

To inefficiency and waste on a grand scale, we can add hypocrisy. Given the posturing and self-righteousness exhibited by many members of Congress, it is ironic that Congress exempts itself, and only itself, from laws it imposes on all other Americans. These exemptions include the Civil Rights Restoration Act of 1988, the Ethics in Government Act of 1978, the Privacy Act of 1974, the Equal Employment Opportunity Act of 1972, the Occupational Safety and Health Act of 1970, the Freedom of Information Act of 1966, Title VII of the Civil Rights Act of 1964 (which prohibits sexual harassment and discrimination on the basis of race, color, sex, religion, and national origin), and the Equal

Pay Act of 1963. In setting itself apart as "a privileged class of rulers who stand above the law," as President Bush has aptly described it, Congress is in effect exempting itself from the most universal, basic moral rule: the Golden Rule.

Americans have witnessed as well the appalling spectacle of senators and representatives, whose private conduct have brought shame on their institution, sitting in judgment of the moral probity of individuals of sound character but also of fundamentally different political beliefs—and in some cases, these congressmen have even led the assault on character. This began in its present form with the character assassination of Judge Robert Bork. But, as the Clarence Thomas hearings so vividly demonstrated, the tactics first used then have now become the coin of the Congressional realm.

In recent years members of Congress and their staff have been responsible for criminal and national security leaks; orchestrated smear campaigns; influence peddling and conflicts-of-interest; illegal kickbacks; the acceptance of hundreds of thousands of dollars in real estate "finders' fees"; check-bouncing scandals; and sexual scandals. There is now a critical mass of outrage and revulsion among the public.

This is not the sum total of Congress, of course, and every institution is going to have its bad apples. In the executive branch, human failings have received widespread attention in the press, some of it deserved. But only now has the spotlight been turned on Congress. The question is, what do you do once these problems have been brought to light? Are there tangible signs that the institution is serious about seeking improvement and reform? Or are we seeing merely a symbolic nod, a feint, in the direction of reform? Unfortunately, not only has Congress demonstrated a marked unwillingness to clean up and police its own ranks but it continues to reward its behavior by voting itself pay raises (often employing a parliamentary sleight-of-hand so members are not forced to go on record in support of pay increases). Little wonder, then, that an October 1991 Gallup Poll showed that the public's confidence in Congress is at its lowest point in the history of the polling organization (only 18 percent of Americans have "quite a bit" or "a great deal" of confidence in Congress). Public doubt is one thing, contempt quite another.

Congressional reforms are desperately needed. Some of the following reforms would help: term limitation; elimination of free congressional mailings; elimination of taxpayer-subsidized press operations; cutting personal congressional staff one-half to two-thirds; limitation of the number of committees and subcommittees; and reforms of campaign financing and political action committees (during the 1990 congressional campaign, incumbent candidates outspent their challengers on the average by more than 5 to 1 while PACs gave less than $7 million to challengers and more than $88 million to incumbents, figures which are indicative of "the money corruption of our politics," in the words of *Washington Post* columnist Mark Shields). It would also help in particular to remove the soft money and gerrymandering that give the House of Representatives more tenure than the Soviet Politburo in the Brezhnev years. When the founders created Congress, they envisioned an institution that would at least partly be kept honest by the constant turnover of seats—a Congress with little resemblance to today's tenured monstrosity.

But the disease runs much deeper than any "process reform" measures can cure. The real solution has to do with institutional leadership. Institutions inevitably reflect the character of the individuals who comprise them. Institutional integrity depends on individual integrity, and institutional corruption is ultimately a product of individual corruption. There is a growing sense that Congress has become increasingly out of touch and that rot is beginning to set in—this in sharp contrast to the Founders' view, that it would "refine and enlarge the public views by passing them through the medium of a chosen body of citizens, whose wisdom may best discern the true interest of their country and whose patriotism and love of justice will be least likely to sacrifice it to temporary or partial considerations."

There is plenty to be disappointed, angry, even furious about in the way politics is practiced in this "Potomac Wonderland." Washington at its worst can be a vicious, sick city. Nothing so captivates the Washington mind as the anticipation of a scandal or that a person in power is about to fall from grace. Washington pundits follow the ups and downs of individual careers in the same way as sports fanatics read only the box scores. This side of Washington was captured best not by any of the "Washington books" but by C.S. Lewis's description of Hell in *The Screwtape Letters*:

We must picture Hell as a state where everyone is perpetually concerned about his own dignity and advancement, where

everyone has a grievance, and where everyone lives the
deadly serious passions of envy, self-importance, and resentment. . . . On the surface, manners are normally suave.
Rudeness to one's superiors would obviously be suicidal;
rudeness to one's equals might put them on their guard before you were ready to spring your mine. For of course
"Dog eat dog" is the principle of the whole organisation. Everyone wishes everyone else's discrediting, demotion and
ruin; everyone is an expert in the confidential report, the
pretended alliance, the stab in the back. Over all this their
good manners, their expressions of grave respect, their
"tributes" to one another's invaluable services form a thin
crust. Every now and then it gets punctured, and the scald-
ing lava of their hatred spurts out.

At the same time, one should heed the warning of the Canadian
novelist Robertson Davies: "Beware of the cynics and the damp-
ers." Washington watchers should be wary of cynicism, too. A
dose of skepticism is always wise. But a retreat into cynicism cor-
rodes the heart of its holder. And it's not warranted—even in
Washington, maybe *especially* in Washington, in that cynicism provides an easy out for those too lazy to get on with the business of
working for and affirming the "true interests of their country." So
wholesale, sweeping cynicism regarding Washington, D.C., and its
denizens isn't the right response. Scattered among the supercil-
ious, the sleazy, the slippery, and the slipshod are a lot of honorable people, too. I have met with, dealt with, negotiated with, and
disagreed with many of them. In Washington, D.C., today, one
finds essentially what Madison, Jay, and Hamilton found in the
politicians of their day: some personifiers of corruption and self-
interest and even conspiracy against the general welfare, but also
some good examples of character and reliability. "This supposition of universal venality in human nature is little less an error in
political reasoning, than the supposition of universal rectitude,"
Hamilton wrote in *Federalist* No. 76.

Shoddy behavior is always disheartening. It is discouraging
to see bad character in persons charged with governing this nation. But this is only one side of the story of current public affairs.

The other side is represented by men and women in both parties who exhibit character. The people whose character impresses

me are true public servants who don't hold their views on the basis of self-interest or political expediency; they hold them primarily because of force of argument, evidence, and a genuine disinterested regard for the common good.

Are there enough men and women of good character in Washington? No, but there is no oversupply of good character anywhere. The point is that it's not true that when you go to Washington you automatically leave your character behind. Not from what and whom I've seen. Nor is it true that you cannot be effective and decent and honorable at the same time in our public arena. You can. "Political ethics" is not an oxymoron.

I have seen men and women of integrity in the House and Senate, in the Judiciary and Executive branches and outside of government, in the press. They demonstrate what should be obvious but, like many great truths, is often overlooked: character is inextricably linked to, is part and parcel of, the individual, not his party or institution; it is something a man or woman either has or lacks. You don't get it from membership; like so many other things, you get it from within.

I have seen people with enough regard for the common good that they merit confidence and praise. And I take pride from having served with colleagues who care deeply about their country and who understand the true meaning of public service, people I know well, such as Jack Kemp, Carla Hills, Dick Cheney, Colin Powell, Howard Baker, Lawrence Eagleburger, Richard Perle, Ken Adelman, Constance Horner, and others worthy of Walter Lippmann's reminder, "Those in high places are more than the administrators of government bureaus. They are more than the writers of laws. They are the custodians of a nation's ideals, of the beliefs it cherishes, of its permanent hopes, of the faith which makes a nation out of a mere aggregation of individuals."

Political leaders should pay more attention to the character as well as the ability of the people they hire (and certainly less to the "contacts" of the applicant). There are lots of smart, experienced people available, but when your administration is involved in controversies, when your political opponents are out to get you, you need people of character as well as skill. You want people whom "nothing can daunt, nothing can bribe," in Learned Hand's phrase, people who won't "grow in office" by becoming more sympathetic to your opponents.

Pericles said the secret of democracy is courage, and I think his words are still right. I was appalled when the Iran-Contra crisis broke out, to witness how silent many people in the Reagan administration, including the Cabinet, were in defense of the President; they headed for the tall grass and waited out events. The first impulse in this kind of situation should be to rally to the defense of your president. Loyalty—personal loyalty—is not in oversupply in this town. If the facts reveal your loyalty is misplaced, so be it. Then say it was misplaced. But the instinct to be loyal to one's colleagues, to one's president, is a good thing, not a misplaced, naive notion.

It is shocking how many people who work in an administration sabotage administration policy by winking at it during congressional hearings or during "background" sessions with reporters. The people who work for a president should be loyal to that president and his agenda. Otherwise, they should resign. Or be fired.

I spent a lot of time during my first year at the Department of Education cleaning house. That's not an easy thing to do, even with people you don't particularly care for, or whose politics you don't agree with. But I had to do it; I had to have my team. On reflection, the Reagan administration should have been tougher in this area.

It should be easier to get rid of high-ranking public officials and Cabinet members than it is to get rid of a corrupt university professor or university president (which is almost impossible to do). A president should ask for the resignation of an official in his administration when he is unhappy with that person's overall performance. I take seriously the phrase, "You serve at the pleasure of the president," and if your actions are not pleasing to the president, he should not be reluctant to ask you to leave. An official should resign when he is doing more harm than good. Sometimes officials will get into trouble that is of their own making, either because of bad judgment, slipshod standards, or inattention. They can become dead weight, and they should go. An administration should not be distracted by controversies that will force it to deviate from its agenda. You shouldn't simply hold ground in politics, you have to gain ground. That is the reality of governing.

*   *   *

"It is impossible to take the politics out of politics," Tommy "the Cork" Corcoran, a close friend and adviser of Franklin Roosevelt, said. You shouldn't underestimate the degree of self-interest and politicization in politics in general, and in the Senate and House in particular. As Justice Brandeis told his daughter, "As soon as you learn that life is often hard, things will be all the smoother for you." This is true in politics as well as life. "Act high, think low, assume their worst, act your best," the historian Gertrude Himmelfarb said to me before I entered public service. Assume there is going to be trouble with everything, that nothing is going to go through unchallenged. And be ready. Prepare more of the case than you think you are going to need, because you are probably going to need it.

Scottish philosopher and historian David Hume wrote, "Though men be much governed by interest, yet even interest itself and all human affairs are entirely governed by opinion." I wanted public opinion strongly on my side. My policy recommendations sometimes fell on deaf ears on Capitol Hill until public support was aroused around the country. Then I got a response. When I first raised a fuss about the price of higher education and the default rate of student loans, many people in Congress didn't want to act. But once public opinion was aroused, Congress began to hold hearings. Now the Congress is being forced to do something. Will they do the right thing? Maybe not. But at least they have to face the issue squarely.

Legislative gains are important, and we did pretty well on that score on the issue of drugs. We would have had many more in education if the makeup of Congress had been different. Our efforts were frustrated by the fact that a lot of committees were taking their direction from the education special interest groups. In addition, we did not go up to Capitol Hill with soft, easy issues. We went up with tough, hard, sometimes radical, proposals. We had no illusions. But we made the case.

For many of the issues I was involved in, legislative victory was not the only or even the most important criterion of success. All the departments I ran took a vigorous posture, and whether or not we prevailed legislatively, we had good success at defining the terms of debate. People had to react to what we were saying, the arguments we were advancing. And hopefully, eventually, they do make their way into policy.

If you are in a prominent position in Washington, the press is a big part of your life, whether you like it or not. Just *how* big depends on several factors, including how important your job is, how comfortable you are dealing with the media, how much confidence you have in your position, how much you have to say, and how interestingly you say it.

Some public officials seek to minimize contact with the press, or perhaps more common, have contact with them only through intermediaries. Washington is filled with media consultants who offer their services when you enter office. What do they promise? That they will help you "handle" the press and "manage" the news. Their assumption is that public officials (because they are naive and unsophisticated when it comes to the press) need handlers. And the press, in their parlance, are something like zoo animals; they need handling, too. These "consultants" will teach you how to talk since you aren't supposed to talk to the press the way you talk to regular people. These "consultants" operate in a bizarre, Byzantine little world, with its own vocabulary (you try to "spin" a story so that it reflects favorably on you). They try to promulgate the idea that they're part of an elite club. They spend hours on the phone with reporters, passing on morsels of "insider" information, collecting IOUs that they can never really cash in on. It's an old trick to inflate one's own value by making the case for one's indispensability—in this case, by promoting the myth that one belongs to the select few who can "handle" the press.

Most of it is utter nonsense. It assumes that the press can be "bought" (or at least rented); that they can be co-opted as allies when they might otherwise be adversarial. All over Washington there are agency officials trying to court the press over drinks and on the phone, all with the hope of building a "relationship" that will insulate them or their superiors against criticism, only to see the political figure they work for carved up in a thousand pieces the next morning, despite all the effort. And at this point the consultant advises the principal to keep his distance from the press.

Keeping distant was definitely not my approach to public life. I viewed the press as an important, even essential part of my work. And while I was aware that a lot of reporters did not share my political or philosophical view of the world, I genuinely liked most members of the press I dealt with. I wanted to "handle" them myself and I thought I could do so without being counterfeit.

Of course, politicians and government officials need to face reality: the press is argumentative, adversarial, and confrontational. It has become (in Charles Krauthammer's phrase) "the official opposition." And this is an appellation it is proud to wear. Washington is full of reporters; many are smart, tough, and aggressive.

The adversarial quality of the press derives in part from one of the oldest and soundest traditions of America: the people's suspicion of government, their impulse toward the diffusion of power, and their wish to scrutinize and keep a close check on government and its officials. The free press acts as a check on government power and sees itself as the protector of the people against the excesses and wrongdoing of government. To the media, the burden of proof is *always* on the government. Overall, that's good. Because as big and as powerful as the press is, government is bigger and more powerful yet.

During meetings with my staff, I would sometimes ask if what we were about to do passed "*The Washington Post* test"—in other words, could we defend our policies and actions publicly? We would ask ourselves, "How would this look on the front page?" As a public official, you begin to *internalize* this, and the self-scrutiny generally works for the good.

It is true that over the last twenty years the adversarial quality has become in some instances out-and-out hostility. With Vietnam first, then Watergate, some of the media such as Bob Woodward and Carl Bernstein became stars, and many others sought to become stars. In some cases, the story took second place to reporters' ambition, the lure of the spotlight and the glitz. The way to big bucks and celebrity status was "investigative reporting," which sometimes became a euphemism for unremitting hostility; healthy skepticism slid into destructive cynicism. The media should be more willing to admit that this has become a problem.

"Major-media journalists have altered their sense of social mission in the last generation," according to S. Robert Lichter. "They see themselves as a kind of permanent opposition. Their job is to get the bad news out. . . . The media have bought into an adversarial self-image, and that affects the way the public looks at social institutions, and how those institutions function." This adversarial self-image, combined with an inflated sense of self-importance, has caused a hemorrhage of trust. One recent poll showed that less than one in five Americans has a great deal of confidence in those "in charge of running the press." Instead of rationalizing this lack of confidence, instead of wearing it as a badge of honor, the press needs to begin a serious self-examination.

Much of the "prestige press" (newspapers like *The New York Times, The Washington Post,* and the *Boston Globe,* newsweeklies like *Newsweek* and *Time,* and the major television networks) tend to hold liberal views. Since the media has a strong interest in maintaining the impression of objectivity, many in the media recoil when they are described as liberal; they will argue that regardless of what their personal political beliefs are, there is no evidence of a discernible political bias in their reporting. But opinion surveys done within the ranks of the largest media organs confirm that liberalism is the reigning political orthodoxy. According to Brit Hume, ABC News' chief White House correspondent, "A great many reporters are liberal. They're temperamentally liberal and socio-economically liberal, but they regard their own political views as middle-of-the-road and neutral. So there's a lot of unconscious bias that seeps into the coverage of things." The liberal leanings among many editors, reporters and television executives has become so obvious as to be virtually uncontested; this is particularly true in their reporting of "social" issues like abortion.

But contrary to the allegations of some conservatives, there is not absolute political uniformity among the press. Nor is there a conspiracy in the press against conservatives, or against conservative government; liberal politicians do not get off unscathed by the press, even by the liberal press. The press tends to be more adversarial than liberal. Ask Teddy Kennedy. Or Gary Hart. Or Jimmy Carter. Or Michael Dukakis.

Nor is it true that conservative views are never given a fair hearing, or that all reporters let their political views affect their reporting, or that it is impossible to overcome a hostile press corps. The political leanings of the press don't tend to get in the way of their interest in getting a story. They need copy, and if you can give them copy they will take it, even if they are not fully sympathetic to your views. My experience is that if you make your case in an interesting, straightforward, and reasonably intelligent way, they will report it. If you do find yourself confronted by an adversarial press corps, you must vigorously defend yourself. And whenever possible, find an unfiltered forum or medium in which you can go over the heads of the press and speak directly to the American people.

The Supreme Court battles over Robert Bork and Clarence Thomas are illustrative. In 1987 Judge Bork, perhaps the most distinguished legal mind in America, was nominated by President Reagan to serve on the Supreme Court. His nomination was rejected by the Senate after a vicious, distorted, and intellectually dishonest smear campaign orchestrated by the left wing of the Democratic party and spearheaded by Senator Kennedy in particular. Unfortunately, the White House did not do enough on Judge Bork's behalf prior to his confirmation hearing. They committed a cardinal political sin: playing defense instead of offense. The terms of public debate were set by the modern-day "Iron Triangle" which consists of liberal special-interest groups, their staffs on Capitol Hill, and their ideological soulmates in the media. Misimpressions about Bork's legal opinions and scholarly writings were allowed to harden into dogma. Bork never had the opportunity to make his case except in the context of answering questions before a generally hostile Senate Judiciary Committee. The Committee Democrats set the ground rules and rigged the game. When confronted with this hard political reality, the White House should have waged a high-profile, full-scale frontal assault on the legal philosophy and political tactics of the left. Robert Bork, an urbane, civilized, and profoundly decent man, suffered because he attempted to engage in a serious legal dialogue while his opponents were doing everything in their power to destroy him. In this instance, the political assassins' bullet hit the mark; Bob Bork was denied the seat on the Supreme Court that he so richly deserved.

Over the last decade a number of other well-qualified conservatives have been bludgeoned by what is euphemistically referred to as "the process" (it's more akin to running a gauntlet or through a minefield). The larger political lessons of some of these incidents are clear: when placed in an adversarial setting, don't become passive; don't bob, weave, pirouette, backtrack, or disavow previously held views in order to appease your opponents (to Bork's credit, he stayed true to his judicial principles throughout the ordeal). The appeasement approach is not honorable and it's largely ineffectual. The implicit deal offered by the special-interest groups and their congressional hatchet men is, Pander and capitulate to us and we will defeat you but resist us and we will destroy you. The proper response is defiance. Be confident, be aggressive, don't retreat and, if necessary, go right down their throats. When you're confronted by thugs brandishing billy clubs and nightsticks, you are not well served if you abide by Marquis of Queensberry rules.

The politics of confrontation is the strategy that Judge Clarence Thomas used so effectively when in 1991 he exposed and exco-riated the Democratically controlled Senate Judiciary Committee as a "circus" and a "national disgrace" trying to conduct a "high-tech lynching." In responding to the eleventh-hour attacks against him, Thomas spoke, angry and unmediated, and his words rang true with the vast majority of the public. This was a seismic po-litical event. The Senate liberals withered under the blistering counteroffensive; the political wrecking ball they set in motion during the Bork confirmation hearings came hurling back on them with a vengeance. Even though much of the "prestige" me-dia mightily tried to derail his confirmation, today Clarence Thomas sits on the high court while the Democrats on the Senate Judiciary Committee (the closest thing the Congress has to en-forcers of "politically correct" thinking) are in disrepute.

The morning of his confirmation vote I phoned Thomas, a friend and a man whom I have long admired. He was as Senator Danforth had described him, a free man, at peace with himself and with God. "Don't ever overestimate the U.S. Congress and don't ever underestimate the American people," I told him. "Clar-ence, I'm damn sorry this had to happen on your back," I said, "but I believe that the country will be better off because of the ordeal you've been through."

One of the lessons of the Thomas confirmation hearings is that conservatives fare much better when the judge and jury are the American people and not the permanent political establishment in Washington.

Overall, on balance, conservatives do get a harder time in the press than liberals, but conservatives need to remember that the world, even the world of the media, is complicated and varied. Television reporters, anchors and executives, print editors, print reporters, and a lot of editorial pages tend to be liberal. But con-servatives have the upper hand in another—and arguably more important—arena, where the battle of ideas, the shaping of the terms of political debate and public discourse, often takes place.

Many of the most influential columnists and most elegant writers are various shades of conservative: William Safire, Charles Krauthammer, George Will, Patrick J. Buchanan, Warren Brookes, Walter Williams, William F. Buckley, James J. Kilpatrick, Thomas Sowell, Ben Wattenberg, Paul Gigot, and John Leo, to name only a few. Some of the best political reporters in Washington are Bob Novak, Rowland Evans, Fred Barnes, and Bill McGurn. The country's most popular radio commentator? The very conservative Rush Limbaugh (with more than eight million weekly listeners). The *Washington Times* is a daily conservative alternative to *The Washington Post*. And conservatives can claim the best and most provocative editorial page in America, that of *The Wall Street Journal*. And as far as influential periodicals, it's conservatives by a wide margin: *National Review, Public Interest, National Interest, American Spectator, First Things, Commentary, Human Events, Policy Review* and *Reader's Digest* (with the world's largest magazine circulation), among others.

Conservatives should also recognize the fact that it was conservative ideas—many of which were advanced in the media—that most profoundly affected the intellectual, political, and public policy debates of the late 1970s and 1980s, in such areas as supply-side tax policy, welfare reform, support for freedom fighters, and a reassessment of U.S. strategic defense doctrine. The most interesting intellectual debates during the last fifteen years or so have been among conservatives and Republicans; even Democrats like Senator Daniel Patrick Moynihan of New York have conceded as much.

The worst thing a public official can do is to fear the press. This plays into their worst instincts, which is to tear a public person down, and puts your political and professional fate in their hands. If you run from them they will pursue you and hound you until you are intimidated from saying anything controversial again. Indeed, more than one would-be Cabinet hell-raiser has been reduced to quiet clerk by a press feeding frenzy. But I was certain that if I knew my mind, did my homework, expressed my views as straightforwardly as possible, I would come out okay.

In the end, some of the press will respect you even if they don't agree with you. In the face of caricature and distortions of what you believe, the key is perseverance; hold shape and keep explaining your views. If you articulate your views well, forcefully, and often, your point of view will gradually get across, even if the messenger (the press) hates the message, hates delivering it, and loves to hate you in print. I remember learning in college that one Irish king had committed suicide because of what the poets had written about him. There are similar, though not quite so extreme, reactions of this sort in Washington. More than one experienced Washington official has dropped into dark despair from a bad review or bad editorial. But this kind of criticism is not terminal. My high school football coach used to tell us, "Today's newspapers are used to wrap tomorrow's garbage."

Politics is like a football game; time of possession counts for a lot. In Washington, you are either on offense or you are on defense. You are never in between. You either have the ball and are moving it against them, or they have the ball and are moving it against you. My philosophy is, move the ball against them, move it at the level of principle, and move it by argument, by your ideas.

High-ranking government officials are typically confronted with a narrow political playing field. According to Mark Blitz of the Hudson Institute, "the field is marked by laws, practices, and hierarchies that structure the bustle of daily politics." Predecessors, holdovers, bureaucrats, and well-wishers immediately tell a new Cabinet official, in effect, "Be careful. Here is the political playing field; you have to play within these lines and by these rules. The accepted way of doing business is meeting with this interest group and that powerful senator, and you have to compromise a great deal with them if you ever hope to be successful." My *modus operandi* was different. I made a conscious effort to enlarge the political playing field by talking about issues directly with the American people. But I did so by ignoring some widely accepted Washington myths:

Myth #1: *Public policy issues are hopelessly complex.* Earlier in this century, Justice Holmes wrote, "At this time we need education in the obvious more than investigation of the obscure." Holmes was right, and what he said is still true. Some intellectuals seem more and more fascinated by the obscure, and make their living by creating obscurities for the rest of us to puzzle over. A friend of mine who was a humanities professor said that in many university courses perfectly sober students pay a lot of money to trade horse sense for moonshine. And a lot of public money is spent in Washington doing the same thing. Congressmen hold endless hearings on the "complex" issue of education and other matters, when much of what evades them are certain simple truths like: homework makes for better learning; the study of Western civilization is important; people who commit serious crimes should go to prison; and public money should not go to support pornography.

I do not want to disparage the joy of working one's mind on complex matters. These are pleasures for the intellect, and discoveries and insights are gained by wrestling with tough problems. It is the tendency or wish to make *everything* difficult that bothers me. It bothers me because it makes a casualty of simple truths. They are simply and utterly true no matter how many mental somersaults one turns to deny them and cast them as problems. They should be preserved because they are valuable; they can be held on to through thick and thin, handles for the mind to grasp in a world in which everything is called confusing and many things are.

Simple truths should be granted not to discourage people from thinking but to encourage them to start thinking about the many things that are truly difficult. All plans—public policies, choices of career—need foundations, and somewhere in the foundations there are simple truths.

Myth #2: *There is special wisdom that comes from being in Washington.* In fact, *nobody* knows better about things in general just because he lives there. You either know better or you don't; Washington has nothing to do with it. Beware of those who take the Washington "insiders" approach. Most of the work of these alleged movers and shakers consists of trying to convince people of one thing and one thing only: there is a Washington "insiders" club, and they are members of it.

Myth #3: *To get ahead, you have to be part of the "network."* Wrong. The most important thing in this city is not so much keeping your network of contacts as keeping your footing. Remember what you believed and who you were *before* you arrived on the scene. Don't forget where the roots took hold. Books and lessons from the past should be your roots. Heed the line from Allen Drury's 1959 best-seller *Advise and Consent:* "Washington took them as lovers and they were gone." As an inoculative against being swept off your feet by "Potomac fever," stay in love with the person you loved when you came. Keep your religious faith and replenish it. Stay home with your family. Stay in touch with old friends. And stick with old routines.

Flannery O'Connor wrote that "Routine is a condition of survival." To the person taking high office in Washington, it's smart to stick to routines established previously in your life. Elayne and I have been going on vacation to the same North Carolina beach since before our children were born. We haven't missed a year. We'll keep going for many more, I hope. It is a way of providing continuity, stability, and perhaps, some sanity to a pretty hurly-burly life. Where there is a lot of change, seek out what's enduring, what's permanent, what provides familiar solid footing.

Almost every weekend of my adult life, I have played a touch football game. With a team of friends and colleagues I gathered (and gather still) on Sunday afternoon at a local high school and play, sometimes among ourselves and sometimes against other teams. We're not great—but we're pretty good. We play hard, we win most of the games we play, and we are proud when we do. It is a good routine; it is also an activity in which being a member of the Cabinet doesn't give you any advantage. You're just a player out there on the field with other players. A good reminder.

Myth #4: *A public official is obligated to attend lots of receptions and eat the food.* In Washington, that means eating mostly poached salmon. I've eaten a lot of poached salmon, and I don't like it— particularly at 10:00 P.M. I never could get used to being fed as if I were a large house cat. My recommendation is to eat home cooking as often as possible. Eat something recognizable. For me, that means beef or chicken. But go home. There is much more there than food.

Myth #5. *If you want a friend in Washington, buy a dog.* Harry Truman's famous piece of advice is funny—it always seems to get a laugh when politicians use it in a speech—but it's false. I left my jobs in government with a lot more friends than when I came here. And they're good ones, too. None of them is a dog.

Myth #6: *To be effective you need to work fourteen-hour days.* In Washington, a lot of people put a premium on having fifteen pink slips in their "call" box at nine in the evening, and on running around looking frantic, preoccupied, and hence very important. In most jobs, as agency or department head, there really is no need to behave that way. You can be both important and courteous. And with very few exceptions, you can go in to work at 7:30 A.M. and be home for dinner. Not everyone can do that, but more can than do.

One of the true tests for an administrator is whether or not he is secure enough to hire the best people he can find, people who may outpace, outshine, and outthink him. Or is he so insecure that he will only hire people who won't blot out his sun, and who will dutifully say "Yes," no matter how bad the directive or idea? Does he hire people who have the courage to challenge the opinion of the boss and the opinions of his colleagues?

I would often gather five to eight of my smartest people together, irrespective of their titles, from an undersecretary to a junior assistant, whenever I had an important public policy decision to make. Sometimes they would have to haul chairs into my office as many as three or four times a day. Once we were assembled, I would lay out the issue and simply ask them, "What should we do?" There were often disagreements, sometimes sharp disagreements, which wasn't surprising, since I had hired very smart, independently minded people. The conversations were frank and direct, and there was no posturing and no pouting afterward. I wanted to hear what was wrong with what I was planning to do *before* I did it, not after I had announced it publicly. If a political leader wants that kind of advantage, he shouldn't hire people who are mainly interested in covering their own behinds and do so, year in and year out, by mumbling acquiescence to what the boss wants. The problem with some of the old Washington "hands" is just that: they're all hands but lack stout hearts. They can't be trusted. They shouldn't be brought on board.

Chester E. Finn, Jr., who was my assistant secretary for research and improvement at the Department of Education, wrote about my team at the education department (many of whom have gone on to hold important posts in the Bush administration):

Bennett assembled a solid team of helpers and associates. I had the privilege to belong to that team for three years and have never had as colleagues a more intelligent, well-read, clear-thinking, dedicated, and compatible assemblage of men and women. To be sure, there were occasions when we ought to have chosen our words with greater care. But this was an extraordinary bunch of people, far less given to "court politics" and backbiting (or stabbing) than is the norm in the upper reaches of government.

We were able to establish an esprit de corps that few other agencies have been able to match. You cannot be indifferent to the personal qualities and loyalties of those whom you hire. I am indebted to the extraordinary people who worked with me—and I owe them a great deal. They speak for you, act for you, represent you. To the world at large, they are in many ways your reflection. Choose well. Choose people with the sharpest minds and best character.

I literally bumped into Ronald Reagan several times—once in a crowd near a school, once after a Cabinet meeting—and I was struck each time by the fact that in knocking into him, I moved him not at all. He was solid, immovably solid. And Reagan on the inside is much like this sturdy outside. This Dixon, Illinois, native had roots too deep and solid to be swept off course by the gusting, shifting political winds of Washington, D.C.

The most important part of Ronald Wilson Reagan, his core set of beliefs and his formative years, can be traced to his hometown of Dixon. He was a product of northern Illinois, not Hollywood. And that was the source of much of his strength and appeal. I have been to Dixon several times (that is where, coincidentally, my best friend was raised). It is a simple place, made up of good people, and simple truths seem to hold there. Dixon is not a place of "advanced attitudes." Ronald Reagan took on a special place in the hearts of his countrymen because he reminded us of our common ideals and aspirations. He represented the good sense, the common sense, of the American people.

Unlike many in Hollywood, Ronald Reagan was never given to debilitating doubt or "psychobabble." To him the abstraction was always made particular by a story, an anecdote, a recollection of things past. He struck me as a man who never experienced an existential crisis, a dark night of the soul. And that's what some of his critics couldn't stand—they wanted melodrama, the "weight of the world" syndrome, a president who showed the "burdens of office." The Gipper never obliged. He was a man at ease with himself and the world.

But some of the crowd that flitted about President Reagan struck me as the twentieth-century counterpart of Robert Bolt's description of the court followers of Henry VIII—he was their lion, they his jackals. These were people who joined the Reagan team—their kind seem to appear in droves with every new administration—not to serve his ends, but theirs. They were interested less in the reform of government than in the "loaves and fishes" of government.

The early months of 1987 were the darkest days of the Reagan administration. The Iran-Contra affair had taken a toll. The administration was wounded, and sharks were closing in for the kill. Critics were hoping for a Watergate redux. Pressure was building. The President was planning to give a televised address to the nation, explaining his role and responsibility. He was getting a lot of advice about what to say, most of it demanding contrition and, I thought, groveling. During a Cabinet meeting on Monday, March 2, I decided to speak up. I told the President that his critics were less interested in having him take responsibility than in having him humiliate himself. My advice was straightforward: explain in the speech what he had done and why, assume responsibility for his own acts, and then issue a call to the American people to unite; it was time to get on with the business of governing the nation.

Two days later, on the morning of his speech, I called Ronald Reagan. "Mr. President," I said, "at the Cabinet meeting on Monday, I said something and I just wanted to be sure it wasn't misunderstood. I said that some people won't be satisfied until you are humiliated and I hope you wouldn't give them satisfaction. I didn't mean to suggest that you were planning to do such a thing."

"I understand, Bill," the President said. "But I do have to take responsibility, and I plan to do it."

"Yes, I know that," I said. "Sure, you're where the buck stops. I guess my point, sir, is that to have you bent or broken isn't what we want. Some people would like to see this break you."

"Oh no," President Reagan said. "Well, this hasn't broken me. I plan to accept this responsibility and move on to other things."

"Yes, sir. Well, I guess tonight is like Dixon High School's game against Rock Falls." (I thought I had once read that Rock Falls was the team the President's school played in the big annual football game in Dixon.)

The President laughed. "Dixon High's big game was against Sterling, Bill, not Rock Falls."

"I stand corrected," I told him. "Thank you for your time, Mr. President."

*   *   *

Ronald Reagan, unfazed and good-humored, always had the gift of being himself. And that self was born and shaped in Lincoln country, not Tinseltown.

The Reagan charm rarely failed. It reminded me of the old Irish definition of charm, "the capacity to elicit the answer 'yes' before the question is asked." Yet for all the charm and good humor, even when I was with Ronald Reagan, I could sense the distance, the detachment. Inside, he had erected a wall that nobody I know, including some of his closest friends and advisers, could ever scale, get through, or get behind. Ask too probing or too personal a question of Ronald Reagan and you hit the wall. This was often covered by the pleasant tilt of the head and the familiar opening word, "Well," followed by a story. That's as far as I ever got. Maybe that's as far as anybody (with the exception of his wife, Nancy) ever gets. So be it.

This man of true and time-honored beliefs, who told simple stories with simple morals, changed the face of the modern world. Early in his administration he called the Soviet Union an "evil empire" and told the world that "the last pages of Communism are being written even now." The critics pounced on him, calling his comments reckless, provocative, and undiplomatic. He didn't flinch. Then the Iron Curtain was raised, the Berlin Wall crumbled, and the Soviet Union dissolved. Ronald Reagan's words and steadiness of purpose were vindicated. Unlike the critics, the people who actually had to *live* under Communist rule cheered his honesty and courage. President Reagan stared down the Russian Bear and in so doing, he dramatically altered history.

Despite considerable efforts over the last few years to discredit him and his achievements, Ronald Reagan's place is secure. His achievements were not due primarily to public relations, clever marketing techniques, lights, mirrors or "Teflon." They were due to a clear, guiding set of principles and the sinew and fiber of leadership. The critics can't bear to admit that he was right on almost all the large, important political questions in recent times. Historians of the twenty-first century (who won't be influenced by their own act of having voted against him) will be fairer to him than many of today's academics and journalists-turned-historians. They will accord him his proper place in history, one of the truly significant presidents in our history, one of the two or three most important in this century.

*   *   *

Before I took the post of drug czar, several people who had worked for George Bush told me that he was the best boss they'd ever had. They told me about his loyalty, accessibility, personal generosity, and genuine interest in his people. They were right. And what was once known to the few is now known to the many. The American people appreciate his palpable decency. With George Bush, familiarity hasn't bred contempt; it has engendered affection and respect among his countrymen. But there is much more to George Bush than merely personal decency; there is also a rare degree of professional competency.

President Bush is a man who, unlike many others and perhaps to their envy, seems to achieve competence, even mastery, effortlessly. To people who are naturally gifted and talented, the world seems to give itself over without a fight; George Bush is so blessed. The apparent ease of effort in his performance makes it seem as if his achievements are less substantial than they in fact are. And that has helped give rise to the notion that he lacks "vision."

President Bush's political and personal disposition is toward consensus, not confrontation. It's hard to imagine a "Bush revolution." His approach to domestic policy issues at least is of a different kind, usually incremental and cautious. His aim is to keep the ship of state on a steady course. He looks to consolidate and build on previous achievements.

His achievements are not effortless, of course; they are a function of self-discipline, a sound intellect, and a seemingly unending supply of good habits—habits of mind and character. He is personally generous, considerate, and a model husband and father (in my later years, I hope I will have the same relationship with my sons that George Bush has with his children). With his children, as with his work, he is comfortable, relaxed, of good humor. And he, like Reagan, has what Robert Louis Stevenson called "the geniality of the world's great men."

There is no deep insecurity in George Bush, no agonistic struggle for self-definition, no angst. When you are with him for a time, you get the feeling this is the way a man is supposed to turn out. (Maybe those New England Yankees knew something about raising leaders after all.) Above all, he is a man of character as Aristotle understood it: reliability, resilience, integrity, wholeness, and a steadiness of disposition.

In the early days as Education Secretary, I took a lot of heat for my early criticisms of higher education. The word around town was that I was one "controversial" comment away from an early exit from government. Before a Cabinet meeting, as we entered and waited for President Reagan, most of my colleagues kept their distance from me—superstitious, perhaps, that if they got too close they might catch my alleged "foot-in-mouth" distemper. It probably had more to do with appearances. They thought I was going to be a failure, and they didn't want anything to do with me. But Vice President Bush made a point of coming over to me to buck up my spirits. "Hang in there, Bill," he told me. "You'll do just fine." It was a small but important gesture at a critical time. I never forgot it.

I suspect that one of the reasons that President Bush had to overcome an "image" problem is that he is not a particularly charismatic figure. Some leaders are larger-than-life personalities; at first glance they are strikingly impressive. At first glance George Bush comes across as intelligent, agreeable, and experienced. But he doesn't make a striking impression. Yet, as many of his early critics are finding out, he grows on you steadily over time. The more you observe him, the more you see just how steady and sure he is. And the steadiness inspires confidence. That is a mark (albeit a somewhat discreet and subtle mark) of presidential leadership. He makes his way slowly, carefully, at his own deliberate speed. But he knows the direction in which he's heading. And once he decides that an important principle is at stake, he's tenacious. When many in Congress and even some in the Administration were in danger of "going wobbly" in the months leading up to the Persian Gulf war, it was George Herbert Walker Bush who remained steady and true.

President Bush is not a particularly strong rhetorician. He happened to follow a president whose strong suit was rhetoric, who evoked powerful images and inspired confidence. Evoking soaring images and inspiring words is not George Bush's style. He is not a poet; he's a good, solid prose writer. Paul Gigot of *The Wall Street Journal* put it well: "George Bush has been underestimated, in part because his own unrhetorical presidency follows the most effective rhetorical president since FDR. Mr. Bush's leadership is personal, discreet, hands-on."

George Bush's most effective communication medium is, not surprisingly, the press conference. It is the extension of the issue-oriented politician. He loves the give-and-take with reporters. This is a man who is competent on almost all questions, masterful at many. There's a reason. This is a man who reads, does his homework, and gets up in the morning to do some more.

As with Reagan, the physical mirrors the psychological. George Bush is perhaps the best, most competent all-around athlete ever to occupy the White House. When the world-champion Detroit Pistons were honored at a White House ceremony, he dropped his first shot at the basket from beyond the foul line. At Camp David, I watched him play nine holes of golf, a set of tennis, shag fly balls, and end the day's activities with some fine putting. We jogged together once in Houston, he in his mid-sixties, I in my mid-forties. We ran three miles and it was all I could do to keep up with him. As we started he said, "Hey, czar, bring me up-to-date on the drug war while we run." I told him, "Mr. President, you have your choice. I'll brief you on the drug war or I'll run with you. But I can't do both." At the end of the run, he was fine. We did some stand-up interviews, and he graciously took a lot of time answering the questions, some of which were directed at me, until I had caught my breath.

During the 1988 presidential primaries, the Dole campaign charged that Bush had "a résumé but not a record." George Bush has both; the résumé attests to the record, and it's a record of success. And now it shows. Should we think less of this man because there is no great character blot, no deep propensity to melancholy, no tragic megalomania? I think not. When I have called on him (as I have on a number of occasions) for help in the drug war, for advice on a policy matter, or even for advice on my life and career, there was always somebody home.

Not all conservatives possess the geniality of spirit that Ronald Reagan and George Bush share. One of the areas that political conservatives need to improve is their disposition. They need to cheer up. Fortunately, over the last several years, conservatism has begun to shed its skin of distrust and defensiveness toward the world in which we live. It has overcome what once was a suspicion, even a dread, of the future. It must now become vigorous, bold, assertive, and cheerful—in a word, fully Americanized. While contemporary liberalism has moved away from—in some cases, even against—the mainstream of American political life, today's conservatism is more at home with the common sense and the common beliefs of the American people. Conservatives should be encouraged about that. Americans are an optimistic lot.

But overall, conservatives are still too dour. There's more to life than scorn and opposition to liberalism. ("One does not become a saint through other people's sins," Chekhov wrote.) There's a great deal in life and in politics to affirm. As one philosopher has said, cynicism, griping, a state of chronic disappointment and complaint about the world is no way to have life work for you or to live it. Conservatives should take into their enterprise what E. M. Foster called "pluckiness," a pluckiness of spirit, good will, and a sense of humor. There are many things to celebrate, not the least of which is the defeat of communism and the victory of freedom (which occurred during a conservative watch and in large measure as a result of conservative policies). Conservatives need to be wary of fretfulness. They need to practice a more affirmative disposition in spirit, in tone, and in attitude. Americans don't want to be led by people who are sour, cynical, negative, or hopelessly pessimistic. Conservatives are properly suspicious of human nature; they understand the complex mix of good and evil that runs through the human soul. But that's no cause for a hangdog attitude. Conservatives should lighten up, enjoy life, and show it. Theoretical pessimism—the belief that in the end, as Isaiah says, "Their works are vanity and naught, their molten images are wind and confusion"—may be in order. But for purposes of action we should subscribe to operational optimism—"What can be done to make things better?" It is better to light a candle than curse the darkness.

Over the course of ten years, I got into political scraps. I took some hard shots. For the most part I think I took them well, if not always cheerfully, then at least without bad will. Certainly I left public life with bad will toward no one. "Through our great good fortune, in our youth our hearts were touched by fire," Justice Holmes wrote. "It was given us to learn at the outset that life is a profound and passionate thing." I have found this is especially true of political life. I enjoyed it a lot—so much so, I may even want more some day. Some of my critics may be able to look forward to having Bill Bennett to kick around some more. Fair enough. I promise to kick back.

EPILOGUE

While writing this book I reflected on my nearly ten years of public service, as chairman of the National Endowment for the Humanities, Secretary of Education, and director of the Office of National Drug Control Policy. During those years I had the opportunity to speak about the condition of our children: in my first job, about the cultural legacy we owe them; in my second, about the structure and substance of the education we owe them; and in my most recent job, about the protection and safety we owe them. The common threads and common themes were the critical importance of cultural questions, the need in public policy to address fundamental matters of right and wrong, and personal responsibility.

Conflict was therefore inevitable. The modern liberal sensibility is quite often allergic to the most serious questions of culture, spirit, and values. Money, technology, and bureaucracy: the liberal-left will talk about and work on them incessantly, vigorously, and enthusiastically. But when the subject is character, personal responsibility, and right and wrong, they tend to grow uncomfortable and diffident.

I understand the discomfort and the diffidence. Ours is a society deliberately and wisely divided into separate spheres of private and public action. Liberty requires it. But as our Founders understood, liberty also requires a strong measure of virtue in each sphere. The public good rests its foundation on the qualities of private men and women. Madison wrote in *Federalist #55* that a government devoted to liberty "presupposes the existence of these qualities in a higher degree than any other form." In America, general liberty cannot survive a dearth of virtue and public policy cannot succeed without addressing the issue of values directly.

Public action should not and need not extend its full reach into strictly private terrain. But the public and private spheres approach each other at many points. And when the private sphere comes forward in partial ill-health, then public *conversation,* at least, should not ignore it by an embarrassed silence. What this means concretely is that we must confront our discomfort and talk openly and candidly about the moral good as an essential part of our lives together.

I know the automatic response from some quarters, since I have heard it more than a few times during my government career: "The Puritans are coming, the Puritans are coming!" But Cotton Mather has been dead for more than 250 years, and this country is hardly at risk of a renewed interest in his thinking. We need to have a calm, complete, and honest talk about some of the most troubling aspects of contemporary American culture. The longer we wait, the more trouble we'll see. The longer we avoid these questions, the worse things will get.

C. S. Lewis wrote in *The Abolition of Man:* "We make men without chests and expect of them virtue and enterprise. We laugh at honor and are shocked to find traitors in our midst. We castrate and then bid the geldings be fruitful." If we ridicule and caricature traditional religious beliefs, standards of decency, and virtue as the hang-up of uptight, obsessive prudes, there will be a cost. It will be primarily to our children.

It needn't be this way. The subject of my most recent government post is a good example. Drug use is a problem with obvious and devastating public consequences, but a problem first and foremost of private behavior, of morality. As I described earlier, our public conversation about drugs was until recently devoted largely to aimless handwringing and expressions of despair. Today, things look very different. Every available piece of evidence suggests that overall the drug problem is getting better, not worse. No doubt that official action has helped. The federal government and many states are now effectively spending record amounts of money on drug interdiction, law enforcement, education, and treatment. We are deploying that money more intelligently and less haphazardly than in the past. All these steps are useful. But something even more important has happened: we have recovered our public mind, our moral clarity, about a dangerous private behavior.

Embarrassment in this area has faded; in fact, it now seems almost antiquated. Taking drugs is wrong. Almost everyone says so, and they say it out loud, and often. Americans want this problem over. And the private voices give strength to the official actions; indeed, they are a necessary condition of the effectiveness of those actions. The result is that fewer and fewer people are taking drugs. It is not a simple process, this "American capacity for self-renewal," as one historian described it. But it is definite, discernible, and replicable. And the first step here, as in so many other areas, involves an open attempt to grapple with moral principles, with principles of behavior and conduct.

The popular press and political commentators often portray cultural issues as a sideshow, a distraction from the more "real" and "pressing" issues we face like, say, the federal budget deficit. A university professor was quoted in *The New York Times* as saying that President Bush had lost his ability to announce any new initiatives that cost money, and "that's why you see these symbolic causes—the flag, abortion, family values." That is a cynical attitude and it is flat-out wrong. Cultural issues are every bit as "real"—indeed, they are more real, more important, and have more impact on the lives of our children.

Nothing more powerfully determines a child's behavior than his internal compass, his beliefs, his sense of right and wrong. If a child firmly believes, if he has been taught and guided to believe, that drugs, promiscuity, and assaulting other people are wrong things to do, this will contribute to his own well-being and to the well-being of others. And if this lesson is multiplied a million times—that is, taught a million times—we will have greater and broader well-being, fewer personal catastrophes, less social violence, and fewer wasted and lost lives. The character of a society is determined by how well it transmits true and time-honored values from generation to generation. Cultural matters, then, are not simply an add-on or an afterthought to the quality of life of a country; they determine the character and essence of the country itself. Private belief is a condition of public spirit; personal responsibility a condition of public well-being. The investment in private belief must be constantly renewed.

During the last twenty-five years, we didn't make much of an investment and we received little return. Many of America's intellectual elite perpetrated a doctrine of *de facto* nihilism that cut to the core of American traditions. While the doctrine never fully took hold among most Americans, it did make significant inroads. A lot of people forgot, and many others willfully rejected, the most basic and sensible answers to first questions, to questions about what contributes to our social well-being and prosperity, what makes for individual character and responsibility, and what constitutes a "good society."

The public has been too quiescent and too accepting about what has been inflicted on them from the upper strata of society and the permanent political establishment in Washington. Too often they elected to sit on the sidelines, in part because legions of officials, special interest groups, professors, and commentators belittle mainstream American values and participation; often they belittle and patronize mainstream Americans themselves. "We know better," the elite establishment said. "Leave it to us, the enlightened experts, and everything will turn out just fine." Too often many people did what was asked of them. The results are now in.

Significant portions of American society have been culturally deconstructed. This has had particularly devastating effects on our institutions: schools, colleges and universities, mainline churches, the legal profession, the Congress, and others. The assault was made primarily by people who held left-liberal political views, who believed that these institutions were corrupt, unsuitable, unworthy and unfit, and so they decided to remake them in their image, for their own purposes.

The good news is that this cultural virus has created its own antibodies. Americans are regaining the confidence to express publicly the common sense sentiments they hold privately. They are learning again that the things a society collectively chooses to affirm and condemn, encourage and discourage, make all the difference. This is true whether we are talking about curricular basics or curricular fluff; welfare or workfare; marriage or out-of-wedlock births; regard or disdain for religion in the public square; color blindness or color consciousness; or drug use as acceptable or unacceptable. This renewed understanding on a whole range of social issues is the critical first step in the "revaluing" of America. Values that were once in exile are being welcomed home. The American people are renewing their commitment to our common principles. And so the task of cultural reconstruction has begun. But it is nowhere near complete, and it is least complete in the institutions that have borne the brunt of two decades of wrong-headed cultural and public policy.

Michael Barone and Grant Ujifusa, editors of the *Almanac of American Politics*, put it this way:

The [domestic] public sector institutions of which liberals have had custody for the last twenty years—the public schools, central city bureaucracies, university governance—have performed poorly. The people in charge of them have a million excuses: they have a poor quality of students or constituents, they don't have enough money, they must do things according to certain rules and regulations because of internal institutional imperatives. These are the same excuses the military made fifteen or twenty years ago. Fortunately, the leaders of the military stopped making excuses and started reforming. Unfortunately, with very few exceptions, the leaders of liberal public sector institutions are continuing to make excuses and their institutions are continuing to perform poorly. . . . Much of the politics of the 1990s will turn out to be a struggle to reform those parts of the public sector that patently aren't functioning.

The time for excuses is over. The returns are in on the Brave New World of liberal social policy, and they are not good. We now know that the left was peddling from an empty wagon. Today fewer and fewer people are swayed by cultural nihilism and leftist social policy. But though the emperor has no clothes, he still has an empire. A number of critical American institutions are still under liberal tutelage.

What, then, to do? The American people face a great and important political task. They need to reassert their influence on their social institutions: elementary and secondary schools, universities, churches and synagogues, the media, the legal profession, federal, state, and local governments, and the arts. Reclaiming our institutions does not mean subjecting them to a narrow or rigid ideology; it means letting these institutions be governed by what works, by what makes sense, and by insisting that they remain true to their original purposes. In short, we need institutions that more accurately reflect the sentiments and beliefs of the great body of the American people rather than those of the cultural deconstructionists. For the citizenry, this requires greater public scrutiny, attention, and action; institutional accountability and reform; more citizen participation (on school boards, church offices, boards of trustees, and the like); political action; and the recruitment of sympathetic talent to take jobs in, and affect the course of, these institutions. In short, we need to pay attention and act.

Those whose beliefs govern our institutions will in large measure win the battle for the culture. And whoever wins the battle for the culture gets to teach the children. This cultural and institutional reclamation project will not be easy. Midge Decter has written that the Reagan election victories set off a response in the liberal community ranging from deep confusion to panic. The reason this occurred, according to Decter, is that his victories

> bore testimony not so much to a wish for radical new policies as to an open declaration of war over the culture. And a culture war, as the liberals understood far better than did their conservative opponents, is a war to the death. For a culture war is not battle over policy, though policy in many cases gives it expression; it is rather a battle about matters of the spirit.

So be it. Reclaiming our institutions is less a political opportunity than a civic obligation. It involves hard work. But it is work of immense importance. At the end of the day, *somebody's* values will prevail. In America, "we the people" have a duty to insist that our institutions and our government be true to their time-honored tasks. In some instances that means that the American people must roll up their sleeves and work to ensure that their institutions and government reflect their sentiments, their good sense, their sense of right and wrong. This is what a democracy—a government of, by, and for the people—is all about. The debate has been joined. But the fight for our values has just begun.

INDEX

California, University of (Berkeley), 185
Call to Civic Service, A (Moskos), 186
Cambridge Criminal Court, 99
Carey, John J., 222
Carter, Deborah J., 201
Carter, Jimmy, 20, 27, 47, 95, 238
  Education Department and, 47, 48
Carter, Lawrence, 181
Castro, Fidel, 221
"Catholic High Schools," 216
Catholics, Catholic Church, 212, 214-217, 222
Catholic schools, 65–66, 215–17
CBS, 31, 221
Center for Media and Public Affairs, 31–32
Center for the Study of Social and Political Change, 221
Centesimus Annus ("The Hundredth Year") (John Paul II), 208
Chambers Elementary School, 82–83
Chapter I program, 64
character, 28, 58–60, 121, 198, 232–233, 253
Charleston, S.C., drug war in, 135–36
checks and balances, 43
Chekhov, Anton, 252
Cheney, Dick, 113, 140, 233
Chesterton, G. K., 211
Chicago, Ill.:
  Board of Education of, 41
  education in, 39–44, 63–67, 69
Chicago Teachers Union (CTU), 41–42
Chicago Tribune, 40–41, 67, 69
child abuse, drugs and, 94, 119
children:
  art's effect on, 33
  drugs and, 92–94, 105–8, 116, 117, 119, 128
  education of, *see* education; schools
  instilling values in, 33–35
  liberal elite and, 33–36
  out-of-wedlock, 190, 192, 197
Christianity, Christians, 206–21
Chronicle of Higher Education, The, 48, 169
citizenship, language and, 54
City University of New York, 207, 216
Civil Rights Act (1964), 187, 229
Civil Rights Act (1991), 190

civil rights movement, 189–92, 196, 202
Civil War, U.S., 43
"Civil War, The," 19
Clark, Joe, 78–81, 91, 101
class size, achievement and, 86
Classroom Management, 79
Closing of the American Mind, The (Bloom), 177
CNN, 115–16
Coast Guard, U.S., 112
cocaine, 95, 126, 141, 146, 149, 150
  babies addicted to, 92–93
  bombing of processing plants for, 102–3
  price of, 114
  U.S. military in war against, 103–4
  see also crack
"Cocaine Alley," 102
Coleman, James, 81, 216
College (Boyer), 177
college freshmen, conservatism of, 148–49
Colombia, in war on drugs, 114, 139–40
Columbia Journalism Review, 220
Columbus, Christopher, 60, 222
Commentary, 30, 61, 190
commitment, 77, 81, 86, 91, 142
Committee on the Arts and Humanities, 32
common school, 57–58
"Confidential Guide, The," 164
Congress, U.S., 65, 97–98, 229–31, 235, 250
  drug policy and, 98, 100–101, 114, 144, 146, 167
  education policy and, 67–68, 167, 176, 215
  see also House of Representatives, U.S.; Senate, U.S.
Congressional Hispanic Caucus, 54
Connecticut, University of, 174
conservatives, conservatism, 186, 238–41, 246–52
  of Bennett, 22, 24, 35–36
  of college freshmen, 148–49
  definition of, 35
  at National Humanities Center, 24
  of NEA membership, 49
Constitution, U.S., 43, 71, 204, 206, 226–27
Conte, Silvio, 144

ABOUT THE AUTHOR

William J. Bennett served as director of the Office of National Drug Control Policy under President Bush and served as Secretary of Education and chairman of the National Endowment for the Humanities under President Reagan. He has a bachelor of arts degree in philosophy from Williams College, a doctorate in political philosophy from the University of Texas, and a law degree from Harvard. Dr. Bennett is currently a John M. Olin Fellow at the Hudson Institute, a Distinguished Fellow in Cultural Policy Studies at The Heritage Foundation, and a senior editor of *National Review* magazine. He, his wife, and two sons live in Chevy Chase, Maryland.